Authoring Interactive Multimedia

ARCH C. LUTHER

AP PROFESSIONAL

A Division of Harcourt Brace & Company

Boston   San Diego   New York
London   Sydney   Tokyo   Toronto

IBM® Ultimedia® Tools Series™ Multimedia Sampler CD
© 1993 International Business Machines Corporation.
All rights reserved.

AP PROFESSIONAL
955 Massachusetts Avenue, Cambridge, MA 02139

An imprint of ACADEMIC PRESS, INC.
A Division of HARCOURT BRACE & COMPANY

United Kingdom Edition published by
ACADEMIC PRESS LIMITED
24–28 Oval Road, London NW1 7DX

Library of Congress Cataloging-in-Publication Data

Luther, Arch C.
    Authoring interactive multimedia / Arch C. Luther.
        p.   cm.
    Includes bibliographical references (p.   ) and index.
    ISBN 0-12-460430-7
    1. Interactive media.   2. Multimedia systems.   3. System design.
    I. Title.
    QA76.76.I59L87   1994
    006.6—dc20   93-48883
                                                             CIP

Printed in the United States of America
94 95 96 97 98 ML 9 8 7 6 5 4 3 2 1

Authoring
Interactive Multimedia

Contents

Preface

In the early days of personal computing (the late 1970s or early 1980s), our computers mostly were used for fun things: to play games, to learn about things, or to develop newly found programming skills. The PC wasn't yet powerful enough to be a practical tool for real work. However, the headlong drive of the semiconductor and computer industries to improve speed, storage, and power quickly took care of that, and we soon learned that word processors, spreadsheets, or databases (*productivity* programs) were valid ways to enhance our work. Thus, the PC became just another object that we associated with *work*, and, for most of us, the fun element of personal computing moved to the background.

At that stage in the history of PCs, we worked with a computer by typing at a keyboard and viewing output on a video screen that could only display text or maybe simple graphics such as lines or boxes. Learning to use a computer involved mastering an array of arcane text-based commands and procedures. It wasn't something for the faint of heart! Unfortunately, the limited power of the computer and the high costs of hardware prevented doing anything fancier in the interest of ease of use.

Today, the power of a desktop PC has grown to the point that the original requirements of productivity software have been met many times over, and computing power now can be devoted to additional features which seemed frivolous or simply impossible in the early days. A major feature in this category is the *graphical user interface* (GUI), where the computer screen displays many objects in addition to text, and the user interacts with them by moving a pointer icon around the screen with some kind of controller and clicking buttons to make selections and to specify actions for the computer. This interface is much easier to learn than the old text-based interface, and a little of the fun element has crept back in; computing has become a little more interesting than just *work*.

But the possibilities for using the apparent excess power of today's PCs are just beginning to be explored. For example, today's computers are capable of presenting video and displaying audio at the same time they are running all the productivity software. That is called *multimedia computing*, or just multimedia, and it can be used to enhance tremendously the user interface and the ability of the computer to present rich information. It also brings back more fun to personal computing, because you now interact with pictures, sounds, and video along with the more mundane numbers and text that used to be all that computers were good for.

Multimedia will soon be a part of all personal computing—whether it is supported by special hardware and software or not. Most new systems, new applications, and updates being done today are offering built-in multimedia features that you will automatically get whether you buy new or update.

This book is about multimedia computing, how to use it to enhance your work, and how much fun it is to do that. But more specifically, it focuses on the tasks of *authoring*—the process of creating multimedia applications. A companion book, *Designing Interactive Multimedia*, deals with the issues of developing the best multimedia approaches to solve specific problems.

This book is directed at the large number of present computer users in industry, education, homes, government, and anywhere else computers are found, who are not necessarily technical experts in computing. You know how to use your computer and the software you have on it, but your main interest is *using* the computer to do whatever your work is. This book will help you face the current explosion of multimedia, and will give you just enough understanding so you can decide how you want to participate in multimedia computing. I can't escape some technical matters—in a new technology like multimedia, technology is rapidly evolving, and not many standards are in place. Therefore, you will face some technical choices, and I will try to explain just enough in simple language so you can make your own decisions.

If you intend to do some multimedia creation—authoring—this book will be especially relevant. It will introduce you to the hardware and software for authoring and lead you through the daunting process of deciding what you need. In doing that, I will stick primarily to fundamentals, and I will not waste your time with details of operating any particular hardware or software. There are plenty of specific books available to take care of that.

I do use specific product examples to help you appreciate some of the fundamental issues. The product examples are chosen to emphasize certain features, rather than to endorse or evaluate the products. In most cases, similar features are available in many products, and I do not try to be comprehensive in listing them. Sometimes you will find that the same product is covered in several different chapters of the book. If you are interested in all the references to any specific product, consult the index to find them. What's important in the product examples is that you learn just enough about a particular *class* or *feature* of hardware or software so that you can read the magazine reviews or look at products in stores without becoming overwhelmed by specifications or hype talk.

Product pricing will be an important factor in your decisions. However, it is impractical for a book like this to discuss actual dollar prices, because they change too fast, and discounts and special offers are often available. I sometimes will use words to convey relative pricing—*inexpensive* means the price is probably less than

$200, and *expensive* means the price is usually more than $1,000. If neither of these words is used, you can assume the price most likely falls between $200 and $1,000.

Programming is usually a part of the creation process for a computer application. It can also be a part of multimedia authoring—but it doesn't have to be. Many software packages for multimedia creation can be used by a person with no programming background at all. However, there are also products that *require* programming knowledge, so this is an important issue to face at the outset—are you already a programmer, or will you learn how to do programming? The book will help you with that question; it is for both programmers and nonprogrammers. There is some programming code in places, but nonprogrammers can pass over that and continue with no great loss.

This book includes a Compact Disc, which was provided with the help of IBM. It contains a large number of examples of current multimedia software from the IBM Ultimedia Tools Series. This will give you a better feeling for the products than any amount of writing I could do. Instructions for using this CD are in Appendix A at the back of the book.

I have always been disturbed by the need to use compound personal pronouns such as he/she or her/his to recognize both genders, since the English language doesn't provide anything simpler for this. In this book I have adopted an approach that I hope won't disturb anyone. In odd-numbered chapters, the personal pronouns are male, and in even-numbered chapters, they are female. So, if at any point you are upset with my use of personal pronouns, just read on to the next chapter.

Multimedia authoring can be very rewarding. I encourage you to become the first one in your department or your company to learn multimedia authoring — this book will help you along the way. You won't be disappointed.

Arch C. Luther

Acknowledgments

A project with the scope of this book cannot be accomplished by the author alone. I would like to especially acknowledge the support of Alan Rose of Intertext Publications, Wayne Jerves and Larry Wheaton of IBM, and Tom Vreeland of Network Technology Corporation. Also, Kayle Luther (my daughter) did much of the artwork and the formatting for the book.

In addition, the following companies provided software, images, or information for the book: Intel Corporation, IBM, Microtek Labs, Macromedia, Autodesk, Gold Disk, Touchvision Systems, Asymetrix Corporation, Kaleida Labs, and Caterpillar, Inc.

1

Introduction

At first glance, a television receiver and a personal computer appear to be similar, because the most prominent feature of each is a video screen. However, we know that this similarity is superficial, and they are really two very different products.

The television receiver is a simple device that demands very little from us—we have only to select a channel and sit back and watch and listen to be informed or entertained. However, we have no control over what we see and hear; it is exactly what is being broadcast or what is on the tape if we are using a VCR; we are simply a passive audience for the program. In spite of that, television has enormous potential for entertainment, information dissemination, or education.

On the other hand, a personal computer doesn't do anything until we provide it with software and a string of commands. But then it can do all sorts of things to help us in business, in school, and in the home. It is *programmable*, meaning that the software can tell the computer to look and act any way that you wish. With appropriate programming, a personal computer can also inform and entertain us, but it still isn't the same as television. The greatest difference is that we are in command of the computer—it is our slave, so to speak—and we can interact with it and control it as much as we wish.

But there are other differences between televisions and computers: The screens don't *look* the same and the sound isn't the same. TV seems realistic and natural, but the computer screen looks blocky and it sounds artificial, even kind of mechanical. This difference is not inherent, rather it is a result of how the personal computer has developed and what the priorities for its use have been. However, that is now changing with the introduction of *multimedia* on personal computers, which is capable of realistic images and sound just like the TV. With multimedia in your computer, you can include realistic images, stereo sound, even motion video, right along with the traditional computer sounds and screens. A new era is beginning that promises to make the computer even more capable of teaching, informing, and entertaining us all—the era of *multimedia computing*.

The greatest excitement of multimedia computing is that you can create multimedia for yourself. You are not at the mercy of what is being broadcast or what is available on tape—you can create your own audio, images, and video using the sounds, scenes, and photographs that are around you, and it is easy! That is what this book is about: how you can create your own multimedia programs for business, education, or entertainment by using the wealth of new *authoring* software that is emerging for multimedia computing, and what you need to do it.

MULTIMEDIA

The word *multimedia* is not new; it was used even before the days of personal computing to refer to a presentation or display that involved more than one method or medium of presentation. For example, using 35-mm slides along with recorded audio is multimedia—the slides are one medium, and the audio is another medium. You could also say that everday life is multimedia, because we receive information from our environment using all of our five senses, each of which can be considered to be a different medium. Similarly, a PC that delivers its output by displaying it on the screen and printing it on paper would be multimedia, because the screen and the paper are different media.

However, in this book I use a more specific definition: A multimedia computer is a computer that uses the normal output media of display screen and printed hard copy *along with* recorded high-quality audio, high-quality still images, animation, or recorded motion video. The words *recorded* and *high-quality* should not be overlooked in the previous sentence—they refer to the capability of the multimedia computer to successfully display images, video, or sound that has been captured from live sources, much like the capability of a television system. Capturing from live sources is in addition to the computer's inherent ability to generate its own pictures or sounds through software, which we refer to here as simulation. This emphasis on *real* or *natural* sounds and pictures is important—it greatly enhances the *realism* of a computer presentation; most importantly, it tremendously expands the sources of materials that you can display or present with a computer. Now, in addition to signing your name to a document, you can use your own photograph or your own voice to "sign." If you want to show a real object as part of your presentation, you simply point a video camera at it and click a button to include that in your work. The possibilities are endless.

Audio, images, and video in real life are *analog* objects—that is, they exist as continuously varying values in space and time. Most of the familiar devices for capture and display of these objects outside of a computer, such as photographic cameras, VCRs, television, or audio tape recorders, are also analog. However, a personal computer is *digital*, meaning that it represents everything as discrete values, carried by groups of bits within the computer. The digital nature of a computer is inherent in many of the unique capabilities of computers, including accuracy, precision, programmability, and flexibility. However, such capabilities will not necessarily apply to analog multimedia objects that are integrated with a computer. In spite of that, many systems have been built using analog devices to present audio and video (in the past analog was easier than digital); however, hybrid analog-digital systems lack the flexibility and sophistication possible with an all-digital approach. This book strongly favors all-digital multimedia; the reasons for that will be explained as we come to them.

Of course, the capability to do photography, sound recording, or videography with a PC calls for the same skills and artistry that we associate with these media in television, sound recording, or films. You need skill (and possibly talent) to get professional results. This is not as hard as it sounds, and it has been covered extensively in other books, including *Designing Interactive Multimedia*, a companion I wrote to this book. This book further assumes that you already have the necessary production skills or have access to someone who does. The focus is on how you go about putting a multimedia story together after you have designed it and after you have captured or acquired the necessary materials.

A multimedia story may be a simple presentation that runs by itself and tells the story, or it may be a complex program involving many paths that can be selected by the user. Either of these (and any of the possibilities in between) is an application of multimedia, and in this book I refer to any multimedia program as an application.

COMPUTER NETWORKING AND MULTIMEDIA

In a large organization with many personal computers in place, there are major advantages to connecting all the computers into a digital *network*, so that they can communicate and exchange data. This becomes even more important when the company also has a large central computing system (sometimes called a network *server*) where all the corporate data reside. Then the network allows the central data to move to and from the PCs as needed to perform the company's business tasks. Such a network is also an ideal environment for multimedia.

Multimedia data objects are often very large (many megabytes), and they are usually time-critical, meaning they must be delivered according to an exact time schedule or the presentation may be interrupted. Modern network capability has grown to the point where distributing multimedia via a digital network is now practical. IBM has articulated a concept, which they call *enterprise multimedia*, where every PC or workstation in an organization (an enterprise) is multimedia-ready, and the network and its servers can handle multimedia traffic along with the other data. Multimedia objects can be stored at any server and made available to users of the network on demand. This multimedia network may be used for corporate communication, training, help, and presentations; it is expected to increase productivity enough to pay for the upgrading of the system and stations. IBM is committed to making this a reality.

Notice that the enterprise multimedia concept depends on the use of all-digital multimedia. A hybrid analog-digital system will not work with the digital network. (Actually, IBM has developed a solution for that problem too, by using a hybrid network that transmits the analog video and audio signals via a form of cable television system that uses the same physical cables as the digital network. It is a very creative approach, but it is expensive and it solves only one of the limitations of analog multimedia—the communication problem. The other difficulties of analog display and manipulation are still present at the PCs and workstations.) The right answer when investing for the future is to choose an all-digital system. Any limitations that this may have today will soon be solved by the ongoing pace of digital system development.

An important possibility, once corporate-wide digital networks are in place, is to use the network for *teleconferencing*. This is simply the holding of business meetings over the network. Each participant remains in his own office, but by means of a digital audio connection through the network, he can communicate with the other participants, regardless of where they are located. Using the other multimedia data types, such as video, graphics, images, or animation, any participant can introduce illustrative material into the meeting to facilitate better communication. Teleconferencing promises to be a major growth area for multimedia technologies.

INTERACTIVITY

With many presentation media the audience has no way to control the delivery of the story. The presentation follows a predetermined path—a straight line—and therefore it is called *linear*. Examples of this are TV programs or movies. Linear presentations are ideal when you have an audience of more than one person. However, if you are working one to one with a computer, you expect to have *control* and to be able to influence what is happening via the keyboard, mouse, or other means of input. This is called *interactivity*, and it is an important feature of multimedia. In many applications of computer multimedia, we want to give the user a choice of what he will do next, or we want to ask a question and get an answer which will affect what the computer does next. Each of these requires interactivity, and such capabilities are built into most multimedia software. There is still a place for linear presentations—often they are contained within a larger shell of multimedia that is interactive; once the user has made a selection, a linear presentation will be constructed and presented based on the selection. At the end of the presentation, control will return to the interactive shell.

Designing an interactive application takes special skill to create a successful product that the user will be able to easily learn and use. This was covered in *Designing Interactive Multimedia* and will not be discussed here except where it relates to specific examples.

AUTHORING

With most computer productivity applications, such as word processors, databases, or spreadsheets, the application itself is a tool that the user employs to create documents or files containing data that he needs for his work. The output from such work is normally *static*, meaning that the documents or files are simply to be read or viewed by the user or his colleagues. The reading or viewing may be done using the same application that created the document, or hard copy may be produced for that purpose. In any case, the output does not behave like a computer program—it is static.

Multimedia is different. Its output is *dynamic*, meaning that it has either a built-in behavior in the form of a sequence or script or an inherent structure that the user can interact with. Multimedia output thus behaves like another computer program—its user can do a lot more than just look at it. This program-like behavior implies that someone had to *program* the output, build the sequences, and tell them exactly what to do in every situation that may be encountered. In addition, the multimedia elements such as images, audio, video, or animations have to be collected or created. All those processes together are called *authoring*, which can be accomplished by actually writing a program with a computer language, or it can be done more easily and quickly using what is called an authoring *system*. A person who creates applications is called an *author*.

An authoring system is a set of software tools for creating multimedia applications. Tools are individual computer programs that perform one or more of the tasks needed to create an application. There are hundreds of authoring tools on the market, for many different purposes and for many different levels of author skill. Some authoring programs try to deliver a compete set of tools in one program—a complete authoring system. While these may be effective for some authors, their functionality in specialized areas is often not competitive with stand-alone tool programs designed just for one specialty area. Most of the material in this book deals with the tremendous range of authoring software and how to select and use it.

Authoring usually requires special hardware for audio and video support, and it also places special demands on the operating system software in your computer. These requirements lead to the concept of an authoring *environment,* which is the total set of hardware and software used for authoring. Figure 1.1 is a block diagram for an authoring environment; it should help you to understand the terminology used in this book. To further clarify the terminology, here are definitions for the terms that define an authoring environment and its parts:

authoring environment   The total set of hardware, firmware (software that is permanently built into the hardware), and software used for authoring.

authoring system   All of the authoring-specific software programs in the environment.

authoring tool   An authoring-specific program that performs one or more authoring tasks.

assembly tool   An authoring tool that arranges multimedia objects into a presentation or an application, dealing with their relationships in space and time.

Authoring is somewhat like making a feature film—a movie—and there are many steps to the process. A typical authoring project may involve the following major steps:

1. Concept—The objectives for the project are defined, and the type of application is specified. In the movies, this is the stage at which the producer decides what kind of movie he wants to make and what the subject will be.

2. Design—This is the process of deciding in detail what will be in the project (what the content material is) and how it will be presented. In the movies, this would include the *script writing, casting,* and *scene design* steps.

3. Obtaining content material—During this stage all the data, audio, video, and images for the project are collected in appropriate digital formats. In

```
┌─────────────────────────────────────────────────────────────────────┐
│                                                                       │
│   ┌───────────────────────┐   ┌─────────────────────────────┐   ┌───┐ │
│   │ PRODUCTIVITY S/W      │   │ AUTHORING SYSTEM            │   │ S │ │
│   │                       │   │ ASSEMBLY TOOL               │   │ O │ │
│   │ SPREADSHEET           │   │ PAINT/DRAW TOOL             │   │ F │ │
│   │ WORD PROCESSOR        │   │ AUDIO CAPTURE/EDIT TOOL      │   │ T │ │
│   │ DATABASE              │   │ VIDEO CAPTURE/EDIT TOOL      │   │ W │ │
│   │ ETC.                  │   │ ETC.                        │   │ A │ │
│   └───────────────────────┘   └─────────────────────────────┘   │ R │ │
│                                                                  │ E │ │
└─────────────────────────────────────────────────────────────────────┘
```

PRODUCTIVITY S/W
SPREADSHEET
WORD PROCESSOR
DATABASE
ETC.

AUTHORING SYSTEM
ASSEMBLY TOOL
PAINT/DRAW TOOL
AUDIO CAPTURE/EDIT TOOL
VIDEO CAPTURE/EDIT TOOL
ETC.

SOFTWARE

OPERATING SYSTEM

CPU
RAM
DISPLAY MONITOR
KEYBOARD
MOUSE

BIOS

MASS STORAGE
VIDEO ADAPTOR
AUDIO ADAPTOR
SPEAKERS
ETC.

HARDWARE
FIRMWARE

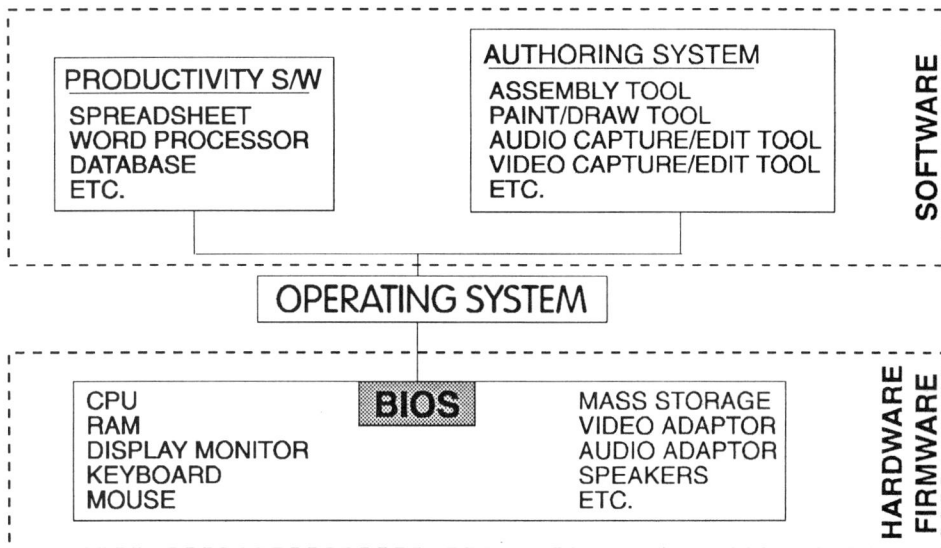

Figure 1.1 Block diagram of an authoring environment

the movies, this would be the *production* stage, where all the scenes for the movie are set up one by one and shot on film.

4. Assembly—In this step, the overall structure of the project is built, presentations are assembled, and any interactive features are built in. In the movies, this is the *postproduction editing* step, although it is much simpler because there is no interactivity in a movie. A tool for this stage of authoring is called an *assembly program.*

5. Testing—During testing, the application is run and checked to confirm that it does exactly what the author intended. In the movies, this is similar to *screening,* where the movie or parts of it are viewed and approved by management people.

6. Distribution—In this step, the application is reproduced and delivered to end users for their use. In the movies, this would be the *release* phase.

As you can see, there is a fairly good analogy between moviemaking and multimedia creation. In fact, it goes further than outlined above, because a multimedia project can create the same excitement as a movie, and it requires many of the same talents and skills as the movies. You can undertake multimedia with a "cast of thousands," like an epic movie, or you can do multimedia on a much smaller scale, where you do almost everything yourself. In that case, multimedia differs from the movies in that there are far more affordable tools available to assist a one-person multimedia producer than there are for someone trying to make a movie all by himself. Anyway, you will be on the right track if you think of a multimedia project like the making of a movie.

USES OF MULTIMEDIA COMPUTING

Of course, you can use the multimedia capabilities of your computer any way you want to; your imagination is the limit. However, a few examples may help to stimulate your thinking. Most applications fall into one of these six categories:

1. Business presentations
2. Training or education
3. Information delivery
4. Sales or merchandising
5. Productivity
6. Teleconferencing

Business Presentations

Business presentations are usually linear, without interactivity except for "next slide" control. Interactivity can be valuable, however, if you have need for backup material that you can pull up to answer questions from the audience. The computer is excellent for this—any backup material that you have can be brought forward at the touch of a button.

Numerous software packages are available for doing presentations; they provide a wide range of styles and approaches that make text, image, and sound presentations easy to create. Typically, they include a complete set of tools in one package. They not only support presentation on the computer monitor, but also allow for creation of 35-mm slides, overhead transparencies, hard copy output, or analog video output. Of course, these alternative output formats (except for analog video) lack the dynamic effects and animations that can be achieved on the computer screen. Several of these "presentation packages" will be covered in detail in subsequent chapters. Figure 1.2 shows screens from a sales report presentation.

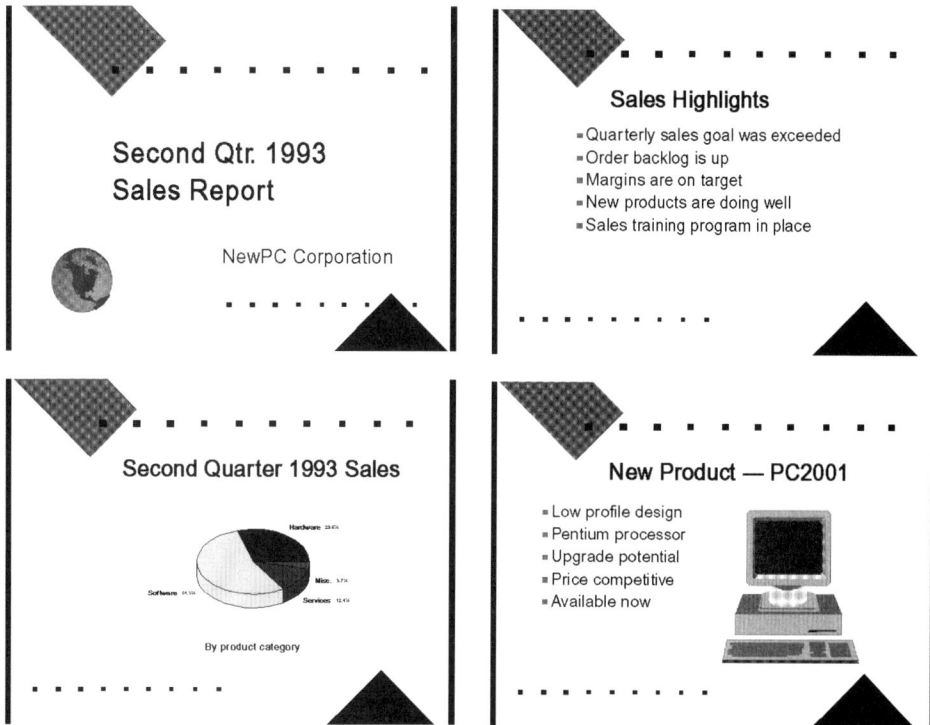

Figure 1.2 Screens from a business presentation produced with Lotus
FreeLance Graphics

Training or Education Applications

A multimedia computer really shines when used for training or education in a
one-to-one situation with a student. The multimedia presentation capability can
show the student material from any kind of source: text, charts, audio, video,
animations, simulations, or photographs. When these are combined with interactivity, an effective learning environment is created. The student has the
opportunity to select the learning material he wants, and the computer can keep
track of the student's progress and tailor the presentation exactly to his needs.
Creation of training applications takes a different kind of software than that used
for business presentations, because a rich interactive environment is needed.

Multimedia training is also extremely effective in teaching someone how to use
a computer program, and many recent releases of productivity and multimedia
programs include multimedia tutorials right in the box.

The inherent complexity of such applications means that creating training
applications is more difficult than doing presentations. However, with the right

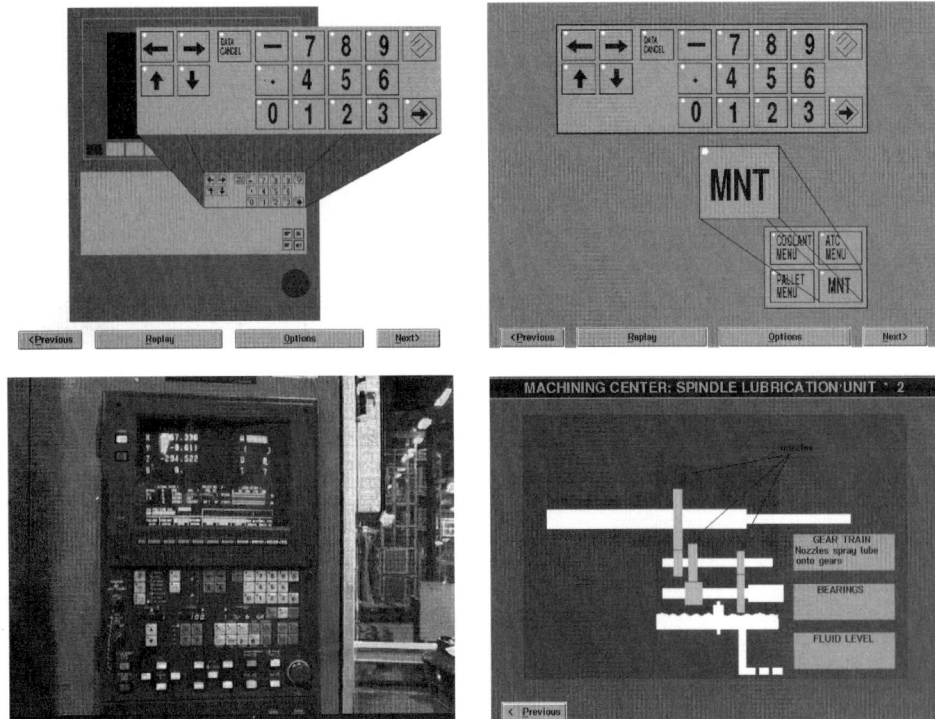

Figure 1.3 Sample screens from training applications — courtesy of Caterpillar, Inc.

software, it is still something that can be done without any programming skill. Figure 1.3 shows some examples of training screens, which were provided by Caterpillar, Inc. These examples are from several applications that teach maintenance procedures for numerical control equipment. The applications were created using the *MEDIAscript OS/2* authoring tool.

Information Delivery Applications

Many multimedia applications exist in order to give a user access to some class of data. Vast collections of data are in the form of books, catalogs, libraries, audio tapes, video tapes, or still photographs. Any of these can be captured in digital format and presented by a multimedia computer; this is called *information delivery*. Because the computer can also manipulate the data or search it, the access and presentation can be much more effective than using the data in its original form.

Authoring for information delivery is a special case, because of the need for handling a large database, and also for the special types of interactivity that are required. There are programs called *retrieval engines*, which can handle all the needs of an information delivery application, but you will be limited to the user-interface style of the retrieval engine. If you want to design your own user interface for an information delivery application, or to combine retrieval with other metaphors (such as simulation or animation), then you may have to program your own application using one of the full-featured language-based assembly packages. Another choice is to combine your authored application with a stand-alone retrieval package using the *interprocess communication* techniques that are a part of the newest operating systems.

Another activity that looms large in creating information delivery applications is the *data preparation.* This is the task of processing the raw data from its original source format(s) into a consistent format that is suitable for access by the retrieval technology of the application. When large databases are involved, the data preparation can grow to be 90 percent of the work of completing the application. There are special tools available for many data preparation tasks.

An important medium for distribution of data for information delivery and other applications is the *CD-ROM* disc. A single 12-cm plastic disc can store up to 650 megabytes of data—that's 250,000 pages of text, up to 40,000 still images, or 72 minutes of full-screen motion video! The CD-ROM disc can easily be 100 times smaller than what it would take to reproduce its contents on paper.

A special class of information delivery application is on-line technical manuals for large vehicles or systems, such as an aircraft or a military system. These systems often require dozens of manuals, filling many shelves. In most cases, a PC system using CD-ROM delivery is actually smaller and lighter than the manuals, making it possible to keep the system on board a vehicle, so it will be available regardless of where the vehicle goes. Technical manuals usually have a lot of text and a lot of visuals in the form of photographs and drawings. A multimedia computer can easily handle all that, and it offers additional access features when compared to print media. A PC can actually enhance the effectiveness of technical manuals by adding animation and video to assist the presentation of difficult concepts or procedures. Finally, the task of keeping manuals up to date is often overwhelming when handled in printed form. With digital media such as CD-ROM, updating can take the form of a new disc at every update time — the user simply inserts the disk and an automatic update takes place. No more fiddling with looseleaf pages or other forms of print updating.

Sales or Merchandising Applications

Selling combines information delivery with other capabilities such as demonstration, quotation, negotiation, order taking, and so on. The information delivery capability is an excellent front end for a program that sells products. A user can browse a database to find out about a range of products; see them demonstrated using audio, video, or simulation; and access specifications and price lists. If the user wishes to buy or order a product, he can then move to a different part of the application to place orders and to arrange delivery and payment. The sale paperwork can be prepared by the computer and, with an interface to the store's main computer, the sale can be consummated. Of course, the computer doesn't have to complete the sale; the system can be designed for a live salesperson to take over at any point in the process.

You have probably seen systems like this in automobile dealerships, shopping malls, and a few supermarkets. They are usually in the form of a *kiosk*, which is a stand alone cabinet containing the computer and a touch-screen display. It is an important application of multimedia, and it's one that is easily cost-justified when placed in a location that gets a lot of traffic by potential customers.

Authoring for sales applications is usually done by programming in an authoring language. This is because these applications combine multimedia information delivery with other computer tasks such as preparing orders, contracts, or invoices. Also, most of these applications are intended for use by the general public, which requires a custom user interface where all computer-style artifacts are hidden. Retrieval engine programs are not usually designed for that kind of user.

Multimedia with Productivity Applications

There are many opportunities to use multimedia with productivity applications. Probably the best of these is using multimedia presentations for on-line help and tutorials. This class of application is a combination of information delivery and training, and it usually requires programming in an authoring language or even in a programming language such as C. Since such applications are done by the developer of the productivity application itself, the need for sophisticated programming is not usually a problem.

Productivity applications such as spreadsheets, charting programs, or database programs create screens that are displayed to show the user's data or calculations. It is valuable if the user can add multimedia objects to these screens so that he can use audio or video to support or explain his screens. If the productivity application has multimedia capabilities built in, this is easy; however, it will be some time before all the productivity vendors do that. Meanwhile, there is another way: using interprocess communication (IPC) protocols such as *Dynamic Data Exchange* (DDE) or *Object Linking and Embedding* (OLE), which are available in *Windows* and OS/2, and which most productivity applications do support.

Interprocess communication is useful when you have two (or more) applications running concurrently. One is your productivity application, and the other is a *multimedia server* application. A server knows all about multimedia and can run audio, video, or other multimedia objects on command from another application via IPC. So, for example, a user can add a button to his spreadsheet to play an audio explanation of the spreadsheet. When someone clicks the button, a command is sent to the multimedia server telling it to play an audio file, which the user recorded ahead of time. Similarly, video can be played by having the server open a separate window on top of the spreadsheet to display the video. When no commands are active for the server, it can make itself invisible by closing or hiding all its windows.

Teleconferencing

Although they are essential to the conduct of many businesses, meetings are expensive propositions, especially when the participants have to travel. Material has to be prepared and printed on paper, and everyone has to interrupt their regular work to attend. The technologies of digital networks and multimedia promise to alleviate may of these problems through what is called *teleconferencing*. With teleconferencing, one can participate in a meeting without leaving his desk or workstation, and he can still obtain the kind of audio-visual experience he would get by travelling to a live meeting.

Teleconferencing has been done for years with a combination of special-purpose analog and digital equipment. However, these systems were so expensive that they were usually built into special rooms where you went to hold a teleconference. Now, the same things can be done with the multimedia PC on your desktop, and everyone can have his own system. The key is a high-speed digital network connecting all systems, and most corporations are installing such networks. Although software for teleconferencing is still scarce, it represents probably the largest potential for the use of multimedia computing in business.

Authoring for teleconferencing is the same as any other use of multimedia if you are preparing the material before the conference takes place. However, the dynamics of a meeting may require authoring on the fly during the meeting; for example, when you want to present something at the meeting but it could not be prepared ahead of time. Therefore, teleconferencing software will need special tools to facilitate presentation of any kind of material during the meeting, whether authored ahead of time or not.

STANDARDS

Before going deeper into the authoring process and its tools, it is necessary to consider the important issue of *standards*. Standards are formally defined objects or systems that can be and are used by many manufacturers. A good example is the IBM PC architecture, which is the basis for the majority of today's personal computers. This is a hardware standard that was originally put forth by IBM, but adopted by many manufacturers of PCs, and now has been enhanced and evolved by the work of several industry groups. The PC standard allowed the market to develop because it ensured that all platforms presented the same interface to application software.

This was accomplished by a two-step process: First, a built-in software module called a BIOS (Basic Input/Output System) allows the machine to interface to *operating system software*, such as Microsoft MS-DOS, which then delivers a standard *Application Programming Interface* (API) to all application programs. A manufacturer wanting to produce a compatible machine creates his own BIOS to provide the standard operating system interface. Other operating systems, competing with MS-DOS, have to present the same interface to the BIOS and the same API to be compatible. Because all of this is standardized, there can be multiple vendors of hardware platforms, operating systems, and application programs.

Of course, multimedia applications benefit from standardization the same as any other applications, but multimedia demands more because it often requires special hardware, and it creates special kinds of data. There are hundreds of suppliers of multimedia hardware and software, and the potential is very high for the proliferation of different hardware and software standards. This problem cannot be solved by a single standard coming at the beginning from one source in the way that the IBM PC started, because there is already a large industry competing to develop multimedia.

However, there are several industry initiatives that are dealing with the standards issues. First, the *Multimedia PC Marketing Council*, an industry group of PC manufacturers, has developed a specification for a *Multimedia PC* (MPC). The MPC specification is a definition of the *minimum* content of multimedia features that qualify a PC product to carry the MPC logo, shown in Figure 1.4. Software products can also carry the logo, if they guarantee to operate on any machine meeting or exceeding the MPC specification. Because the MPC spec is a minimum, PC manufacturers can compete by offering more than the minimum, and

Figure 1.4 The logo of the Multimedia PC

software vendors can make their products so that they will perform better on hardware that exceeds the MPC minimum requirements. The MPC specification is described further in Chapter 3.

Another multimedia standardizing initiative comes from the way operating system developers such as Microsoft and IBM are creating their systems. The objective is to have a single API presented to all applications for multimedia, regardless of the hardware that is contained in the system. Applications should be able to tailor their operation to the available hardware of the system in which they reside, and users should not have to worry about this problem. This is done by creating an open-ended multimedia interface in the operating system. Without getting into too much detail, this is done by a special operating system module called the *Media Control Interface* (MCI) and by using a software module called a *driver* with each piece of hardware. The hardware's driver connects the hardware to MCI, and MCI connects to the application program. The result is that if you install the correct driver with each piece of hardware you install, any MCI-knowledgeable application will be able to talk to your hardware.

The data format part of the multimedia standards issue is more difficult. There are already dozens of formats for image data, audio data, and video data, which have been developed by different companies over the past ten years or so. Each of these worked in the particular arena addressed by its parent company. However, multimedia now is reaching broader markets, and the various niche approaches are incompatible. Major players, such as Microsoft and IBM, have published their formats for anyone to use, and other companies are in the business of selling conversion software.

A third initiative, which may help sort out the data format issue, is the IBM Ultimedia Tools Series program. (Ultimedia is IBM's trade name for multimedia products.) In the Tools Series program, a group of multimedia authoring, presentation, and editing product vendors, led by IBM, have designed a unified specification, which guarantees that authoring products will work together and will have a degree of uniformity in their author interfaces. (Each product of course retains its own unique metaphor, but *generic* tasks should be uniform between products.) Already, a large number of vendors have joined the program. IBM also has set up a centralized marketing and customer support organization for the Ultimedia Tools Series program. The Ultimedia Tools Series documents could well be the basis for future multimedia authoring standards which would be supported throughout the industry.

SUMMARY

Multimedia on personal computers is creating a new opportunity for PCs to become even more effective in business, education, and the home, while at the same time becoming easier to use and more friendly. By the use of authoring software, anyone can create presentations that embody realistic audio, images, and video along with traditional computer data and graphics. New industry standards are emerging that will soon lead to multimedia capabilities in every PC.

2

The Authoring Process

In the previous chapter, the authoring process was likened to the making of a movie, and the major steps of the process were outlined. In this chapter, that discussion extends, covers the steps in more detail, and begins to characterize authoring software relative to each of the authoring steps.

WHY AUTHORING SOFTWARE IS NECESSARY

You may be wondering why special programs are required to work with multimedia when the same capabilities can be addressed through normal programming languages, or by adding multimedia objects to productivity applications such as spreadsheets, word processors, or databases. For programming, the answer boils down to the inherent complexity of working with multimedia. If an author has to deal with all of the details of multimedia, as is required when using a programming language, it becomes a formidable task. When adding multimedia objects to productivity applications, the approach works well with one or two multimedia objects at a time, but it becomes difficult to create complex multimedia screens this way. The objective of an authoring program is to make all that easy: To allow an author to create multimedia objects, sequences, or entire applications without having to worry about the details of programming for multimedia. The attainment of that objective also depends on answers to other questions, such as: How skilled is the author, what type of application is intended, and how complex is the application? These factors can conflict, so an authoring system designer often has to make tradeoffs between them; that is one reason there are so many different authoring products on the market. For example, an authoring program designed to be used by an author with limited skills will have a hard time supporting the most complex types of applications, because the most complex applications are best addressed by the use of programming concepts, which an unskilled author probably cannot handle.

Eventually, all productivity applications will have built-in multimedia authoring—you will be able to call up multimedia objects directly from your spreadsheet or word processor. However, waiting for that will hold back the growth of multimedia. Multimedia companies, which have the most to gain from the success of the technology, are making the investment to design authoring systems so multimedia can be used immediately. This is not as bad as it sounds because modern operating systems have ways for multimedia programs and productivity programs to run simultaneously.

It has been said that the integration of multimedia into productivity programs will make authoring tools unnecessary. That is an oversimplification, because it will not be practical to build complex interactive applications using productivity tools—authoring programs will still be needed for that. Once a complex multimedia object has been authored, you will be able to call it up from your spreadsheet or your word processor. Authoring will not become obsolete!

STEPS OF AUTHORING

The broad steps of authoring (from Chapter 1) are:

- Concept
- Design
- Collecting content material
- Assembly
- Testing
- Distribution

These steps are not always followed in the order shown. Especially in large projects, different steps for various parts of the application may be proceeding in parallel. Authoring is an *iterative* process, and steps may be repeated as the testing process shows that changes are required. However, in all cases, the planning steps (concept and design) must occur first. I will discuss each step in detail.

Concept

The objectives for the project are defined at the concept stage. This includes identifying the application audience, the kind of application (presentation, interactive, etc.), the purpose of the application (inform, entertain, teach, etc.), and the general subject matter. Ground rules for the design stage should also be set at this time; things such as style, application size, target platforms, etc., may be specified. The usual output of the concept stage is a *treatment* document, which is a narrative description of the proposed project.

There are not many ways that authoring software can help the concept-defining task. Mostly it is the author and/or her management who must decide about these things, and all it takes to create the treatment document is a word processor.

Design

The purpose of the design stage is to specify in detail the project architecture, the styles, and all of the content material that will be needed. The objective should be to generate enough detail so that the following stages of content collection and assembly can be carried out without more decisions. However, it doesn't often happen that way, and it is common for new material to be selected or parts of the application to be added, deleted, or changed at very late stages in the project. One measure of an authoring system is to see how well it tolerates that sort of revision.

Authoring software begins to be valuable at the design stage and it is convenient to place the design parameters into the authoring system as they are being determined. Then the authoring system can take over the task of documenting the design, and it can keep that information in a form that can move directly into the content collection and assembly stages without any further manual entry. Authoring features that help in this way include: outlining, storyboarding, flow charting, and scripting. Many of these features have been highly developed in authoring packages intended for business presentations. For example, most presentation products have a "storyboard" or "slide sorter" view that shows the screens of a presentation arrayed in the order in which they will be presented. An example is shown in Figure 2.1. Typically, a storyboard view allows the order of the presentation to be changed by dragging around the screen icons, and sometimes you can go directly into the editing of a screen by double-clicking on its icon in the storyboard view.

Presentation software usually offers the choice of an outline view to enter and edit the content of a text bullet chart presentation, as shown in Figure 2.2 for Lotus Freelance. Storyboard or outline views are easy to understand for linear presentations, but they become awkward to represent an application containing interactivity and branching. In that case, a flow chart view is more useful, although even that breaks down when the interactivity becomes complex, because you get too many crossing lines. At that point, a simpler representation may be better;

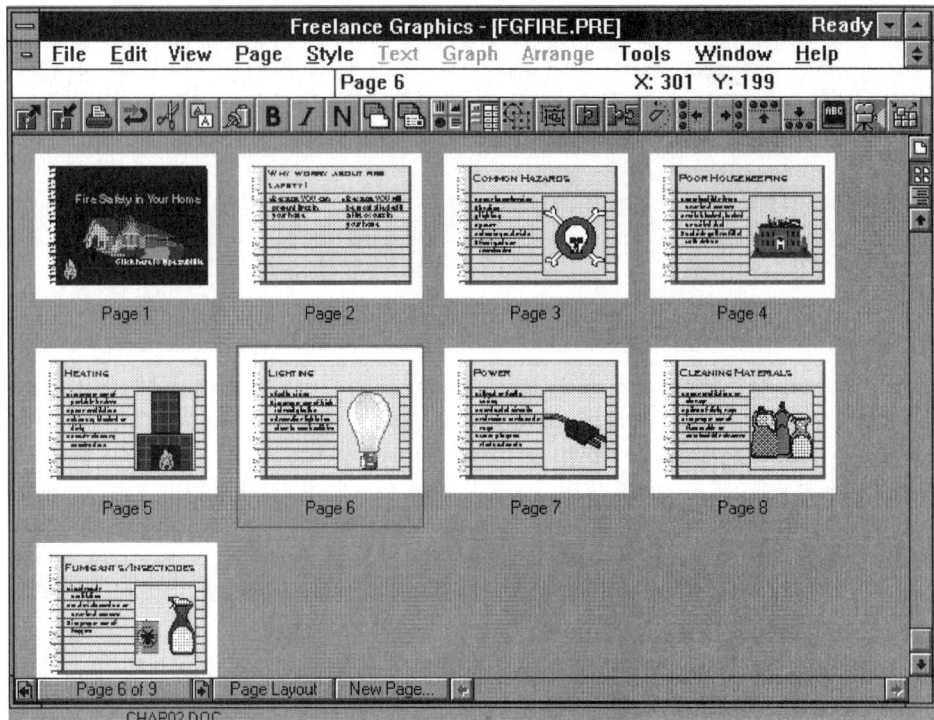

Figure 2.1 The storyboard view from Lotus *FreeLance* presentation authoring software

for example, the network node view used by the *MEDIAscript* Organizer, shown in Figure 2.3. In this view, you can navigate the application by clicking on the left and right arrows. The figure shows an application that starts with the script "begin", which is a menu having six choices. Each choice launches another script; when those scripts end, control return to "begin".

The other task in the design stage of a multimedia project is to decide about all the content material, including text and database files, audio, video, and still images. The objective should be to generate lists of the material to be acquired, found, or created so that it can all be collected in the next stage. Authoring software typically does not help much with this task, although some systems allow you to enter dummy file names, which can be followed up later with real files. If you can use dummies, then the authoring system will keep track of the content for you, and the objective of the next task is simply to remove all dummy content names from the project. If this will not work for you, then you should manually generate lists of content, which will serve to manage the content collection process.

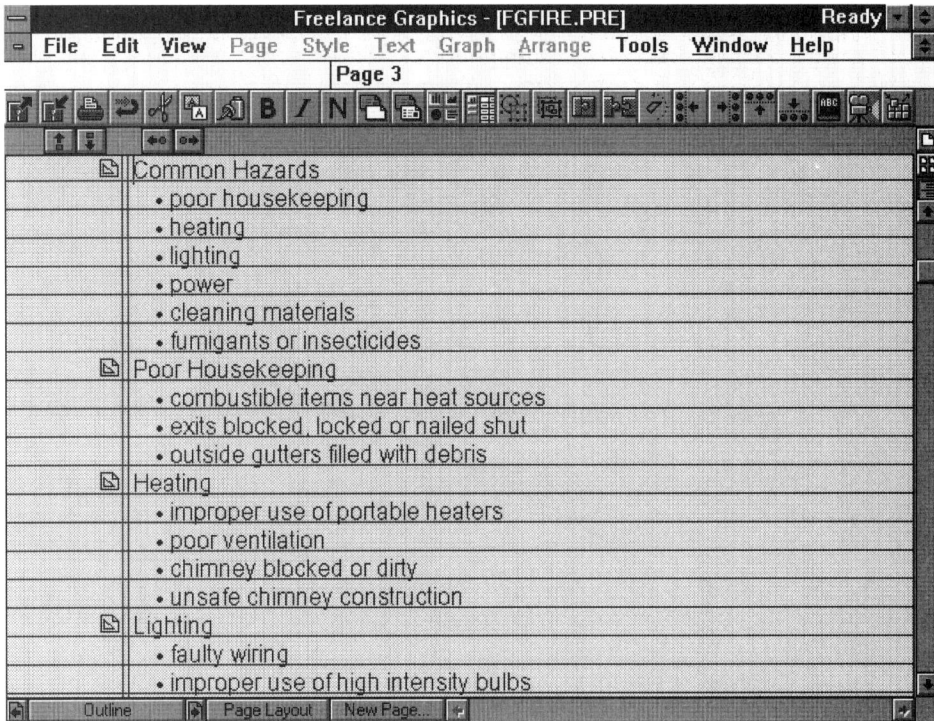

Figure 2.2 The outline view from Lotus *FreeLance*.

Collecting Content Material

Working from the content lists created in the design stage, an author or her helpers must collect all the content material for the project. This can often be done in parallel with the assembly stage, especially if the authoring system allows dummy content to be used until the real files are available. Content material is obtained either by selecting it from available internal sources or libraries, acquiring it from outside sources, or creating it in-house specifically for the project. Authoring systems assist these tasks in several ways.

When you are selecting existing content either from internal or outside sources, you don't need any creation tools; however, you may need file conversion or editing tools to conform the foreign material to the formats required by your system. Authoring systems vary in the amount of support they offer for these tasks, and it is important to make sure that you will be able to work with the material that you get. There are also many stand-alone software packages for file conversion, image processing, audio or video editing, and text processing. With a multitasking operating system such as DOS/Windows or OS/2, you will not have

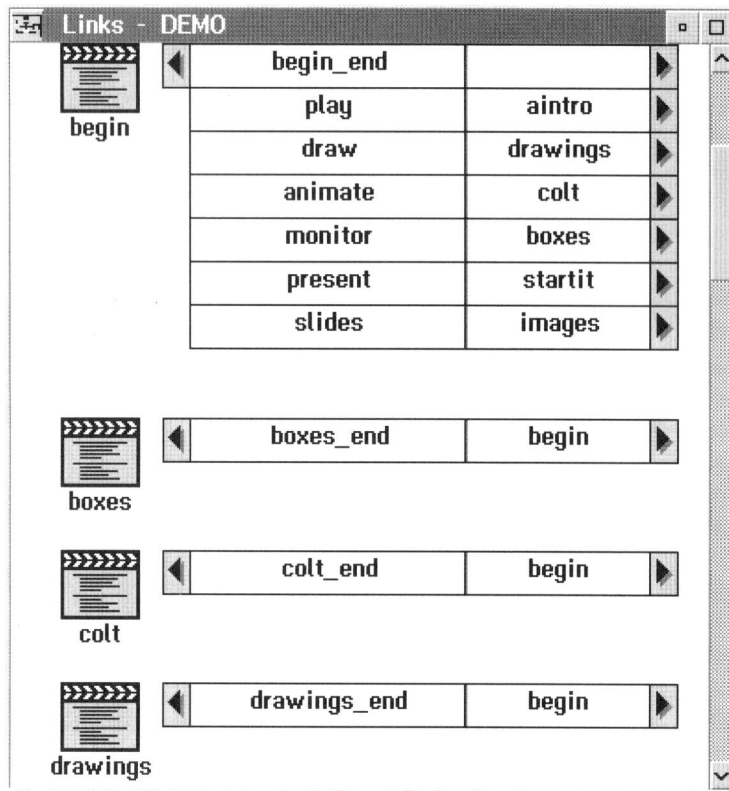

Figure 2.3 The network node view used in *MEDIAscript*

any trouble or inconvenience from selecting stand-alone tools for these tasks, because the tools can coexist on your desktop with your principal authoring package. The operating system will allow you to move rapidly between working in the authoring system or working with a separate media tool, and the multimedia files can move between applications via the hard disk.

Creating your own content poses some additional problems. Besides having the necessary hardware and software, you also must have the appropriate skills to do the creation task. For example, if you are going to create your own drawings, you must have some artistic skill and experience. Some authoring systems, particularly for presentations, give you templates, "master" screens, or clip art libraries so that you can create illustrated sequences without any drawing skill. These are good for giving you a quick start but, in the long run, you may find that your output always looks the same and starts getting boring. You have to make your own decision about that.

Creation of text objects requires word processing software, images require paint or drawing software or image capture hardware and software (to acquire images from real scenes or from hard copy), audio requires audio capture hardware and software, video requires video capture and compression hardware and software, and animation requires animation software. Some authoring systems have certain of these features built-in, but typically they will be limited when compared to stand-alone programs for the purpose. For the best results, you will want stand-alone tools for the objects that are most important to your work. Again, in a multitasking environment, these tools can be readily integrated with your other authoring software. Later chapters will cover audio, video, image, and animation authoring in much more detail.

Assembly

The entire application or project is put together in the assembly stage. Depending on the amount of support that your authoring software has given to the earlier stages, there will be practically no work in this stage, or you will have to do it all. Presentation packages, for example, do their assembly while you are entering the content for the various screens. Once you have defined all the screens and placed then in order, the presentation is ready to run. The price you pay for this convenience is that you will have no or little interactivity, and there will be some limitations about what can be on any one screen. On the other hand, if you don't need anything more, then certainly use a presentation authoring program. You will get professional results with very little effort.

If your authoring package has flowcharting features that you used for the design stage, you will also find that most of the assembly is already done. The authoring software will build the program structure from the flowchart, and your work will consist mostly of plugging content material into the screens shown on the flowchart.

When your application involves a lot of interactivity and very complex or dynamic screens, you will find that most authoring will revert to detail work, sometimes almost programming. If you need to create this kind of application, you must have the necessary skills yourself or work with someone who does. There is a limit to what any authoring package can do to simplify complex or diverse tasks. You can alleviate this problem somewhat if you can characterize your intended applications as a series of modules that are similar.

Most high-end authoring software packages, particularly those that have a full authoring language, can be operated in a modular mode where a skilled programmer can create custom modules that fit the specific needs of your applications. Once this is done, you can pull up the modules as you need them, plug in the appropriate content material, and have your application. The custom programming has to be done only once. This mode of operation is especially valuable when a large application has one or more procedures that occur over and over with the only difference being the content data that is used. For example, an application based on a large database of related information will need display routines that show groups of data selected by the user. Often an engine program can be written to display the data exactly as you want it, based only on some file names, record numbers, or other pointers to the specific data to display. In this kind of application, once the engine programs are built, the only other assembly task is the organizing of the database for access.

Testing

Once the application is built and the content material is plugged in, you need to test it to be sure that everything works and looks the way you want it. In fact, you will probably do a lot of this while you are assembling the application, and it is very important that an authoring system allow you to easily view and check your work as you go along. Fortunately, most systems have extensive features for testing, letting you "run" your application partially or fully, and reporting errors that occur while running. For example, if you call for a data file that is missing, the authoring system will tell you about that, and maybe even help you find it on your hard disk.

More sophisticated authoring requires advanced features like single-stepping, reporting of variable values during execution, or tracing program flow. The high-end systems have such features, but of course they require more skill to understand and use. You need this only if you are doing the kind of sophisticated work that requires it.

An important issue in testing is to make sure the application works in the actual environment of the end user, not just in your authoring machine. Typically, when you are creating applications for use by others, they will not have the same computing environment that you do, and often their environment will be less powerful than yours. In these cases, you must test your application in the actual target environment to be sure that everything is OK. Since your users should not have to own the expensive authoring software that you do, most authoring systems offer an inexpensive or free runtime module that allows an end user to run an authored application. If you are using this approach, you should also be sure to test your work with the actual runtime module.

Finally, your testing should take account of the possibility that your end user is not as skilled in multimedia as you are. You should test with typical end users to make sure that they can use your application by themselves. This is especially important for interactive applications, which inherently have some form of user interface; you must confirm that your user can understand and use the interface you provide.

Distribution

If your application is intended to be run by someone else on a different machine, you must deal with the problem of copying or transmitting the application to one or more other machines. You may be concerned with floppy disk, CD-ROM, tape, or network distribution, and your authoring system needs to include the features to make this possible. An application typically will include a number of different files—sometimes a very large number of them—and you need ways of collecting all the files for an application and placing them on the desired distribution medium. Some authoring systems help you with this, some don't. Often you can solve this problem yourself simply by the way you arrange the material on your hard disk. If you can group all the files for a project into a single directory, then the subsequent management of that data will be simple.

CHOOSING AN AUTHORING ENVIRONMENT

As you can see from the foregoing discussion, authoring may require special hardware and one or more special software packages. The combination of all that is called an authoring *environment.* Before you can do any authoring, you must create your own authoring environment. It should be tailored specifically to you and the kinds of things you want to do. In fact, the two most important factors that affect the choice of your authoring environment are:

- The kind of applications that you want to author
- You

The hardware and software that you choose must be able to create applications containing the features *you* need, and it must be able to do that with *you* at the controls. Beyond that, you are looking at factors such as price, support, personal preference, etc. These are also important and you must evaluate them, but the two major issues above will typically let you narrow the choice down to a smaller number of possibilities before you consider the less important factors. Chapter 11 discusses the characterization of your applications and yourself, in order to develop a specification for the authoring system you need. That chapter also discusses how to evaluate potential authoring systems against this specification.

TYPES OF AUTHORING SOFTWARE

In the discussion of authoring systems, some characterizing terminology must be defined. The first level of this is to define the *style* of authoring. The style is the basic metaphor that an author works with when using the system. There are two styles: *command* and *object*. These have nothing to do with whether the system is graphical or text-based, rather they refer to the underlying organization of authoring. Many authoring systems will use both style types, often in different places or at different levels. The following describes each in more detail.

Command Style

In a command-style authoring system, an application is built by stringing together lists of *commands* or *keywords*, just like a programming language. Most commands will require *parameters* that tell the system about arguments and options for that command; this also is like programming. Any programmer would be comfortable with this style, but nonprogrammers may not be. A full-featured system will have 100 or more commands, which an author has to learn how to use and place them together. Usually, the rules for combining the commands are similar to programming logic, simply because there are a lot of people who already understand that.

Authoring of anything more than a linear presentation requires a means for *conditional program control*, in order to build structures other than straight lines. For example, menu selection requires a *branching* method, and many applications will require *loops* or *subroutines*. In command style, the natural way to do these things is to use well-known programming constructs such as *goto, if-then-else, while, do,* and *for*. Of course, this leaves the nonprogrammer behind.

A command-style system is easily implemented with a textual interface, where the commands are typed into an editor. However, command style can also be implemented with an icon-based interface by defining one icon per command. Typically, each icon will have an associated window for selection or input of arguments and options.

The key indicator of a command-style authoring system is the existence of the large list of commands. If a system has such a list that authors must learn, then it is a command-style system. The advantage of command style is that the large number of commands gives extreme flexibility to create any kind of application.

Object Style

An object-style authoring system typically operates at a higher level than command style. There will be a number of *objects* that the author works with, not more than 20 or 30. Each object carries a set of *properties* and a *behavior* that allow it to perform a complete task. For example, an audio object will do everything needed to play a clip of audio. Similarly, an image object will do everything needed to display an image. The authoring process becomes one of selecting objects, defining their properties and any nondefault behavior, and placing them together in the order that they should be executed. You might say that this is the same thing you do with commands, but with objects you do it at at a higher level, and you have fewer types of objects than commands to learn and use.

Object-style authoring system design becomes most creative when addressing the need for conditional program control. This is difficult to do without introducing some programming concepts, but many systems have tried it. Most have defined some special objects for this, with varying degrees of success.

Because objects have a less abstract nature than commands, it is natural to represent them as icons rather than text. Thus, most object-style authoring systems use icons. Each object icon usually has a window behind it where the characteristics are entered for that object. It is also useful for each object to have *default* characteristics, which will apply if the object is placed in an application without defining any unique characteristics. For example, for an audio object, you must specify the name of the audio file to play (this is a *mandatory* characteristic), but the other aspects of behavior could be defaulted to cause playback at maximum volume to both left and right channels and to play the entire file from start to finish. The defaults would be changed if the author deliberately specified them.

Object-style authoring is typically easier to use than command style. However, the object organization may limit flexibility, and all kinds of applications may not be addressable. Object-style systems are best when they are designed specifically for certain classes of applications, rather than trying to design them to be everything to all authors.

AUTHORING INTERFACE TYPES

As mentioned above, another dimension of an authoring system is whether it uses a graphical or a text-based interface. Again, the approach may be different in different parts of the authoring system. Each of these is discussed in more detail below.

Text-Based Authoring Interface

A text-based interface simply means that the author enters information into the system by typing it from a keyboard, and the display shows a text screen. This type of interface may also use a mouse for things like menu selections, but the mouse is not the primary tool for the main input procedures.

Of course, there are parts of authoring that cannot avoid the use of text. For example, when the object being input is text itself, there is no way the author can avoid working with text, and the keyboard is the best tool for entering or editing text. Presumably, the author knows what she wants the text to say in the application, so there is no special learning process needed for her to enter the text.

However, when the task at hand does not involve text, such as choosing colors or defining windows or rectangles, a text interface becomes more difficult because the author must know some type of language or syntax to type the text that will specify a window, for example. These tasks are more naturally graphical, and text becomes a burden. However, even in graphical tasks there is a place for type-in input. It occurs when the author is entering physical dimensions and she wants a certain exact relationship to apply. For example, she may wish to create several windows of an exact size so that they will fit together into a pattern. Although there are graphical approaches to this also, it is often much more straightforward to simply provide type-in boxes where the author may (optionally) enter the exact numbers she desires. Another use for type-in is to enter variables or expressions that will allow a parameter to be calculated at runtime of the application. Thus, many authoring systems will provide both text and graphical input techniques for the same parameters.

Graphical Authoring Interface

The most common metaphor of a graphical interface is *drawing*. When drawing, the author uses a *pointing device* such as a mouse, touch screen, or graphic tablet to position objects on the screen. The technology for this is highly developed and becomes very intuitive once you learn a little about it. It is definitely the best approach for creating objects that are themselves graphical, such as windows or drawings.

On the other hand, if the task is to enter text, typing with a pointing device is very awkward. Thus, a graphical interface will usually still have a keyboard which will be used when the keyboard has an advantage. In fact, the best graphical interfaces will have a keyboard way to do *everything*; the author can choose which method to use for any task. As an author becomes familiar with her system, she will find that it is usually valuable to begin learning the keystroke commands instead of using the mouse for everything.

Because there are so many ways to build a graphical interface, the issue of *standards* becomes important. Graphical interface standards will help an author move between different authoring systems or applications, and she will learn how to operate the different interfaces simply by trying them. In the PC world, the most comprehensive graphical interface standard is presented in the *Object-Oriented Interface Design: IBM Common User Access Guidelines* (usually called the CUA Guide) document published by IBM. It is written for application designers and it describes a standard graphical interface and how it should be used. With version 3.1 of Windows, Microsoft has also published a similar document called *The Windows Interface: An Application Design Guide.* These two documents are very similar; if all multimedia application designers would follow one or the other of them, we would be close to having a graphical user interface standard for all PC software.

AUTHORING OPTIONS

Regardless of the type of authoring system or the type of author interface, there are different ways that authors can approach the task of application development. These different techniques may also affect the selection of authoring tools. One major dichotomy is whether an author chooses to build the application structure before or after obtaining all of the content material. It may seem awkward to try to build an application before you have all its ingredients, but it is possible, and it has some interesting advantages.

To author in this style, the author will specify dummy material for all of the content for the application. She will set up a naming convention at the outset, so that data file names can be placed into the application structure as it is being built. All of the data files (that haven't been created yet) are copies of dummy files, which may simply be empty, or they may be special dummies that identify themselves when displayed or played. The major advantage of this is that a working sample of the application can be built at the same time the structure is being designed; in fact, the structure authoring tool can be used to document the design.

Once the structure is built, the application can immediately be run for testing, using the dummy material. Bugs that may exist in the structure design can be seen and weeded out. Further, since the content material creation is usually the most expensive part of an application design project, it is valuable to do as much testing of the application concept as possible before the full investment is made in content material. That way, if the structural testing affects the choice of content material, no actual content that is already made gets lost. It takes a little planning to use the dummy material approach, because you have to set up your naming conventions and create a set of dummy files with those names. Not all authoring tools lend themselves to this approach, and therefore you have to consider this when choosing your tools.

Of course, if you are creating an application where the content material already exists, such as when you are using an existing database, then you can do all of the assembly authoring with the real content, and if something gets thrown out at a late stage, you haven't lost any new work. Many authors feel that assembly authoring is easier when all the actual content material is at hand, even though this approach precludes the assembly and testing having an effect on the content unless you will accept redo of content.

SUMMARY

The authoring process was described in detail, and the way that authoring software can help at each step was pointed out. It was also shown that the principal determinants for choice of authoring software are (a) the intended applications and (b) the author herself. Beyond that, the decision is more subjective.

Authoring systems may be divided between command-driven and object-driven styles. They can have text-based or graphical authoring interfaces. Of course, there are many other characteristics of an authoring system, based on the details about whether and how a system handles each of the many parts of authoring. This will be treated in depth in later chapters.

3

Platforms and Operating Systems

The platform underlies the multimedia authoring environment—it is the hardware and the system software that is common to all the applications or tools you use. Even though we usually think of the PC as a standard, there is an unbelievable selection of options from which we must choose our particular system. In fact, for many authoring situations, we must choose two systems—the system we will use for authoring, and a target system (sometimes called a delivery system) that will run our authored applications. This distinction is important, as you will see, because authoring requires all the system power and resources you can afford, but it may not take all that to simply run multimedia applications. When you are authoring applications that will run on a number of target systems, those systems can be less expensive than the one you use for authoring.

Some of the hardware and software choices become very technical, which is beyond the scope of this book. This chapter discusses hardware and operating systems without getting too technical. When technical considerations come up (and they will because this is a complex subject), I try to define the terms first, choosing language that will be easy for you to understand. For those of you who want more technical details, the Bibliography will lead you to more information.

HARDWARE PLATFORMS

A block diagram of a typical personal computer is shown in Figure 3.1. The units of the computer are connected to a system bus, which provides for digital data flow between all units (although not simultaneously, as described below).

CPU

The "heart" of the PC is the Central Processing Unit (CPU), which is an integrated circuit (IC) chip that performs digital processing under software control. The CPU works closely with the system memory (RAM) and the mass storage. All of these together determine the system performance, not just the CPU. In "IBM-compatible" PCs, the CPU is a member of the Intel x86 family (386, 486, etc.) or its equivalent from other manufacturers. CPUs come in different speeds, which are indicated by their clock frequencies—25 MHz, 33 MHz, etc. Larger numbers indicate faster CPUs, everything else being the same. The original design of the IBM PC/AT was a 16-bit system, but it used the 80286 CPU, which had 24-bit addressing capability. This meant the CPU could access up to 16 megabytes of system memory. However, the system software available at that time (DOS) limited the addressing to 20 bits, so only 1 megabyte of memory was actually usable by applications. With the introduction of the 386 CPU, addressing was increased to a full 32 bits, giving an address space of 4 gigabytes, although most system software still could not use that. Today, however, software is available or coming out that uses the full 32 bits, and for this reason you should not consider a system with less than a 386 processor.

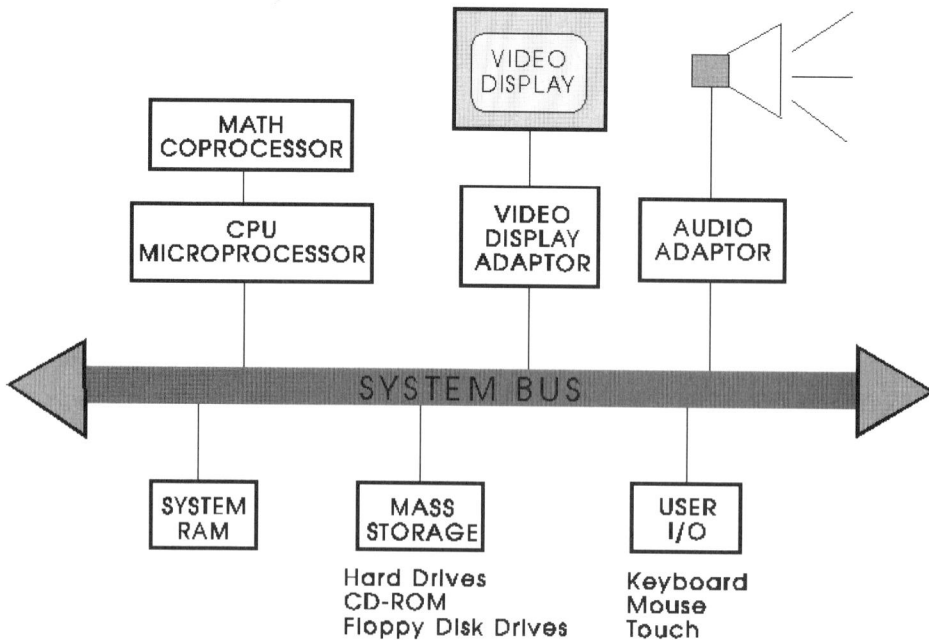

Figure 3.1 A block diagram of a typical PC system

RISC and CISC

The x86 series of processors described above are CISC (Complex Instruction Set Computer) microprocessors. The *instruction set* of a microprocessor refers to the native commands that the microprocessor understands. A microprocessor instruction set is always in the form of binary codes (numbers) that make up the program running on the chip. CISC means that the instruction set contains a large number of instructions, and a single instruction may take more than one CPU clock cycle to execute. There are other processors called Reduced Instruction Set Computers (RISC), which are designed with a simplified instruction set in which every instruction executes in one clock cycle. RISC processors are often used in engineering and graphics workstations, which require more processing power. However, the software for these platforms is different from PC software and it is not compatible with x86 software, nor will x86 software run on RISC platforms without some form of conversion or emulation process.

Microsoft has announced the *Windows NT* operating system, which has versions that run on different processors, including some RISC machines. Application software designed for Windows NT should run on any platform that runs NT, regardless of the processor type. This is called *cross-platform* compatibility, and we can expect to see more of it in the future.

Pentium

Intel has announced their successor to the i486 CPU, called *Pentium*. This chip is the latest result of the continuing progression of integrated circuit technology that has made possible the astounding growth of microprocessor power over the last 25 years. Pentium promises to more than double system performance compared to today's best 486 machines. All present x86 software will run on Pentium, and there will be a considerable performance improvement, but to get the most from Pentium, software optimization (changes) will be needed. This is because Pentium has two complete processors within the one chip, and software has to change to achieve full loading of that parallel architecture. Pentium is just another step along the road for microprocessors. The next step is in the engineering laboratory today, and the step beyond that is being developed. We can expect to have to find ways to utilize more CPU power for some years to come.

RAM

The CPU works closely with the system's random access memory (RAM), which is an array of IC chips for temporary storage of digital data. RAM storage is called *volatile*, because it depends on power being continuously supplied to the RAM chips; if power is interrupted or turned off, all data in RAM is lost. For this reason, all computers have some form of permanent storage, called *mass storage*. Data to be accessed or processed by the CPU must first be brought into RAM. For example, if you need to process an image, the entire image is first moved from mass storage into RAM; the CPU then processes the image, often by making another copy of it in RAM. When the process is complete, the new image may go back to disk, or it may be copied to the video display so the user can see it. Processing and displaying large images takes large blocks of RAM, and the more you have, the more your system can do. RAM storage is specified in megabytes (MB), which are millions of bytes. Typical RAM sizes for multimedia range from 4 to 16 megabytes. RAM storage is much faster than disk, and its speed is limited mostly by the system bus speed.

Mass Storage

For permanent storage of data, the computer has mass storage, which is usually disk storage—floppy diskettes or hard disks. Magnetic hard disks have the greatest capacity and the fastest speeds, and all PCs today have hard disk storage. Storage capacity is specified in megabytes, and hard disk speeds are specified by access time (how long it takes to find the start of a specific block of data), usually given in milliseconds (thousandths of a second—ms), and by data transfer rate (how fast the block of data can be moved into RAM), usually given in megabits per second. A typical hard disk unit might store 100 MB and have an access time of 18 ms. The data transfer rate is not widely specified for hard disks and, in fact, it is a characteristic of not just the hard disk, but also its interface, determined by its controller. Typical PC hard disk transfer rates range from 1 to 15 megabits/second.

The most common hard disk interface is the Integrated Disk Electronics (IDE) system. A faster interface is the Extended System Disk Interface (ESDI), and this is often used for the larger hard disk sizes. However, the best interface for multimedia is the Small Computer System Interface (SCSI—pronounced *scuzzy*). A SCSI controller creates its own bus, separate from the system bus, on which you can install up to eight SCSI devices. The devices may be hard disks, CD-ROM drives, image scanners, or any other devices having a SCSI interface.

The CD-ROM drive is a most important mass storage device for multimedia use. Based on the familiar audio Compact Disc (CD), it can hold up to 680 megabytes of digital data on a 12-cm (4.5") plastic disc that costs only a few dollars to replicate. In multimedia terms, 680 megabytes of data means 250,000 pages of text, thousands of still images, tens of hours of audio, or even an hour or more of full-motion video. CD-ROM drives are significantly slower than magnetic hard disks—access times are 200 ms or more, and data transfer rates go only up to 300 kB per second. Also, the CD-ROM is a read-only device—you cannot write your own data onto a CD-ROM disc. Therefore, you still need another kind of mass storage for read/write use — usually a magnetic hard disk; but CD-ROM is a fantastic medium for distribution of multimedia data.

The magnetic hard disk is currently the most satisfactory kind of read/write mass storage; it is fast and reliable. However, other read/write mass storage devices are on the market; they usually offer some advantage compared to magnetic disks, such as removable media or greater storage capacity, but there is usually a tradeoff in access speed and often the price. Typical of these are the *Write-Once, Read Many* (WORM) drives that are optical like CD-ROM and can be written only once at any location. There are also optical drives that can create a disc that will play in a CD-ROM drive—these are expensive, but they are important tools in developing for CD-ROM or for doing small-quantity distributions.

Video Display

For multimedia use, the most important part of the PC is its video display capability, which includes the video display monitor, and a video display adaptor board, which provides the interface between the computer and the display monitor. There are many variations of video display; some support good multimedia, and many don't. Most PCs today have a VGA (Video Graphics Array) display system, which is a standard format that displays 640 × 480 pixels with 16 colors for each pixel. (A pixel is a single point in the image—640 × 480 means that the entire image is displayed by an array of pixels that has 640 pixels across in a line, with 480 lines of pixels vertically, a total of 307,200 pixels.) The size of the pixel array is called the resolution, and, superficially, you can say, the more the better.

There are several things that are significant about the numbers 640 and 480. Since the video display is processed by a digital computer that works most efficiently when things are related to powers of 2, most resolution numbers will resolve to powers of 2 in a simple way. (Neither 640 or 480 is an exact power of 2, but the relationship is still simple.) But a more important consideration is that the numbers 640 and 480 are in a 4:3 ratio. That is because 4:3 is the ratio of the width to the height of a standard display screen, called the *aspect ratio*. When the pixel resolution numbers are in the same ratio as the aspect ratio, you get square pixels. There are some display systems that don't have square pixels (512 × 480, for example), and these work just fine. However, there are some problems when you try to use the same image data on both square and nonsquare pixel systems.

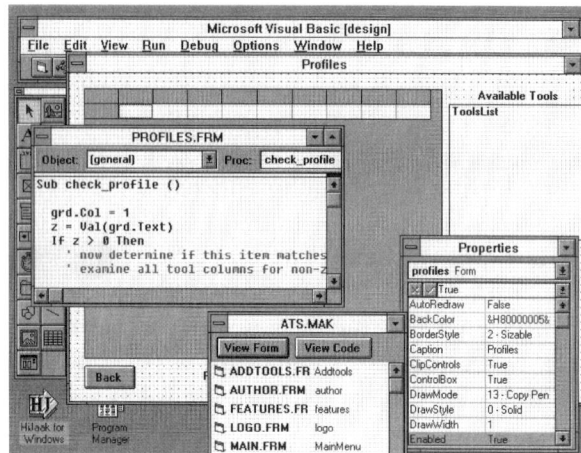

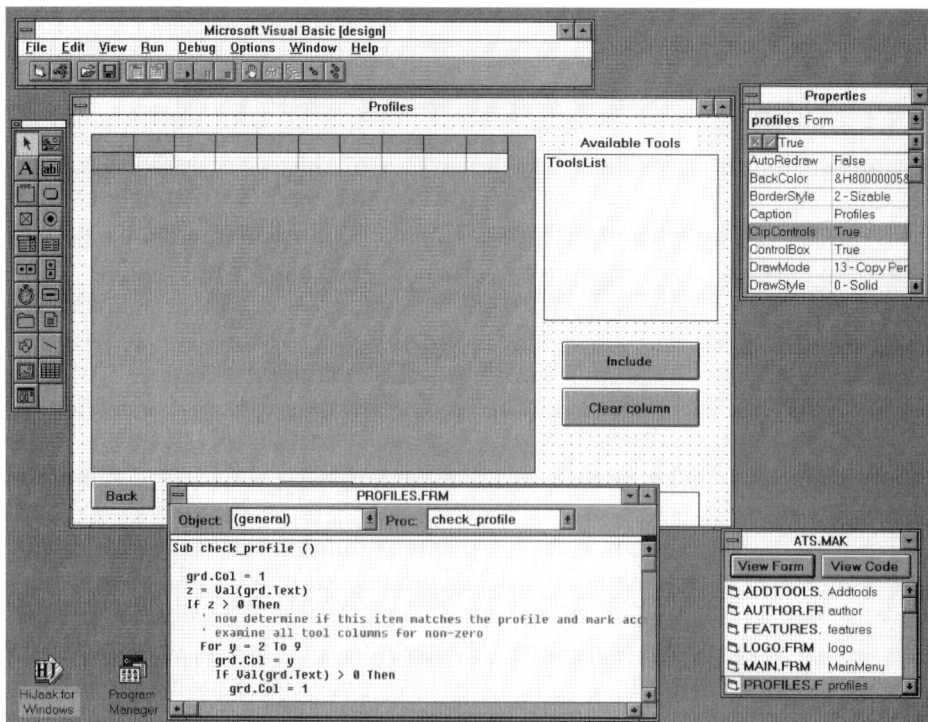

Figure 3.2 The same authoring environment shown on VGA (640 × 480) and super VGA (1024 × 768) screens.

The industry is moving toward everything having square pixels, but you should be aware of the distinction.

Because the amount of data required to fill the screen increases with higher resolutions, more resolution is not always better. More data means that higher-resolution screens will be slower, everything else being equal. Also, higher resolution means more RAM, and more mass storage is required. For normal viewing in a desktop situation on display screens up to 14", 640 × 480 pixels is enough resolution. It provides clean images without pixellation (when the pixels themselves become visible as tiny blocks making up the image). In an authoring situation, however, there are advantages to using a larger display screen with higher resolution. In particular, it gives you space on the screen to display more windows at once, or even to display a 640 × 480 window representing your application screen, along with other windows for authoring purposes. Therefore, for authoring you might want to consider super VGA (SVGA), which has resolutions up to 1024 × 768 pixels. Figure 3.2 shows a typical authoring environment (Visual Basic) on a 14" VGA or a 17" SVGA display. You can see that the SVGA gives much more room for multiple authoring windows.

Note that SVGA requires a larger display monitor screen for effective use. A small display may not have enough resolution to effectively show SVGA. The parameter of display monitors that affects this is the *dot pitch*, which gives the size of individual color dots on the display screen. Most small displays have a dot pitch of 0.28-mm or so, which is sufficient to show 640 × 480, but not enough to show all the detail in super VGA resolutions. Also, you have to get too close to a small screen to see more than 640 × 480 resolution, and that is uncomfortable. A comfortable viewing distance for most people is around 18"; with SVGA, that means the screen should be at least 17", and a 0.28 mm dot pitch at that size is OK. (Note that different monitor manufacturers have different interpretations of screen size numbers—when you are buying monitors, take along a ruler!) Of course, larger screens cost more, too, and you have to decide whether the advantages of higher resolution are worth the price.

Another solution to the problem of finding enough space on a display for all the things you want to look at during authoring is to use two display monitors. A few environments support this; usually, you use one screen for authoring dialogs and the second screen is just used to show your application running. Of course, you need two video display adaptors to do that. For most people, a single high-resolution screen will be a more reasonable solution—it's cheaper, and it takes less space on your desk.

When considering higher resolutions, you should avoid display systems that have interlaced screens. Interlacing means that the display updates only half of its lines of pixels for each vertical scan—every other line. The remaining lines are filled in on the next vertical scan. This allows the scanning rates of the display to be reduced, thereby lowering costs, but it has the disadvantage that it will show flicker on fine detailed edges or lines on the screen. Paying a little more for a noninterlaced display is worth it.

The number of colors displayed by the VGA is another serious problem. Although VGA colors can be specified to be anything, there are only 16 available at any one time. The usual choice is to make them the brightest colors available (red, green, blue, yellow, cyan, magenta, black, white), and each of the same colors reduced to half brightness. These colors make the prettiest computer screens, although they are not very useful when you want to display a natural image such as a photograph. There is a feature in most GUIs called dithering, where the system approximates other colors by creating patterns of the pixel colors which average out to a different color. This works well if you don't look closely, but on close examination of a dithered image, you will see the patterns and the image will look coarse. (Colors are discussed further in Chapter 6.)

Therefore, the first thing you should look for in a platform for multimedia use is a capability for displaying more colors at 640×480 resolution. (VGA can display 256 colors per pixel by reducing the resolution to 320×240, but that also looks coarse, and 256 colors is still not enough for realistic imagery.) Display adaptors are now available to support 32,768 or 65,536 simultaneous colors—16 bits per pixel (bpp), or even 16,777,216 colors (24 bpp) at VGA resolutions or higher. A 16 bpp system is sometimes called high color and 24 bpp is called true color.

The 16 bpp and 24 bpp formats are fundamentally different from the 4 bpp (16 colors) and 8 bpp (256 colors) used with VGA adaptors. The difference is that 16 and 24 bpp do not use a color palette, sometimes called a color lookup table. With a palette, the pixel values represent an index into the palette; the palette is a table that contains actual RGB (red, green, blue) values for the colors to be displayed. This way, you can display any color that the pixel depth of the palette supports (often 18 bits—262,144 colors), but you can use only as many different colors at a time as represented by the 4-bpp or 8-bpp pixel depths. Although you can sometimes display realistic looking images with a 256-color palette that has been chosen to match the image being displayed, you have to create a new palette for every image you show. This process becomes doubly awkward when you want to show more than one image at a time. You somehow have to construct an average palette that will reproduce all the images in a reasonable way.

All those problems are eliminated with 16 bpp or 24 bpp, because each pixel value represents an RGB color directly—there is no color lookup process. With 16 bpp, the bits are often proportioned with 5 bits for each primary color—this gives 32,768 colors. The 16th bit is unused or is used for a flag bit. Another 16-bpp format sometimes used is 6,5,5 (G,R,B), which gives 65,536 colors. With 24 bpp, 8 bits are used for each primary color.

The 24-bpp system gives 16 million colors, which is more than there are pixels in most images—but why would anyone need so many colors? Well, of course, we don't need more simultaneous colors than there are pixels, but we often want to choose the current colors from a larger range in order to match natural colors, and especially to reproduce smoothly shaded colors, such as flesh color. If there are not enough colors available to correctly reproduce smooth shading, the shaded area will show an error called *contouring*, where the transitions between adjacent colors become visible. On a smooth shaded region of an image, you can sometimes see the difference between 16 bpp and 24 bpp, but for most purposes, 16 bpp will be sufficient.

Using 16 bpp or 24 bpp also increases the amount of data required to refresh the screen, and it causes additional slowdown of display functions and also requires more memory and storage. The slowdown can be addressed by the use of an accelerator on the video display adaptor. An accelerator is a special IC chip, which operates directly on the display memory to perform common graphics functions. Because it does not have to go through the system bus as the CPU does, it can go as fast as the video display hardware can support. With resolutions or colors higher than VGA, an accelerator is essential.

You need 16 or 24 bpp for multimedia, and you should have higher resolution at least for authoring. To avoid slowdown, you also need a graphics accelerator. Numerous display boards have already been introduced with these features at attractive prices. However, video display is a rapidly moving field, with more new boards being introduced and prices still coming down.

Audio

Audio is the second most important multimedia capability after video display. Most PCs have limited audio capability—a small built-in speaker is controlled by a 1-bit driver. That does a good job of making beep sounds as needed for the computer to warn the user, but it is not at all capable of realistic speech, music, or other natural sound reproduction. However, a number of reasonably priced add-in boards are available that offer realistic sound reproduction, even stereo. A multimedia PC requires such a sound board. New PCs that are offered as multimedia PCs either have a board bundled in the package or, in a few cases, the capability is integrated onto the motherboard. We will see more of that in the future as multimedia grows in popularity.

Digital audio reproduction is accomplished by digitizing analog audio, in a format sometimes called WAVE audio. This requires a lot of data, sometimes as much as 100 KB per second. When the need is for music only, there is a better method—MIDI. This acronym stands ford *Musical Instrument Digital Interface*, and it is a technology developed in the music industry for digital control and communication between musical instruments such as synthesizers, keyboards, drum machines, etc. The MPC audio specification defines a MIDI synthesizer interface that can play instrumental music from multimedia data files. This takes from 10 to 50 times less data than digitizing the audio itself. Most of the audio add-in boards contain a synthesizer chip that meets or exceeds the MPC specification, making MIDI music a valid multimedia format.

Motion Video Capability

As we know from watching television, motion video can be a very powerful medium, and many multimedia applications would be much more effective with motion. You can easily add motion video to a computer by adding an analog video source such as a laser video disc or a VCR, along with a video overlay board to integrate the analog video into the computer display. This hardware approach has been in use for many years in the computer-based training (CBT) field, where video capability is extremely important.

However, analog video overlay needs the extra hardware (and the extra storage media used by that hardware), and the computer cannot do any modification or manipulation of the analog video. The video on the video disc or video tape must be exactly as it will be in the application; if you need simple variations, you must record each one separately and then select them while your application is running.

A much better approach is to use digital motion video, where the video data is just like any other computer data—stored on computer disks and capable of being processed by the computer to do anything you want with it. However, digital video is extremely demanding of both computer data capacity and processing power, and it is only recently that is has become practical at all on desktop systems.

The video display hardware already described can be used for "software-only" digital motion video, where we simply do everything needed to display video in software (remember—software can do anything!), but CPU processing power and bus data rates will limit the performance to only small windows, small numbers of colors, and low frame rates. Even so, software video is usable for many applications and, of course, performance will improve with future generations of systems that have faster CPUs and buses. However, if you need full-screen, full-frame rate motion video right now, you have to go to hardware assist to get it. There are several approaches on the market; one of the leading products is DVI Technology, developed by Intel and IBM.

DVI Technology is based on a chip set, manufactured by Intel, and called the i750 processors. These chips are programmable devices that can perform motion video compression and decompression in real time. Video compression of up to 150:1 is achievable, meaning that full-screen motion video at 30 frames per second can be delivered from CD-ROM discs, which have a data rate usually limited to 150 KB per second. The DVI chips have been packaged onto add-in boards by several companies, for both PCs and Macintosh computers. One board, marketed by IBM, is called *ActionMedia II*. It is a single-slot board, which includes the i750 processors, video RAM, an audio processor, and a special video display adaptor. It is available for most PC-compatible and IBM PS/2 computers.

ActionMedia II is usually used in combination with a VGA adaptor to create a very flexible system that can display motion video in any size window up to full screen, while all the normal VGA capabilities operate completely independently. The ActionMedia II board creates its own separate video display signal, which can be shown on a separate display monitor, or (preferred) it can be keyed into a standard VGA or XGA display to show everything on one screen. With the ActionMedia II keying, any area of the VGA display that is filled with a particular color (usually black) will show the DVI display. Thus, a black rectangle on the VGA screen becomes a DVI window. With this architecture, and the right operating system software, DVI video can be integrated seamlessly into any application, even ones that never heard of DVI Technology.

System Bus

Within the so-called "standard" IBM personal computer, there are three major categories of hardware, based on the type of system bus. The system bus connects all of the units of a computer, as shown in Figure 3.1, and it allows digital data to flow between any two units of the computer at a time, rapidly switching connections to support other pairs of units as needed by the task running on the computer. Because of this time-sharing of the bus, it can become a bottleneck when a lot of data has to be moved between units. Since multimedia computing uses large data objects for audio and video, bus performance is an important issue. Each bus type has its own unique hardware connections, so you must choose add-in boards that fit the bus type in your machine. The three bus types are:

1. AT-bus—This is the 16-bit bus originated by the IBM PC/AT, and it is the most common. It is also known as the ISA (Industry Standard Architecture) bus. The largest number of add-in boards fit this bus.

2. Microchannel—This is the bus introduced by the IBM PS/2 product line. It is a higher-performance 32-bit bus that has been used mostly by IBM. (32

bits means that 32 bits—4 bytes—of data are passed on each cycle of operation of the bus. This is a wider bus than 16 bits, and it is inherently faster.) The Microchannel bus is slightly more expensive than ISA, but is still considered to be in the same price range. However, few manufacturers other than IBM make boards for the Microchannel bus.

3. EISA—This is the Extended Industry Standard Architecture bus, which was developed by a consortium of companies to compete with IBM's Microchannel bus. It is a still higher-performance 32-bit configuration, but it is definitely more expensive and is the least common bus architecture. Most EISA machines also have some board slots in ISA format, so you are not locked out of using those boards. However, because of the cost of EISA machines, they are primarily used for applications such as network servers, which require the highest possible mass storage performance.

For most multimedia applications, the ISA bus is the best choice, unless you are going with IBM—then you should consider Microchannel. All multimedia developers are working to make their hardware and software run within the performance of the ISA bus, simply because it represents the largest potential market. By the way, most software will run on any of the bus configurations—the bus is mostly a hardware issue.

Another issue regarding the system bus is how many slots are left free for add-in cards, such as video display, audio, modems, network interfaces, etc. The smaller system packages may have only three slots available, whereas larger packages can offer six to eight free slots. For multimedia use, three slots is not enough, unless features such as audio and video display are built in elsewhere in the package and not taking up slots.

When a system provides for a number of add-in card slots, you also must make sure that the system power supply is large enough to power the devices in the slots. Power supplies are rated in watts, and a good number is 200 watts. Anything less than 150 watts is likely to prove marginal for multimedia applications.

Local Bus

Because of the industry preference for the ISA bus, where bus performance is sometimes limiting, variations have been developed to solve specific problems. In particular, graphical user interfaces, such as those employed by Windows and OS/2, require a lot of data traffic between the CPU and the video display adaptor. To make this traffic run faster than the main bus, and at the same time unload it from the main bus, many platforms are using a local bus architecture, as shown in Figure 3.3. This local bus is simply a separate connection between the CPU

```
                    ┌──────────┐
                    │  VIDEO   │
                    │ DISPLAY  │
                    └──────────┘
```

┌─────────────────┐   ┌────────┐   ┌──────────┐   ┌──────────┐
│   MATH   │   │ HARD │   │ VIDEO   │   │ AUDIO   │
│   COPROCESSOR   │   │ DRIVE │   │ DISPLAY │   │ ADAPTOR │
└─────────────────┘   └────────┘   │ ADAPTOR │   └──────────┘
┌─────────────────┐   └──────────┘
│   CPU   │
│ MICROPROCESSOR │
└─────────────────┘

◄══════════ **LOCAL BUS** ══════════►

◄══════════════ **SYSTEM BUS** ══════════════►

┌──────────┐   ┌──────────┐   ┌──────────┐
│ SYSTEM │   │   MASS   │   │   USER   │
│   RAM   │   │ STORAGE │   │   I/O   │
└──────────┘   └──────────┘   └──────────┘

                 Other Hard Drives   Keyboard
                     CD-ROM   Mouse
                 Floppy Disk Drives   Touch
                                        Pen

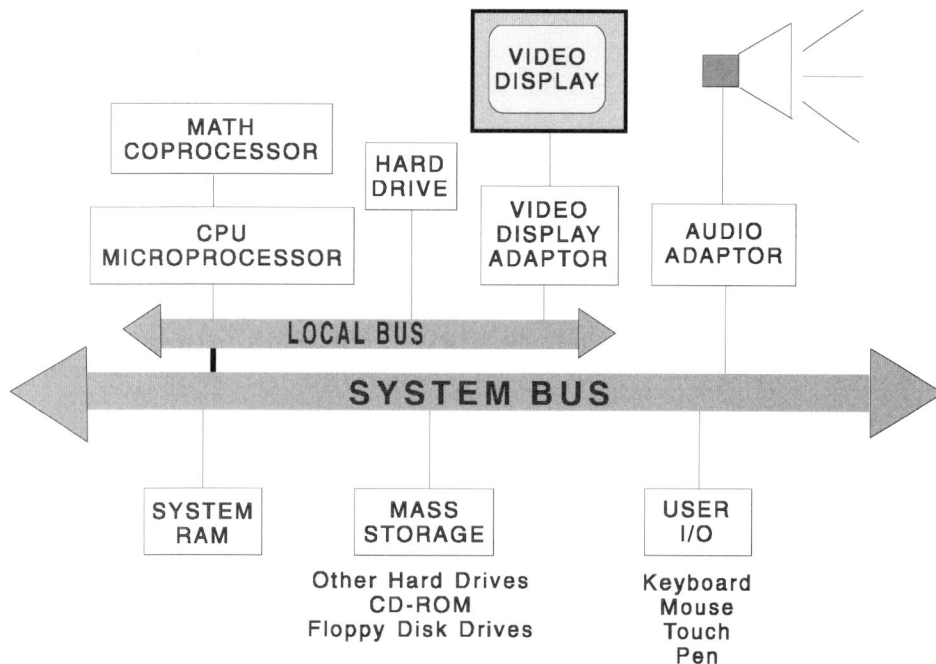

Figure 3.3 Block diagram of a typical PC system showing video local bus   architecture

and the video display adaptor—designed for higher speeds. It is almost always 32 bits wide; in fact, some variations are going to a 64-bit data path. The local bus must be built directly on the motherboard, which means that you cannot add it to an existing computer except by replacing the motherboard.

There is an industry standard for a PC local bus, called the VL-bus, which was developed by the Video Electronics Standards Association (VESA). The VL-bus has special slots for adaptor boards, up to a maximum of three. Video display adaptors for the VL-bus are on the market, and some systems also use VL-bus hard drive controllers.

PCMCIA

Another specialty bus is the PC Memory Card International Association interface (PCMCIA), which was developed for expansion slots in ultra-small notebook and handheld PCs. This bus provides for credit card size expansion modules for mass storage, modem, or other uses. Because of the unique capabilities of some of these modules, PCMCIA slots are starting to appear on desktop PCs as well.

It is not necessarily a good idea to put a lot of things on the local bus, because as you add other items to the local bus, it has to time-share them, meaning that everything can slow down. Once you start doing that, it may be better to go to an inherently faster main bus such as EISA. You can get EISA machines with a local bus, too, if you really want to have everything!

MULTIMEDIA HARDWARE REQUIREMENTS

After all that discussion, the question is, What hardware do you really need for your multimedia work? A baseline for a delivery-only system is the MPC minimum specification of the Multimedia PC Marketing Council. That is a 16 MHz 386 SX processor with VGA display, audio board, and CD-ROM. For very little extra cost, you can go to a faster (33 MHz) 386 DX processor, and it is worth it; but better still, you can even consider 486 SX machines in a similar price range. If you expect your delivery system to display realistic images, you will have to go to super VGA instead of VGA—that adds cost for the display adaptor and the monitor.

For authoring purposes, you will benefit from having as much power and capability as you can afford in CPU, RAM, storage, audio, and video. The best way to do that is to think in terms of the major hardware items. However, few people have a blank check, so this section discusses the tradeoffs.

- System—As already mentioned, an ISA-bus system is probably the best choice based on price/performance. The IBM PS/2 with Microchannel is also a good choice at only slightly higher prices. Your system should have five or six open board slots and a 150 watt or larger power supply.
- CPU—Although many multimedia objects can be played satisfactorily on a 20 MHz 386SX CPU, that one task will use up all of your system, and if you want to do other things while multimedia is playing, or if you want to run multiple applications at the same time, your system will slow down seriously. Today, 486 systems have come down so much in price that I recommend that you go for at least a 25 MHz 486SX, and you will still see major performance improvements in multimedia by going to a 486DX CPU or still higher clock frequencies. Advanced systems based on the Intel Pentium, the IBM/Motorola PowerPC RISC processor, the DEC Alpha AXP RISC processor, and the MIPS R4400 RISC processor are being introduced, but prices are high. However, since the need for still more power is there, such systems will rapidly invade the high end of the market, and you can expect prices to drop within a year or so. It's premature today, but a year from now, I would probably recommend that you buy one of these systems for authoring.

- RAM—The price of RAM chips is a bellwether of the solid-state industry. As of this writing, 1993, RAM is about $40 per megabyte, and you can expect that this will continue to fall as larger chips are brought to market. Although you can run a GUI system (Windows or OS/2) with 4 megabytes of RAM, it isn't very satisfactory in terms of speed and responsiveness. For multimedia, 8 megabytes is the minimum that you should consider, and if you are running more than one thing at a time, you should go to 12 or 16 megabytes. RAM is not quite the same as CPU, in that you will reach a point with RAM where you have enough so that all of your work can remain resident in RAM all the time. When that happens, additional RAM will no longer improve performance. For today's multimedia applications, that point is probably somewhere between 8 and 16 megabytes of RAM, but of course application designers will learn how to use more as soon as you give it to them. On the other hand, a faster CPU always improves performance and you can use all you can get.

- Mass storage—I've already said that multimedia data objects are large, so it should be no surprise that you can also use all the mass storage you can get. Similarly, large objects can take a long time to read from storage, so you should also have the fastest data transfer rate you can get. Usually, the best choice is to get a system with a SCSI interface and a SCSI hard disk, because you will need a SCSI interface for CD-ROM, and you have to have a CD-ROM drive.

- Audio—A multimedia computer should have an audio board that will do WAVE audio and MIDI, both in stereo. The board should be interfaced to a set of stereo speakers. Most audio boards also support audio digitizing (capture), but you should check this out if you intend to capture your own audio.

- Video—You also need a video display adaptor that will support 16- or 24-bit VGA or super VGA resolution. If you are planning to do motion video, you should also consider a board that supports video compression and decompression, such as the IBM ActionMedia II board or the Intel Smart Video Recorder board, which is a capture-only video board using the same i750 processor chip that is in ActionMedia II. Video accelerators and local bus features are also valuable options. Selection of video boards will be discussed further in Chapter 7, "Still Images."

As you can see, multimedia is a hog for almost all aspects of system performance, capacity, and speed. This is the reason that multimedia has not become important before now. Most of the multimedia ideas have been around for years, but they were too expensive for general use. Now that you can buy affordable systems with the kind of performance numbers mentioned above, multimedia is suddenly practical in terms of hardware. Multimedia software is also catching up to that.

OPERATING SYSTEMS

In addition to selecting the basic hardware for your system, you have to consider software. In some respects, software selection should come first—you choose the software you want and then choose the hardware that will run it. However, when you are starting from scratch, hardware and software should probably be selected at the same time, iterating between them until the complete system suits your needs.

The only software that is built into your system is the *Basic Input/Output System* (BIOS) module, which is usually in read-only memory (ROM) in your computer. The BIOS provides an interface between the hardware and the first level of installed software, the operating system (OS). The BIOS is custom tailored by the hardware manufacturer to deal with the specific nature of the hardware, and brings the interface up to a more or less standardized level that can be recognized by OS software. OS software, of which there are several choices, will then access the BIOS interface and bring the interface up to a level that is fully standardized for that OS—the *Application Programming Interface* (API). Application developers write their programs to access the API to reach all the system resources managed by the OS. The combination of BIOS and OS serves to hide most of the peculiarities of each system's hardware, making the API simpler and more standard than if all applications had to talk directly with the hardware.

This environment of BIOS and OS is also designed to be extensible, meaning that there are strategies available to add new features to the system without affecting the operation of what is already there. It is done by providing methods in the architecture by which new hardware can extend the BIOS. It also supplies the means in the OS for installable modules, which can make that hardware accessible as part of the API. Modules that perform such tasks are usually called *drivers*, and any special hardware that you intend to add to your system must come with its own driver software to install into your operating system.

Choices

Fortunately, the number of operating system choices is much smaller than the hardware choices. At this writing, there are three major possibilities, and maybe a dozen other lesser prospects, which mostly apply to certain niche markets. The three major systems are: *DOS* (and *Windows*), *OS/2*, and *Windows NT*.

DOS

DOS (Disk Operating System) is the operating system that has grown up with the IBM PC family. That means its roots go back more than ten years, which is a very long time in the PC business. The biggest problem caused by this heritage is that DOS was designed originally as a single-user single-task operating system, meaning that it does one thing at a time on the assumption that a single user needs only one thing at a time, and it is perfectly all right for him to wait for each task to complete before going ahead to the next task. In multimedia there is often more than one thing happening at a time (for example: audio playing in the background while other things are being displayed on the screen), and a single-task operating system makes this very difficult.

Another problem with DOS is that it is still a 16-bit operating system with 20-bit addressing (as was the original PC/AT), and it cannot directly utilize system memory beyond 1 megabyte. Many hardware and software schemes have been developed over the years to get around the memory restrictions of DOS, especially when the 386 or higher processors are used; however, these still require special programming in applications. Many applications do not include the special programming in their code and therefore cannot benefit from the memory extenders.

It is a testament to the ingenuity of programmers that they have been able to make multimedia work on DOS systems anyway. But the limitations are still there, under the surface, and the flexibility and performance of DOS multimedia is limited. The modern solution to this problem is called a multitasking operating system.

The current version of DOS is 6.0, and it is still a 16-bit system, meaning that it will not make use of 32-bit features that may be in your hardware. It runs fine in a 32-bit system, but no advantage is being obtained from the advanced hardware. DOS application programs can be written to use 32-bit features, but they will still go to 16 bits whenever they call a DOS function.

Windows

Microsoft *Windows* is not technically an operating system—it is an extension module that sits above DOS. It provides a graphical user interface (GUI) and as much multitasking as can be accomplished with DOS still present. That was enough to make it one of the hottest software products recently, and more than ten million *Windows* packages were sold in the first year after version 3.0 came out. (Windows actually goes back about seven years, but versions before 3.0 were not widely accepted.)

Because of its GUI, *Windows* has a different API than DOS, and *Windows* applications will not run under DOS without *Windows*. The reverse situation, however, has been provided for in the design of Windows, and most DOS programs will run under *Windows*. Version 3.1 of *Windows* includes some built-in multimedia capabilities, such as the MCI API. It handles audio very well, but the limitations of the underlying DOS begin to show up when you attempt motion video. That works well only if you limit the other simultaneous things the system is doing.

Windows is a 16-bit system, the same as DOS, although Microsoft is in the process of providing 32-bit extensions, which will be able to benefit from 32-bit hardware. It will require special programming in applications to take full advantage of the 32-bit features.

OS/2

OS/2 is an IBM product that was originally developed in collaboration with Microsoft. OS/2 was designed from the start to be a true multitasking system, where the operating system manages how the computer resources are allocated to a multiplicity of simultaneously running tasks. Unlike *Windows*, it does not require the use of DOS. With version 2.1, it is fully a 32-bit system. *OS/2* was initially marketed as a premium OS, and this reduced its acceptance. That is no longer the case, and *OS/2* is considered to be IBM's standard OS for PCs.

However, because it has a smaller market, there are fewer application programs for *OS/2* than for DOS-Windows, and this continues to slow the growth of *OS/2*. In versions 2.0 and 2.1, IBM dealt with the applications availability problem by making *OS/2* also run Windows programs. Thus, an *OS/2* user can enjoy all the *Windows* programs as well as the *OS/2* programs; in fact, you can multitask between them—*OS/2* and *Windows* programs running simultaneously.

OS/2 is an excellent platform for multimedia. The current versions have multimedia extensions, using the MCI approach similar to *Windows*. *OS/2* multitasking works very well, and multiple multimedia activities can run smoothly, up to the limits of the hardware.

Windows NT

NT means New Technology. Like *OS/2*, *Windows NT* is a complete operating system—it does not require DOS. Therefore, all the limitations of DOS are gone. Many other features are built in to make it a strong competitor to *OS/2*: true multitasking, network features, true 32 bits, running DOS-Windows programs, etc. Although, at this writing (1993), NT is just entering the market, Microsoft seems to be making the same mistake that IBM did initially with *OS/2*. They are proposing it as a premium system, probably to keep it from disrupting the *Windows* market. I expect that will soon change. The recent preannouncements of *Windows 4* may indicate a step toward a low-cost version of *Windows NT*.

Windows NT is even more demanding of system resources (memory and storage) than *OS/2*, requiring more than 8 megabytes for minimum running and taking upwards of 50 megabytes of storage just for the system and its features. However, those kinds of hardware needs are being met at lower and lower cost, so there is nothing wrong with using a lot of resources if the performance matches the cost (and it seems to). *Windows NT* will also be an excellent platform for multimedia work, and certainly will be in the same performance league with *OS/2*.

OPERATING SYSTEM FEATURES

Regardless of the operating system you choose, there are certain features that you must consider. These are discussed below.

Multitasking

As already defined, multitasking is the capability to run more than one application program at a time. The operating system does this by managing the use of memory for all applications to make sure that it is shared without conflict, and by switching the CPU rapidly between the applications to create the impression that they are running simultaneously. However, this strategy may not work properly unless the applications involved have been properly designed. The greatest issue is that applications must not hog the CPU by running long processes without allowing the operating system to regain control. Under Windows, this is a problem because the OS cannot always take control and do a task switch unless the running application lets it by periodically calling a system function. DOS itself has the same problem because the disk file system cannot be interrupted until it completes a task. It becomes the application's responsibility to break up time-consuming disk tasks into small blocks so that the system can take control and run pieces of other applications during a long disk access.

There is a solution—*preemptive* multitasking. In such a system, the OS can interrupt any task at any time. Both OS/2 and Windows NT have preemptive multitasking. In such an environment, an application designer ensures that an important multimedia function will get attention simply by giving it a high priority in the system. Then the system will see that the task regularly gets CPU cycles, regardless of whatever else is happening, and the programmer does not have to worry further about it.

Multimedia Services—MCI

It is not reasonable to build a lot of specific multimedia features into the OS's API because there are so many choices, and the field is growing so rapidly. A better OS strategy is to create a multimedia API that is general, but can be configured ad hoc by installing proper drivers. This is the concept of the Media Control Interface (MCI) developed by Microsoft with a consortium of software manufacturers. MCI is an OS API feature that can pass an arbitrary command string to any installed driver module. To activate a special piece of hardware, a driver module is installed to connect that hardware to the OS's MCI interface. The driver knows a command syntax for that hardware, and an application program can know the same command syntax. When the application wants to use the special hardware, it makes an API call to MCI, specifying which driver it wants, and passing it a command string that tells the driver what it wants the hardware to do. The result is that we can control any hardware, simply by having a driver for the hardware and by having applications know the command syntax for the driver.

MCI goes a little further in two ways:

1. The use of a command string is not always the most efficient way to pass data between software modules, so MCI also provides for a function-call interface between an application and a hardware driver. In this case, the application knows the proper function-call parameters to send to the driver, and MCI makes the connection.

2. In the case of the command-string mode, there are many common aspects to the language for different multimedia. For example, both audio or video would have commands for play, pause, stop, rewind, etc. Therefore, MCI proposes some preferred commands, so that hardware drivers that have common functions will all use the same command syntax. Although this is not mandatory, its use will make it possible for an application to use the standard commands to talk to all audio boards, even one that was designed long after the application was designed. As noted, Windows, OS/2, and Windows NT all support MCI.

Interprocess Communication

An important feature of multitasking is that you can simultaneously run applications (processes), and they should be able to communicate with each other. Therefore, all multitasking systems (*Windows, OS/2,* and *Windows NT*) provide for *interprocess communication* (IPC). These systems have IPC features available in their APIs, which will provide efficient communication whenever an application needs it. API features have to be programmed into applications at design time, so they are useful only for features that are fully defined when the applications are designed. There are two IPC methods that are general (like MCI), and they can be used later to implement connections that the application designer may not have thought of. These are *Dynamic Data Exchange* (DDE) and *Object Linking and Embedding* (OLE).

DDE

Applications that know about DDE can set up their own communication paths at runtime. DDE is an IPC protocol for establishing a connection between two or more applications, which can then be used to pass any kind of data in either direction. The applications were programmed when they were designed to support DDE, but the actual connections and data formats do not have to be set up until the applications are run.

A typical example of this is expressed by the concept of a multimedia *server*. A server is a program that can be running in a dormant state, but on command it will come alive and perform a specific service. For example, an audio server would play a particular audio file when you told it to. An application that needs audio does not need to know anything about playing audio, it only needs to know how to use DDE to access the audio server. In fact, using this approach, you can play audio from an application that you have been using for years, simply by adding audio hardware and a server for it. As long as your old application knows DDE, you can create a macro in the application to access the audio server. Most Windows programs support DDE, so you could play audio (or video) from your Windows word processor, spreadsheet, or database applications.

Some multimedia authoring programs are server-based. *MEDIAscript OS/2,* by Network Technology, for example, uses a single server for all its multimedia functions. If the *MEDIAscript* Server is installed in your system, you can tell it via DDE to run a particular script of commands. With scripts, you can create windows, display text and graphics, play audio or video, display images, do animations, or specify anything else the Server can do. Note that the Server is an *OS/2* application, but *OS/2* will run *Windows* programs, and those can still access the Server via DDE. Another server-based application is *AddImpact!* by Gold Disk, which can deliver animations to other *Windows* applications using DDE or OLE.

OLE

DDE communication requires that applications specifically send messages whenever something has to happen. But it would be better to have a connection that will automatically update information in multiple applications whenever it changes, with all the messaging handled invisibly within the system. You also might like to be able to bring an object from a first application into a second application, but still be able to edit the object while you are in the second application without having to deliberately open up the first application and do the edit. This is what *Object Linking and Embedding* (OLE, pronounced "oh-lay") is all about. An example will clarify the concept.

You are using a word processor to create a flyer for your business, and you want to include a drawing (an object) that you have made with a separate draw program. You could simply have the word processor access the file for the drawing on your hard disk, but this would mean that you would still have to work on the drawing and the document separately in two applications. You can do it a better way with OLE. Again, you identify the file to your word processor, but rather than inserting it into your document, you tell the word processor to link it. This sets up an OLE connection where the word processor now knows not only about the file, but also about the application that created it. The drawing will appear in your word processor as it usually does, but now you can double-click on it and the creating application for the drawing will pop up so you can edit the drawing. When you are finished with that, you close or minimize the drawing program, and you are back in the word processor with the latest changes showing in the drawing.

A different concept is to *embed* the drawing in your document. When you do this, a *copy* of the drawing is stored in the word processor document. You can still edit the drawing by double-clicking on it in the document window, but now the only thing changed is the copy of the drawing that is in the document. The original source file for the drawing is unchanged.

THE ULTIMEDIA TOOLS SERIES

Chances are you will need a number of different applications in your authoring environment to accomplish all the tasks you require. It is important for you to choose a set of applications that will work together, with compatible file formats and consistent user interfaces. IBM has created the Ultimedia Tools Series to solve just these problems. A group of suppliers of authoring software, working in a committee called the Ultimedia Tools Series Architecture Council, has established a set of architecture documents that define a consistent framework within which authoring products can work together.

The Tools Series Architecture provides a consistent way for tools to specify what they do and what platform characteristics they require. It also defines protocols for interprocess communication, both DDE and OLE, and rules for how the tools' graphical user interface should look and operate. Finally, it defines a set of data file formats for consistent multimedia data interchange between tools. The Architecture specification is written so as not to limit any other features or formats supported by the tools—it defines just enough so there will be a subset of tool functionality that works with other tools.

The suppliers that have joined the Tools Series are committed to deliver products meeting the specifications. IBM has set up a marketing operation to sell the Ultimedia Tools Series products. The present product list (fall 1993) is shown below. There are already more than 90 tools in the list, which attests to the complexity one faces in choosing authoring products.

Tool Type	OS	Tool Name	Vendor
Assembly	Win	IconAuthor	AimTech
Assembly	OS/2	IconAuthor	AimTech
Assembly	DOS	Quest 4.0	Allen Comm.
Assembly	Win	COMPEL	Asymetrix
Assembly	Win	MediaBlitz!	Asymetrix
Assembly	Win	Multimedia Toolbook	Asymetrix
Assembly	DOS	Multimedia Explorer	Autodesk
Assembly	OS/2	MultiMaster	Commix SP
Assembly	DOS	LinkWay Live!	IBM
Assembly	DOS	Storyboard Live! 2.0	IBM
Assembly	OS/2	Ultimedia Builder/2	IBM
Assembly	Win	MediaDeveloper	Lenel Systems
Assembly	Win	Multimedia Works	Lenel Systems
Assembly	Win	Action!	Macromedia
Assembly	Win	Authorware Professional	Macromedia
Assembly	DOS	Studio XA	Mammoth
Assembly	DOS	TEMPRA Media Author	Mathematica
Assembly	DOS	TEMPRA Show	Mathematica
Assembly	DOS	TEMPRA VISION	Mathematica
Assembly	DOS	MEDIAscript DOS	Network Tech.
Assembly	OS/2	MEDIAscript OS/2 Desktop	Network Tech.
Assembly	OS/2	MEDIAscript OS/2 Pro.	Network Tech.

continued

Tool Type	OS	Tool Name	Vendor
Assembly	Win	Q/Media for Windows	Q/Media Software
Assembly	DOS	Media Master	Vision Imaging
Assembly	DOS	Multimedia Studio	Vision Imaging
Graphics	Win	Adobe Illustrator	Adobe Systems
Graphics	Win	Adobe Photoshop	Adobe Systems
Graphics	DOS	Crystal 3D Designer	Crystal Graphics
Graphics	Win	Fractal Design Painter	Fractal Design
Graphics	Win	Fractal Design Painter X2	Fractal Design
Graphics	Win	Fractal Design Sketcher	Fractal Design
Graphics	Win	Professional Draw	Gold Disk
Graphics	OS/2	Ultimedia Perfect Image/2	IBM
Graphics	DOS	TEMPRA Access Plus	Mathematica
Graphics	DOS	TEMPRA GIF	Mathematica
Graphics	DOS	TEMPRA Pro	Mathematica
Graphics	OS/2	Color Tools	Time Arts
Graphics	DOS	Lumena	Time Arts
Graphics	DOS	PC Paintbrush 5+	Wordstar International
Graphics	Win	PhotoFinish	Wordstar International
Animation	DOS	Animator Pro	Autodesk
Animation	DOS	Crystal Desktop Animator	CrystalGraphics
Animation	DOS	Crystal Flying Fonts!	CrystalGraphics
Animation	Win	AddImpact!	Gold Disk
Animation	Win	Animation Works Interactive	Gold Disk
Animation	DOS	TEMPRA Turbo Animator	Mathematica
Animation	DOS	StrataVision 3-D PC	Strata
Audio	Win	SuperJam!	Blue Ribbon Soundworks
Audio	Win	Encore	Passport Designs
Audio	Win	Master Tracks Pro	Passport Designs
Audio	Win	Music Time	Passport Designs
Audio	Win	Trax	Passport Designs
Audio	Win	Wave for Windows	Turtle Beach Systems
Audio	Win	AudioView	Voyetra
Audio	DOS	Sequencer Plus Gold	Voyetra
Planning	DOS	Collaborator II	Collaborator Systems
Planning	OS/2	DisplayMaster	Commix SP
Planning	DOS	CUE MASTER	Comprehensive Video
Planning	DOS	LOG MASTER	Comprehensive Video
Planning	DOS	MOVIE MASTER	Comprehensive Video
Planning	DOS	SCRIPT MASTER	Comprehensive Video
Planning	DOS	Mannequin	HumanCad
Planning	Win	Mannequin Designer	HumanCad

continued

Tool Type	OS	Tool Name	Vendor
Planning	OS/2	Ultimedia Workplace/2	IBM
Planning	Win	MediaOrganizer	Lenel Systems
Planning	Win	MpcOrganizer	Lenel Systems
Planning	Win	Virtus Walkthrough	Virtus
Video	Win	Adobe Premiere 1.0 for Windows	Adobe Systems
Video	OS/2	SPLICE for OS/2	Digital Media Int'l
Video	Win	SPLICE for Windows	Digital Media Int'l
Video	Win	VideoDirector	Gold Disk
Video	OS/2	Jasmine Clipper	Jasmine Multimedia
Video	OS/2	Montage 3 Picture Proc.	Montage Group
Video	Win	Montage 3 Picture Proc.	Montage Group
Video	DOS	D/Vision	TouchVision Systems
Video	DOS	D/Vision Pro	TouchVision Systems
Video	Win	OZ-1	Videomedia
Video	Win	OZ-2	Videomedia
Control	DOS	COST TRACKING	Quantum Films
Control	DOS	SCRIPT SCAN	Quantum Films
Control	DOS	TURBO AD	Quantum Films
Control	DOS	TURBO BUDGET	Quantum Films
Distribut'n	OS/2	Person to Person	IBM
Distribut'n	DOS	TEMPRA CD Maker	Mathematica

THE MULTIMEDIA PC

Because there are so many variables in selecting hardware for a multimedia platform, a group of companies formed an organization called the Multimedia PC Marketing Council in 1990 to set minimum standards for multimedia hardware. This led to the publication of the Multimedia PC (MPC) Level 1 standard, which called for a minimum of a 16-MHz 386SX CPU with 2 MB of RAM, a CD-ROM drive, an 8-bit sound card, and at least a 30-MB hard disk. Systems meeting or exceeding these specifications can be licensed to display the MPC logo (shown in Figure 1.7). Software vendors can also license their products with the logo, indicating that the software will run on an MPC platform.

By today's standards, the Level 1 standard is too low, a fact that has caused the Council recently to introduce a Level 2 standard that substantially ups the ante for multimedia systems. Level 2 specifies (a minimum of) a 25-MHz 486SX CPU, 4 MB of RAM, a double-speed CD-ROM drive, a 16-bit sound card, and a 160-MB hard drive. It also specifies a 640 × 480 16-bpp video adaptor. The interesting thing is that today a typical Level 2 system will cost less than a Level 1 system did in 1990! That shows how rapidly the price performance of personal computers is improving. In this book, a Level 2 MPC is a satisfactory delivery system, but I recommend a more powerful system for authoring.

SUMMARY

Multimedia authoring requires as much computing power and resources as you can give it. A reasonable recommended system for authoring today consists of an OS/2 or Windows NT platform, including:

- a 486DX CPU at least 33 MHz
- at least 8 MB of RAM
- at least 200 MB SCSI hard disk
- a CD-ROM drive (also SCSI)
- a 16-bit audio board
- a VL local bus
- a true color video board
- a mouse

4

Author Interfaces

The purpose of authoring software is to simplify the inherently complex task of creating an interactive multimedia application. This is usually accomplished by providing an author interface that conveys a simpler metaphor than the resulting application itself will have. The metaphor helps the author to think about what she is doing and makes the work seem less abstract. At the same time, an author interface helps the author by keeping track of many details for her, making sure that she does not make mistakes, and performs other important tasks such as file management. This chapter discusses the things that an author has to do in creating an application and then explores some of the ways that authoring software makes them easier.

AUTHORING TASKS

An authoring project involves a myriad of tasks. For example, to author a simple linear presentation you may have to do the following:

File management—Creating a file or files that hold the authored application. Also, loading and saving files during authoring.

Screen building—Creating the individual screens that make up the presentation. This is the most complex part and it can include selecting backgrounds, colors, and styles; entering, formatting, and positioning text; capturing or creating images and graphics; and importing, sizing, and positioning images or graphics.

Sequencing—Arranging the parts of the presentation into the proper order for display.

Adding dynamics—This includes selecting transitions between screens, adding animations, capturing audio or motion video, and placing audio or motion video in the sequence.

Editing—Once a presentation has been built, it should be possible to revisit any part of it and make changes.

Testing—Running the presentation with all its elements to confirm that it works the way you want it to.

Delivering—The completed presentation is shown to the target audience, either onscreen or in the form of hard copy output such as paper, 35-mm slides, or overhead transparencies.

Packaging—When you have to move the presentation to another platform, you have to output it in a form that can run without the authoring environment.

That is just for a linear presentation. When interactivity is required, you can add the following steps to the list:

Architecting—Defining what happens for each interactive choice by the end user and specifying where the program instructions are kept for each part.

User controls—The buttons, menus, and other controls used by the end user must be selected and built.

Variables and calculations—In applications that reqire them, variables have to be defined, and their contents calculated and maintained.

Conditionals—When the application must respond to an accumulation of conditions (not just direct user input), the logic involved must be designed.

I/O—Applications that involve communications or hard copy output must have those functions programmed.

For even more specific application classes, the list could go on. The point is: Even a simple interactive application involves a lot of different things. To repeat, authoring is inherently complex.

TOP-LEVEL INTERFACES

The principal I/O medium of an authoring interface is the video display screen. Because authoring involves complex operations on a number of things at the same time, a windowed video display, such as produced by *Windows* or *OS/2*, is usually preferable. Recognizing that no one tool program is going to do every-

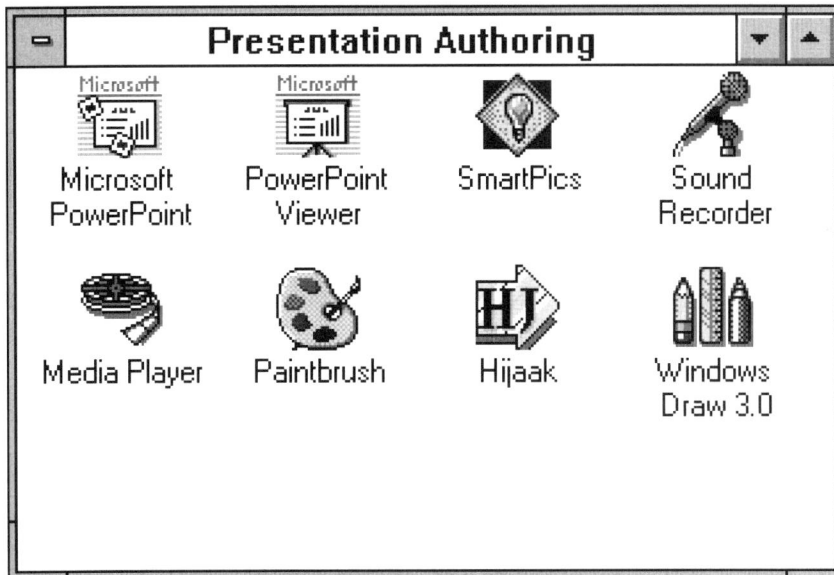

Figure 4.1 A DOS/Windows group box showing icons for all the authoring tools in an environment

thing you need in authoring, most environments will include multiple tool programs. Usually, the interface to individual programs will be handled by the windowing operating system, and your tools will appear as icons in one or more group boxes. Figure 4.1 shows an example of this for presentation authoring based on Microsoft *PowerPoint.* The Presentation Authoring group box contains icons for *PowerPoint* along with a collection of drawing and sound-recording tools that you also need to create content for presentations assembled with *PowerPoint.* Therefore, the top-level interface for a multiapplication environment is the operating system. This is where multitasking pays off—you can have several tools running at once and easily and quickly switch between them. The tools can also communicate data via interprocess communication, so you don't have to worry about that either.

Of course, each tool has its own top-level interface, and one of the difficult aspects of choosing an authoring environment is finding a set of tools that have similar interfaces. You can't always achieve that, and you may have to learn several different interfaces. Standardizing initiatives such as the Ultimedia Tools Series are trying to solve the problem of a standardized author interface.

The author opens the tools she needs by double-clicking on their icons in the group box. Each tool starts up its own window on the screen. These can be minimized to icons, or they can be sized and arranged to coexist on the screen at the author's choice. At this point, all the tools are being multitasked by the operating system, and each is using some system RAM. Obviously, the amount of RAM you need will depend on the number of tools you plan to use simultaneously. (The alternative is to start each tool only when you need it—this is also workable, but if you change tools often, you will waste time waiting for tools to start and close.) Note that, if you wish, you can set it up so the operating system at boot-up will automatically open and configure the tools you regularly use.

Within one tool, the top-level interface has to allow the author to move between the different parts of the tool easily and quickly, without confusing her, and without losing any of her work. It also should guide her through the process so that she performs the steps in a logical order and doesn't leave anything out. With today's tools, the top-level interface is usually accomplished by some form of menu structure, such as a pull-down or drop-down menu bar, menu lists, or a toolbar. These are easily understood devices, but it may not always be easy to understand what the menu items themselves mean. That can be a problem whether the menu items are words or icons. One of the first steps in mastering a new interface is learning the meanings of all the icons and words.

THE SLIDE SHOW METAPHOR—*PowerPoint*

Because a linear presentation is the simplest structure you can author, let's examine the issues in the interface for a presentation package. We'll use Microsoft *PowerPoint* as an example; its interface, shown in Figure 4.2, embodies most of the principles expressed above. *PowerPoint* provides a complete environment for authoring presentations, including tools for assembly, drawing, formatting, charting, and many I/O options. As a result, it has a large number of features, but it is organized to still be easy to learn and use.

PowerPoint uses the *slide show* metaphor. Each screen of a presentation is seen as a slide object that you can separately create, edit, and arrange. The top-level interface in *PowerPoint* is a menu bar, which shows across the top of Figure 4.2. There also is a toolbar just below the menu bar and a tool palette (down the left side of the screen), both of which can change depending on what you are doing. When menu items change this way, it is referred to as *moding* (having *modes*). Moding is not necessarily a good thing—it would be better if everything in the interface always looked the same way and always did the same things. However, sometimes it turns out to be simpler to use modes than to try to keep everything the same all the time. Anyway, if you choose an interface with modes, make sure it has a clear way to tell what mode the system is in at all times so you won't get confused.

Figure 4.2 The author interface of Microsoft *PowerPoint* in the slide view

In *PowerPoint*, you can choose any of four different view modes (all using the slide metaphor) for working on the presentation you are authoring. A selection of views is valuable because it lets you emphasize different aspects of your presentation at different stages of the authoring. View selection is made by clicking one of the icons at the bottom of the screen or by making a selection from the view pull-down in the menu bar; the choices are:

- slide view (shown in Figure 4.2)—In this view, you can see one slide at a time, displayed full screen at a selectable magnification. The magnification is chosen from the view menu or from the selector at the right end of the toolbar. This view is most valuable for working with the details of the slide layout.
- slide sorter view (shown in Figure 4.3)—In this view, you can see icons for all the slides in the presentation arranged in their order of presentation. You can edit the order by dragging the slide icons around on the screen. The magnification controls can be used to adjust the display to fit the screen

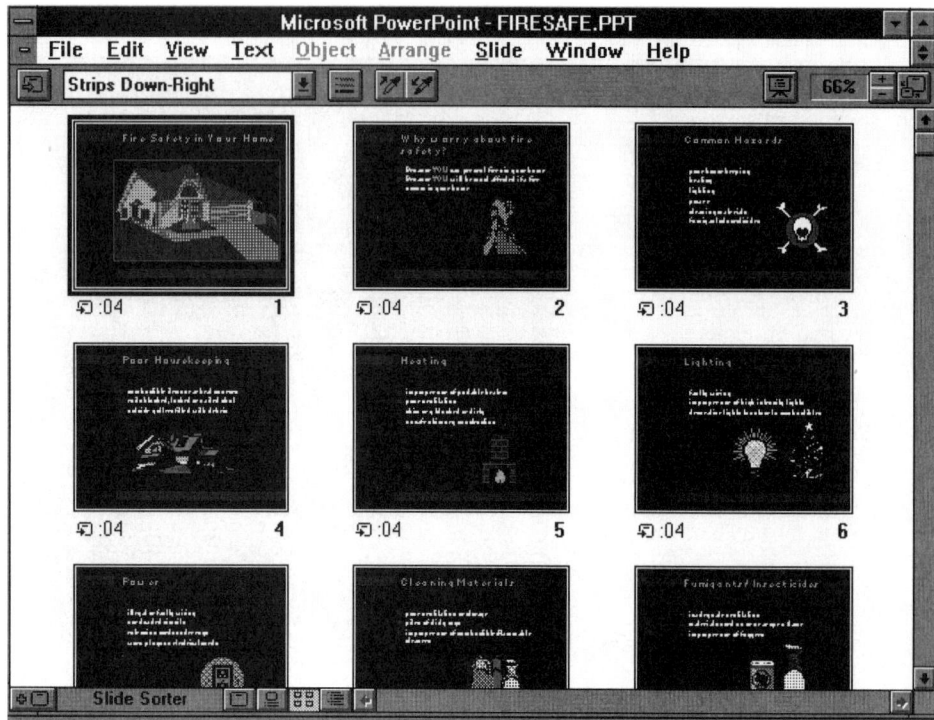

Figure 4.3 *PowerPoint* shown in the slide sorter view

or to zoom in on one area of the presentation. This view is most valuable for arranging the order of slide presentation.

- notes view—This is another single-slide view. It shows the slide itself along with any notes that you wish to attach to it. When making hard copy output, you can specify a format that prints the slide with its notes (or not). Figure 4.4 shows the notes view. This view is most valuable for entering notes that you want to attach to each slide.
- outline view—This view shows the text of all the slides arranged into an outline format. This view is most valuable for initial entering or editing of the text content of a presentation. Figure 4.5 shows an outline view.

The screen looks so different in the four views that you will never be confused about what mode you are in.

You can begin authoring a presentation in any view of *PowerPoint*, but it is probably best to first use the outline view, because that will help you organize your thoughts as well. You can view your presentation at any stage of authoring, even just after entering an outline. However, before you view your presentation the

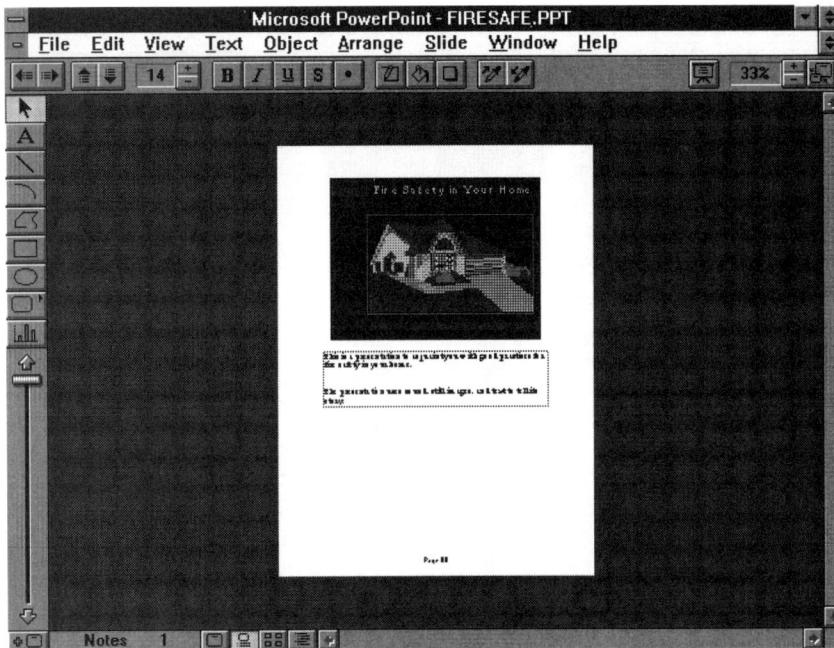

Figure 4.4 *PowerPoint* shown in the notes view

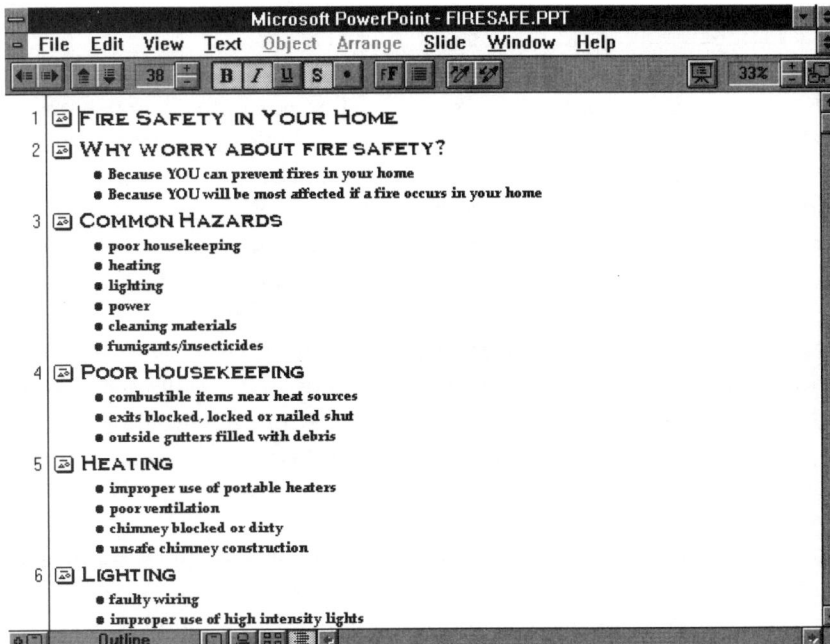

Figure 4.5 A *PowerPoint* presentation shown in the outline view

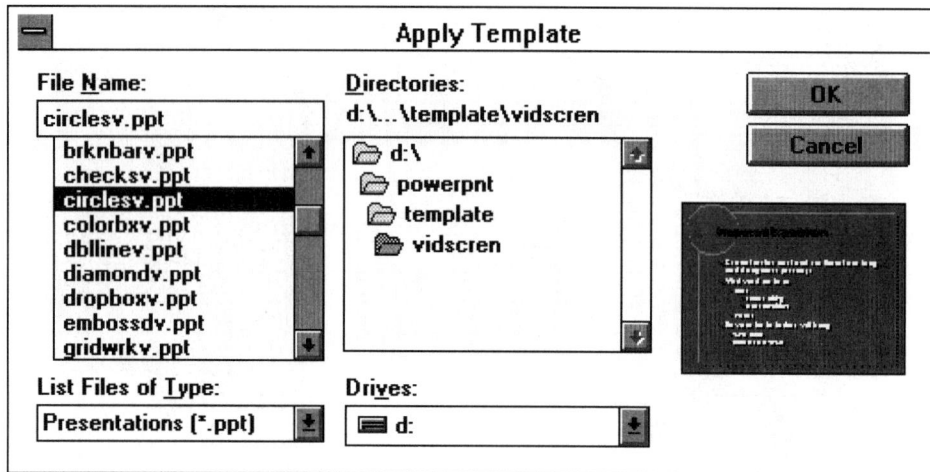

Figure 4.6   The *PowerPoint* dialog for selecting a presentation template

first time, you will want to choose a *template* for the screens. Using a template will give your screens a uniform look. *PowerPoint* gives you a selection of more than 160 templates, accessible under the Apply Template... item of the File menu. Figure 4.6 shows the dialog for selecting a template. The currently selected template shows in thumbnail form at the right of the dialog. You can also create your own templates and add them to the list of choices.

In addition to or instead of using templates, you can draw each slide individually with the draw tools built into *PowerPoint.* Another possibility is to use images on the slides. There is a clip art library built in to *PowerPoint,* containing hundreds of drawings of familiar objects. These objects can be selected, resized, recolored, or modified for inclusion in your presentations. The clip library is in the form of a number of slide presentations made up entirely of drawings. You choose a subject from the dialog shown in Figure 4.7, and a slide show of drawings for that subject is loaded into a separate window.

The clip art presentation can be viewed in any of the four views the same as a presentation you create yourself. Figure 4.8 shows the clip art library for common household objects. The coffee cup image selected in the clip library window at the right has been copied into a slide in the presentation window at the left. The text font and sizing have been changed to create the slide and the image itself has been reproportioned to suit the slide.

Another feature of *PowerPoint* that is very easy to use is specifying transitions between slides. Figure 4.9 shows a slide sorter view of a presentation with the Transitions menu dropped down. By selecting from this menu, you can specify

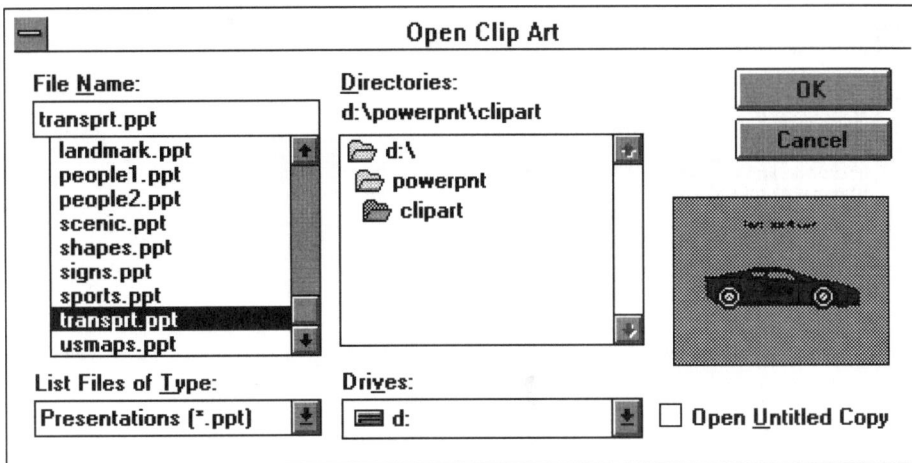

Figure 4.7   The clip art dialog from *PowerPoint*

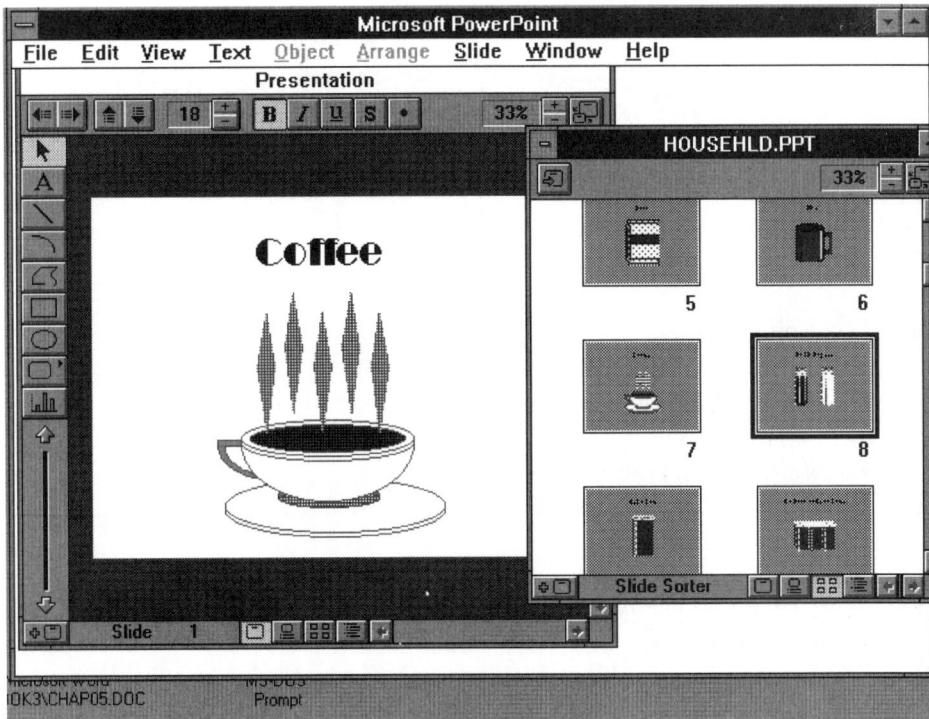

Figure 4.8   The clip library for household objects from *PowerPoint* is shown to the right with a presentation window at the left

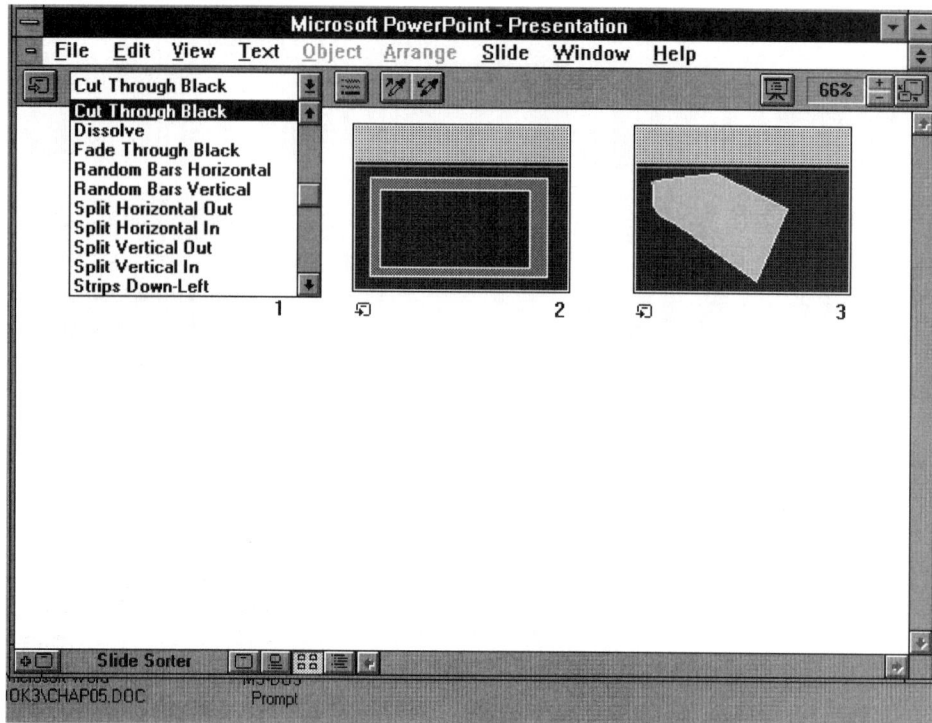

Figure 4.9 *PowerPoint* transition selection

a dynamic transition effect for each slide in a sequence. There are dozens of choices.

Many other presentation authoring products use the slide show metaphor, including Lotus *FreeLance* and Software Publishing's *Harvard Graphics*. While this approach is excellent for authoring linear presentations, it is not optimum when random interactivity is needed, because you are constrained only to jumping around in a straight line of slides. In interactive situations, some of the other metaphors are better. A full example of authoring a presentation with the slide show metaphor is given in Chapter 13.

THE BOOK METAPHOR—*ToolBook*

The slide show metaphor does not lend itself to a rich interactive application. The only interactivity you can achieve is jumping between points in the linear sequence of slides. For better interactivity you need to build a multidimensional structure. One metaphor for that is the *book*. In this metaphor, you think of an application as a book containing any number of *pages*. Each page is a screen shown in its own window, which can contain any number of multimedia objects and any amount of interactivity. A page is a richer architecture than a slide because you can arrange interactivity within the page. *ToolBook* displays only one page at a time, in a single window, and you navigate the application by displaying different pages.

A page in a book can also start other books, so an even more complex hierarchy can be built. When you start another book, you are actually beginning another *instance* of *ToolBook*, so each book can exist in a different window, with its own characteristics. Multiple instances is one of the advantages of a multitasking environment, and it is not as wasteful as it seems, because only one copy of the tool's executable code is required; all instances run from the same program code. Using multiple instances, you could, for example, begin with an application that you called Bookshelf, and include all of your individual subjects as separate books in the Bookshelf. (*ToolBook* has a sample application like that.)

All window and dialog generation in *ToolBook* can be done graphically with the mouse, including drawing objects, choosing colors, and placing text objects. Standard objects like pushbuttons and check boxes, etc., have a default behavior built in, which provides the standard highlighting features of *Windows*. However, to assign custom behavior to a control or other object, you write a *handler* in the *OpenScript* language. Handlers are code modules that define the response to any *event* that occurs in the application. Events result from user actions, or they can be created by the application itself. Each object has an associated script, which contains any handlers that object requires. Although *OpenScript* is an easy-to-read language, it is a full-featured programming environment, and elaborate *ToolBook* applications will take a lot of programming. The result, however, is that extremely dynamic applications can be built.

The *ToolBook* authoring environment, shown in Figure 4.10, has a main window with a menu bar that provides access to all functions. There also is a tool palette, shown at the left, and a number of other palettes that can be optionally displayed all the time; the colors and patterns palettes are shown at the right. The command window, shown at the bottom of the figure, allows *OpenScript* commands to be typed in and immediately executed. The authoring environment also includes some aids for writing scripts, such as a recorder that can create a script from actions you do with the mouse. There are also many sample books provided with the product, from which you can cut and paste objects, pages, or even entire books to build your own books based on the *ToolBook* samples.

Multimedia ToolBook supports audio, video, and animation by using the MCI and DDE interfaces of *Windows*. These take some significant scriptwriting, but there are good sample multimedia books included with the product that make

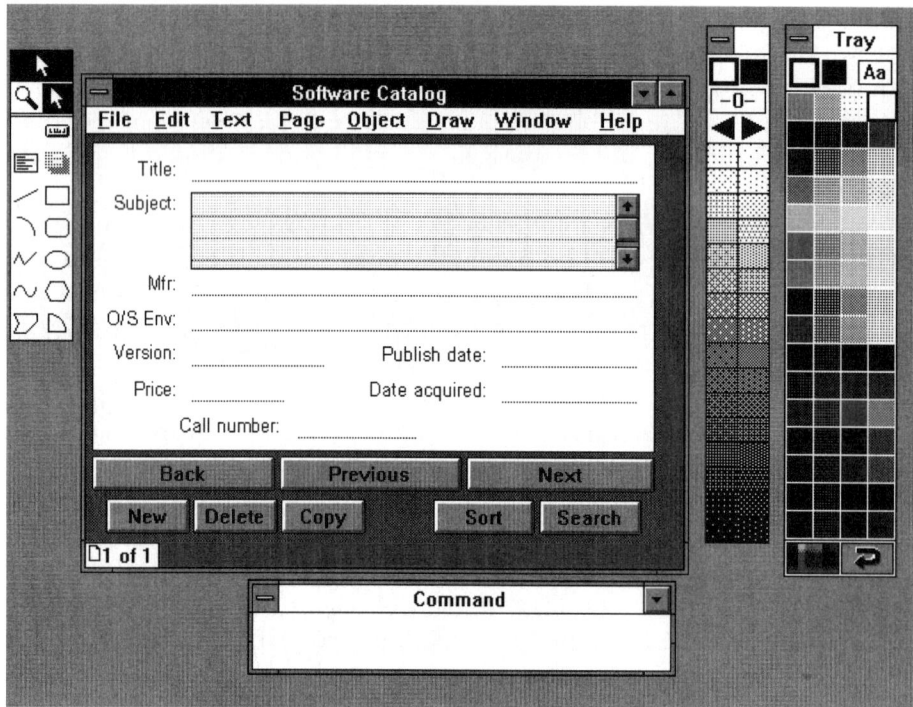

Figure 4.10   The authoring environment of *Multimedia Toolbook*

it relatively easy to import the objects and scripts you need into your own work. Although *ToolBook* can be used by a nonprogrammer, accessing the real power of it requires programming skill—you will be severely limited without that. A full example of an interactive application done with *ToolBook* is given in Chapter 14.

THE WINDOWING METAPHOR—*Visual Basic*

Applications in *Windows* and *OS/2* use the windowing metaphor for their user interface. This is also a valid approach for multimedia authoring. A window is an on-screen object that the user interacts with. Objects and controls in the window are all considered to be children of the window and receive their control via the window. This concept provides a hierarchy for multimedia objects by requiring them to be grouped into windows, and requiring the windows themselves to be arranged into a hierarchy or parent-child relationship.

It is important for a *Windows* or *OS/2* authoring system to be able to author windows in any configuration desired and as many times as desired. *ToolBook*, just described, can author only a single window per instance of the program. But the

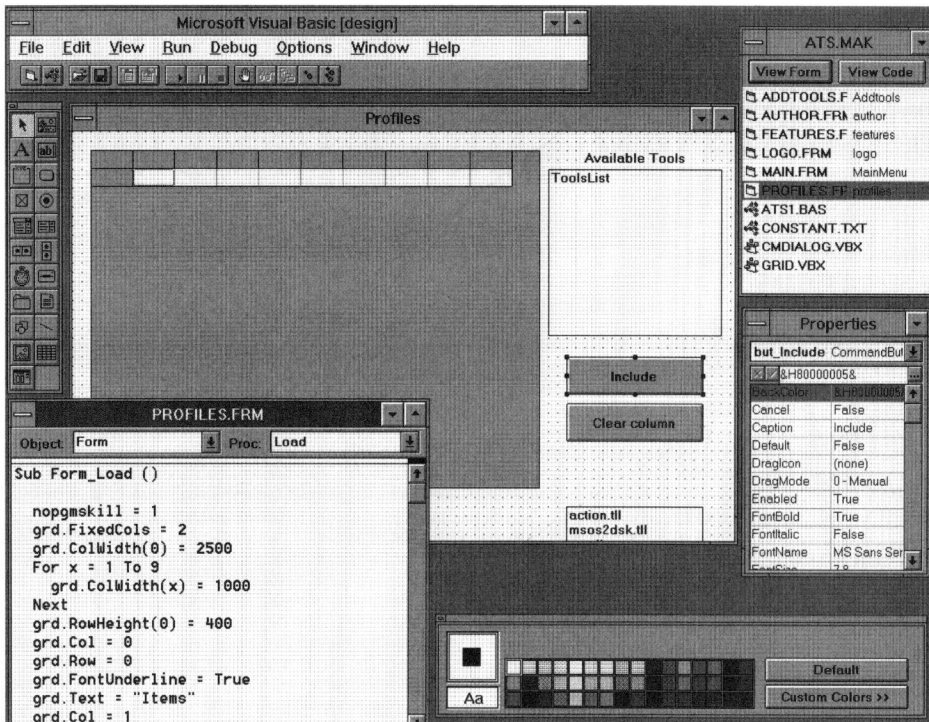

Figure 4.11 The authoring environment of *Visual Basic*

metaphor of *ToolBook* is really the book-and-page concept, and the window required for each book is a secondary concept. On the other hand, Microsoft's *Visual Basic* uses the window as its metaphor and its architecture—all the features of authoring are tied to one or more windows. It has many similarities to *ToolBook*, but there is no book-and-page architecture built in. This is both good and bad—good, because it means you are not limited to book and page, but bad because you don't have a predetermined structure to depend on, so you have to build something equivalent for yourself.

Visual Basic is a language-based assembly package that offers graphical author-ing of windows and their contents (objects), and then provides language-based authoring of the behavior of the objects. (In this latter respect, *VB* is similar to *ToolBook*.) It is very easy to create the windows—as many as you need for an interface and, if you are a programmer, it is moderately easy to attach code blocks to any kind of event for any object that requires custom behavior. Major interac-tive applications can be built with this environment. The environment provides a good set of debugging tools, and when your application is complete and correct, it can be compiled into a standard *Windows* executable format so it will run by itself under *Windows*. The author interface of *Visual Basic* is shown in Figure 4.11.

The main menu of *Visual Basic* is shown at the top of Figure 4.11, along with a window (Profiles) that is currently being authored. (*Visual Basic* calls each window a *form*.) Other windows of the environment include a tool palette at the left, an index of all the files in the current project (ATS.MAK), a color palette at the bottom, a window (Properties) listing the properties of the selected object (but_include), and a code window for some code (PROFILES.FRM) that is attached to the Profiles form. That code runs every time the Profiles window is started up.

The environment provides tools for creating windows, adding many types of objects to windows (shown in the tool palette), specifying attributes for each type of object, drawing and adding text to windows, and attaching code to all kinds of events that could happen with a window or an object. The system takes care of almost all of the structuring of your application's code—you only have to write the individual code modules. However, the large number of possibilities for where you can attach code means that you have to keep your wits about you, or you can get lost in a large project.

THE TIMELINE METAPHOR—*Action!*

Some applications, or parts of applications, lend themselves to timeline authoring. With this metaphor, you work with a time scale diagram and you place objects and events on the time scale in correct relationship to each other. This is especially valuable when you are dealing with a lot of animation or other dynamic activity. Macromind *Action!* is a good example of a presentation assembly program that contains the timeline approach. The timeline screen from *Action!* is shown in Figure 4.12.

Action! builds a presentation as a sequence of *scenes*. The scenes are treated the same as slides are in slide-oriented presentation authoring—they can be individually created and arranged in a slide sorter. The difference with a scene is that it is an animation in which you can control separately the behavior of every element (if you wish). Each scene has a timeline that details exactly when each part of that scene takes place and for how long. By double-clicking on an object in the timeline, the Edit Object dialog comes up for that object, as shown at the left in Figure 4.12. With the dialog, all the properties of the object and its behavior can be entered or edited. The control panel window at the lower right of the screen allows the presentation to be previewed at any time. Objects are selected from a tool palette, shown at the extreme right of the screen.

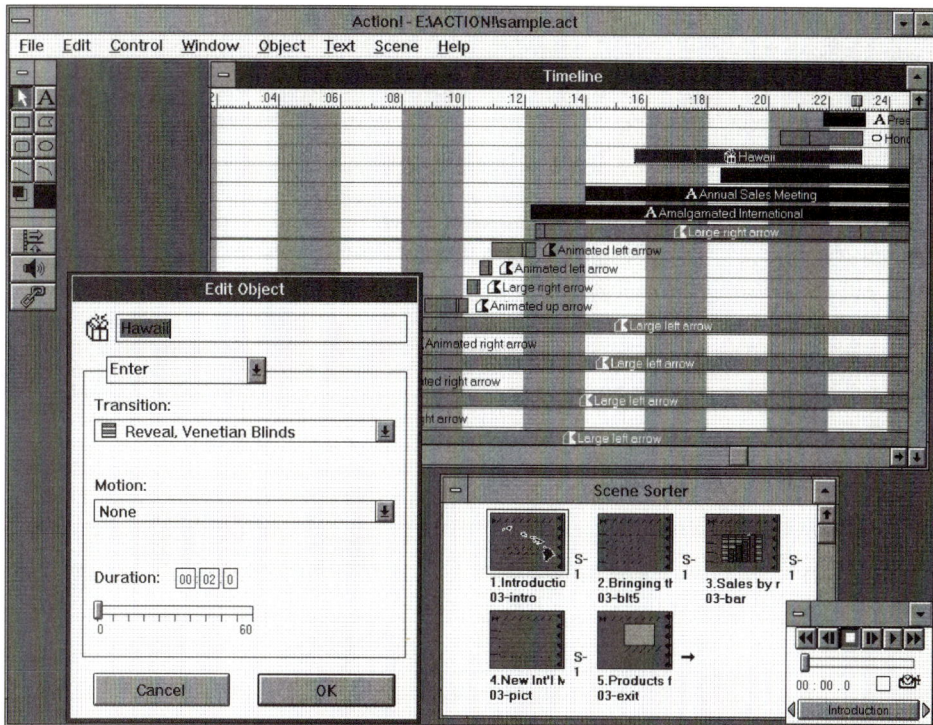

Figure 4.12   The authoring environment of *Action!*

Action! provides interactivity by allowing any object in a scene to become a *button.* When the user clicks a button, control can be sent to any other scene. Thus, you can build an application with a number of scenes, and your user could random access to any scene.

THE NETWORK METAPHOR—*MEDIAscript*

The ultimate interactive application would allow the user to move from any object in the application space to any other object without restriction. This is full random access, and maybe you wouldn't want all of it very often, but it is the most unrestricted concept of interactivity. Many assembly tools use hierarchical models of some sort, but these cause restrictions in that you must move between objects via the paths in the hierarchy. For some kinds of application you would like to have a more free environment that has no restrictions on where you can go. An approach to that is the network metaphor.

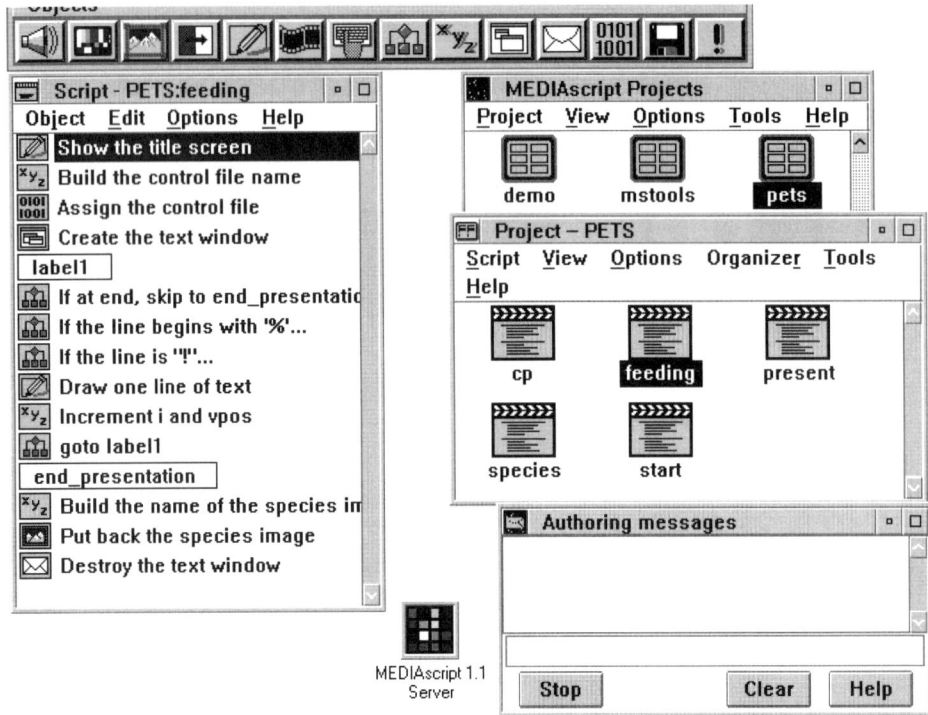

Figure 4.13 The authoring environment of *MEDIAscript*

The network metaphor can be built with any programming language, but it requires that the author be a programmer, and it provides no help to her in maintaining the organization of her application. An assembly program should provide that kind of help to an author.

One authoring package that implements the network metaphor is *MEDIAscript* from Network Technology Corporation. In *MEDIAscript*, an author builds a group of multimedia objects or functions in the form of *scripts*, which can be interconnected in a completely general fashion. A script is an executable object; it can be simple or complex. Scripts are built from a set of multimedia objects, 14 types in all, that support all of the functions of a full-featured programming language. However, the authoring interface is graphical: Objects are selected from a palette and placed into scripts, and the characteristics and behavior of each object are authored via dialog boxes. This environment is shown in Figure 4.13. A script window is shown at the left of the figure and the palette of objects is shown across the top of the screen. There are only 14 object types, but that small number encompasses all the capabilities of the full-featured authoring language that lies behind *MEDIAscript*'s graphical authoring interface.

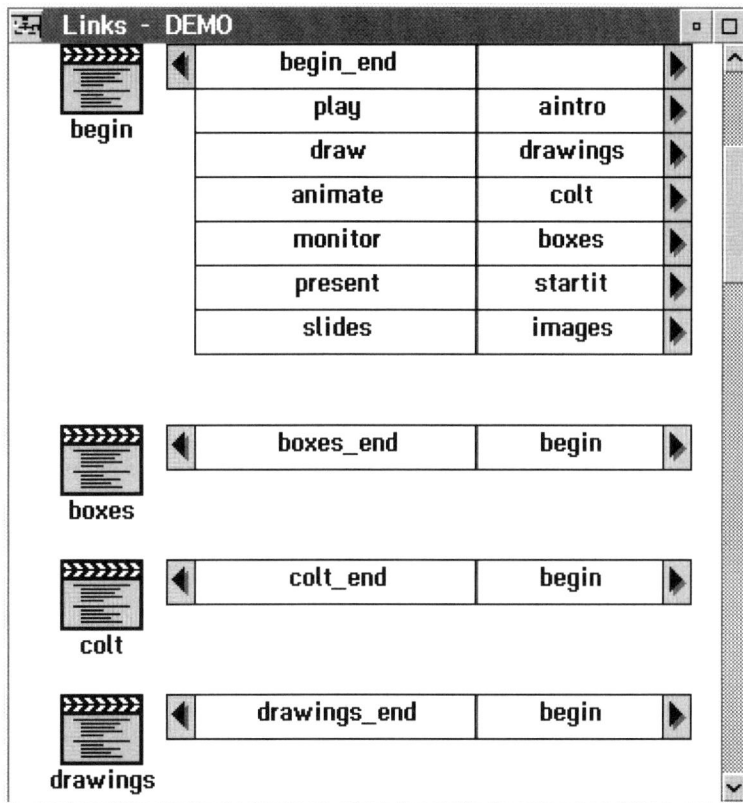

		begin_end		
		play	aintro	
		draw	drawings	
begin		animate	colt	
		monitor	boxes	
		present	startit	
		slides	images	
boxes		boxes_end	begin	
colt		colt_end	begin	
drawings		drawings_end	begin	

Figure 4.14 The *MEDIAscript* Organizer window

Scripts in *MEDIAscript* are connected by using its Organizer tool, shown in Figure 4.14. A script always runs from the beginning, but it can have any number of exit points, called *links*. Each link is given a name during the authoring of a script, and those names appear in the Organizer window as an item next to the icon for its parent script. In the Organizer, the author connects each exit point to the start of another script. There are no restrictions on this process, so a network of any degree of complexity can be built. Each link and its connection in the Organizer window has arrows that allow the author to traverse the network either forward or backward to see the application structure. A full example of an application authored in *MEDIAscript* is given in Chapter 15.

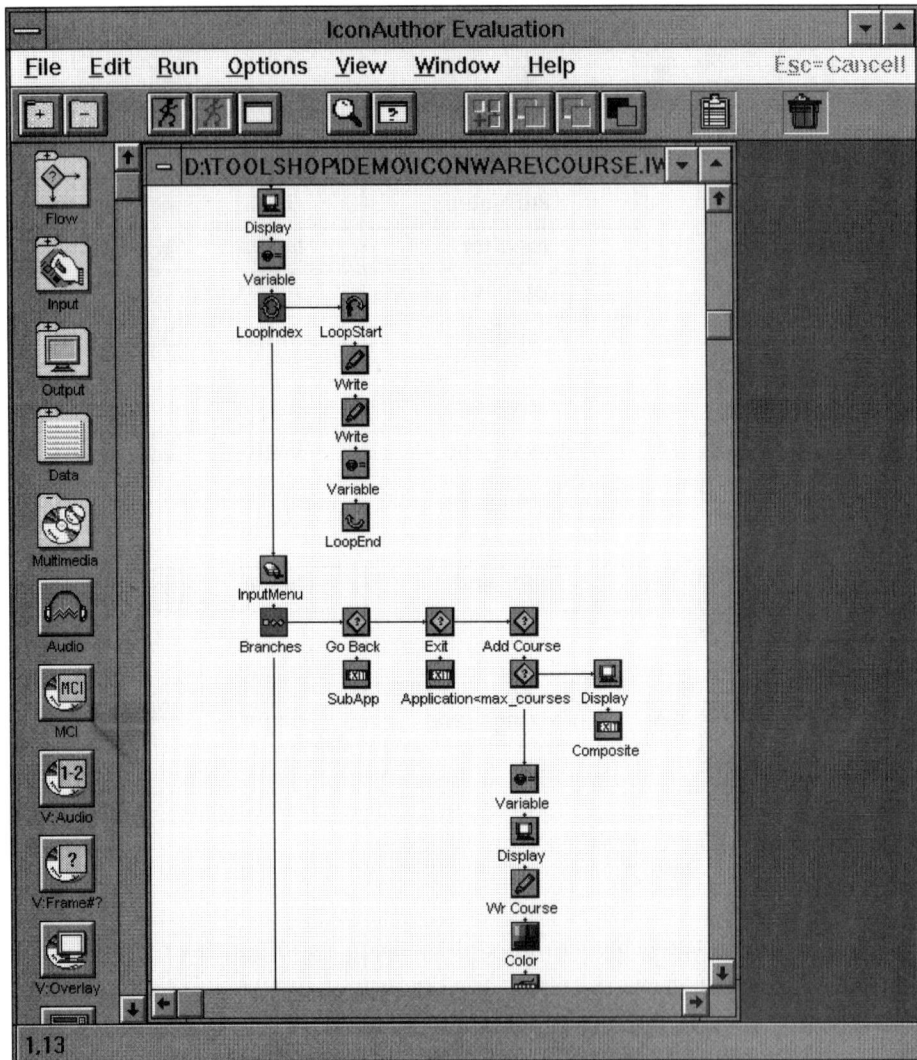

Figure 4.15 The authoring environment of *IconAuthor*

THE ICON METAPHOR—*IconAuthor*

An authoring metaphor that is particularly suited to authoring by nonprogrammers is the *Icon* metaphor. This metaphor is the basis for Aimtech's *IconAuthor* product, whose authoring environment is shown in Figure 4.15. In *IconAuthor*, an application structure is built by dragging icons from an icon palette into the application workspace and connecting them to create the logic of the application.

This is usually done as a flowchart. Then each icon is "opened" to reveal a dialog box that allows the properties and the content of that object to be defined. No scripting is required, and there is no language.

There are about 50 types of icons in *IconAuthor*, which provide support for nearly all computer functions and all multimedia functions. Audio, video, and animation are supported via MCI. DDE is also supported. Most of the flexibility of a language is provided in *IconAuthor*, without requiring any programming. However, developing sophisticated applications is still a difficult and complex task, but the author can concentrate on the application logic and content rather than on the details of programming and language syntax. But concentrating on logic still embodies some of the structural concepts of programming—an author planning to do complex applications will need training in the concepts of conditions, loops, data structures, nesting, etc. You still need to learn to think like a programmer to master the logic of a complex application.

SUMMARY

The authoring process encompasses many different tasks, which usually require an environment of tools to accomplish. Various authoring software products take different approaches to the organization of the environment and the way that applications are structured—this is called the metaphor of authoring. The following metaphors were discussed in this chapter:

- the slide show metaphor
- the book metaphor
- the windowing metaphor
- the timeline metaphor
- the network metaphor
- the icon metaphor

Each metaphor has advantages and disadvantages; the choice between them depends on the kinds of work you will be doing and on your personal preferences.

5

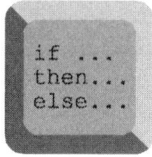

☐ Authoring Languages

All computer programs involve some kind of language or code to carry the commands that tell the computer what to do. The CPU microprocessor in the computer has its own language, often referred to as the CPU's instruction set. Ultimately, any other language will be resolved into an instruction set for running on the microprocessor of the target system. Although the instruction set means everything to the microprocessor, it it likely to be quite unintelligible to a human programmer, which leads to the need for different languages for use by programmers.

Languages become an issue in multimedia authoring because a language is a valid metaphor for the assembly stage of authoring. A well-designed language can allow an author to include in his application *anything* that his target system is capable of doing, and he will not be restricted by any predetermined limits built into the assembly tool. On the other hand, working with a language is *programming*, and not all of us are (or want to be) programmers. But there will be times when a feature you need in your application can only be achieved by using a language. Don't be put off by that, because many assembly tools include authoring languages that are surprisingly easy to learn and use.

This chapter discusses computer languages and focuses on languages specifically designed for multimedia authoring systems.

WHAT IS A LANGUAGE?

A language is a means for transmitting information—in this context it is information that gives instructions to a computer. *Programming* languages are languages that have been designed specifically for a person to use in building a program; they differ from the computer's instruction set in that they are easier for a person to read and understand. To use a programming language, you usually write text in the language using a text editor or word processor. This text, called the *source code*, is eventually converted by your language tools into CPU instructions for execution on the target platform.

With modern authoring tools, much authoring can be done without ever using or seeing a language. However, there are such vast possibilities for what you might do with multimedia, that no nonlanguage authoring tool will be able to do everything you might think of. If you intend to be as creative as possible in your multimedia development, you will want to know about authoring languages. That doesn't necessarily mean that you have to become a professional programmer; but, depending on what you want to accomplish, you may need to learn some programming techniques.

LANGUAGE LEVELS

The *level* of a programming language refers to how easy the language is to use. The lowest-level programming language is assembly language, which is a set of words or statements (sometimes called *mnemonics*) that resolve one for one to a CPU instruction set. The statements of a language are called its *syntax*. Assembly language allows a programmer to work with words that read like English, and by using a special software tool called an assembler, the language is converted directly to CPU instructions for execution or testing. Assembly programming is complex and difficult, but because it gives the programmer direct control over the CPU instructions, it can produce the fastest and most powerful programs. Because of its difficulty, assembly programming is rarely used except in limited parts of an application where the ultimate in processing speed must be achieved.

Another limitation of assembly language is that, because the programmer works directly with mnemonics that represent the CPU instruction set, the language is inherently CPU-specific. This means that if you want your program to run on several platforms having different CPU types, you have to rewrite your program for each platform.

High-Level Languages

Nearly all programming is done with *high-level* languages, which are designed to simplify programming by making each language statement perform a complete logical task. This usually makes each statement produce more than one CPU instruction. High-level languages require a special process to convert language statements into the correct groups of CPU instructions. This processing may be done as part of the programming process, where it is called *compiling*, or it may be done at runtime, where it is called *interpreting*. A major advantage of the high-level language approach is that the same program can be *ported* to different CPU platforms simply by having a compiler or interpreter for each platform. Then, a program you write in the high-level language can be run on several types of platforms—this is called being *portable*. Of course, there are limits to portability because different platforms may have different features.

A compiler converts language statements into CPU instructions in an *executable* format that can be run by the microprocessor. However, it is different than an assembler in that there is not a one-for-one correspondence between the language and the instructions. In fact, the relationship may become very complex in that compiled programs may include loops, jumps, and other sophisticated code constructs as a result of very simple language statements.

An interpreter has to do the same thing as a compiler—convert language statements into instruction sequences—but it does it at runtime. The interpreter uses the microprocessor to read each language statement and immediately to output additional instructions to the microprocessor to perform the tasks specified by the language. Because the microprocessor must share the work of interpreting and execution at the same time, it will run the program slower. Also, in the interest of not being too slow, an interpreter usually will take a simpler approach than a compiler, causing it to produce less than fully *optimized* code. These are major disadvantages of an interpreter. On the other hand, an interpreter makes programming faster because you do not have to worry about the compile step during programming and testing, which means that when you write a line of source code, you can execute it immediately.

There are numerous variations and combinations of the compile and interpret techniques. For example, compilers can be built to perform their work while you are entering language statements or editing them, so that a compiled instruction stream is available almost instantly at any time during programming—this is called *incremental compilation*. It helps to reduce the waiting that a normal compile step requires. Also, a composite approach is possible where the compiler produces an *intermediate code* , which is then interpreted at runtime. The advantage is that an intermediate code can be designed to interpret very efficiently, and thus eliminate much of the slowness of an interpreter, while still retaining most of the convenience of the interpreter approach.

Authoring assembly tools often use an intermediate code, so that they can be portable across platforms. Each platform has its own version of an interpreter for the intermediate code. Some tools use a text-based intermediate code that is accessible by the author—it is their authoring language.

General Programming Languages

Most professional programming is done with general-purpose (g-p) high-level languages, such as C, Pascal, BASIC, FORTRAN, etc. All languages come in compiler form, but BASIC is often available in interpreter form, too. The BASIC language, which was built into most of the early PCs, was interpreted, and many people have learned programming with it. A g-p language contains statements that address all normal programming constructs, but they deal only with general data types. Typical constructs in a general-purpose language are:

- *functions*—These are blocks of language statements that can be *called* to run from another place in your program. When the function completes, it returns to the next statement in the program that called it. In some languages, functions are called subroutines. The advantage of functions is that the same code can be used repeatedly in different parts of your application, and they can be used to impose an organized structure on your program.
- *data types*—A g-p language contains a variety of predetermined data types for storing numerical values, strings, or more complex information structures.
- *conditionals*—One or more data values are tested against a *condition statement*; if the condition is true, a specified action takes place; if it is false, a different action can be specified. In most languages, the conditional construct is of the form if-then-else.
- *loops*—A loop is used when the same process must be repeated a number of times. The number of repeats may be determined before the loop begins, or it can be determined dynamically by using a conditionl statement within the loop. Typical language constructs for looping are for, while, or do.
- *jumps*—Sometimes you need to move to another part of your program as the result of a conditional. This is called a *jump*, and the most common language statement for this is goto.
- *I/O*—Most languages provide statements for file input/output, access to CPU ports, serial and parallel devices, etc. Thus, the language is capable of accessing any device in the hardware environment.

There are other programming constructs not listed here. They are all general, applying to almost any kind of end use. You use data types to represent your unique information in the system. Data types in a g-p language are very general. Typical ones are:

- *integer* (int)—This is a data type for storing a number that has only integral values. Most systems also have a long data type, which is an integer that has a greater numerical range. Typically, int is a 16-bit value, having a signed range of –32,768 to 32,767, and a long data type is a 32-bit value having a signed range of –2,147,483,648 to 2,147,483,647.
- *float*—Most languages support *floating-point* numerical values, where the internal digital values represent a mantissa and an exponent. This is particularly valuable for scientific work or for working with precise graphical models, such as in a computer-aided design (CAD) program.
- *string*—Text is represented in a computer as a string value. Most languages support this data type.

There are other g-p data types in most languages, and some languages allow for the programmer to create his own special types. In some languages you can create elaborate data *structures* to represent complex data objects. However, this is entirely a responsibility of the programmer, and the language simply facilitates doing it. With a g-p language, the programmer must create all the code to tell the complex type how to behave.

The list below gives you a summary of language features. Except for the last item, it applies to any programming language—it lists all of the things that a "full-featured" language should have. A language must deal with each of the issues in this list if it intends to allow every part of the computer system to be accessible from within an application and any type of logical structure to be built.

Category	Capabilities
Program control	loop, branch, conditional, exit
Windows	create, manipulate, destroy windows and dialogs
User input	keyboard, mouse, touch input
Graphics	vector drawing, text, colors
File I/O	read/write data, random access, directory
Copy, cut, paste	use of the system clipboard
DDE, OLE	use of the system IPC
Printer access	use of the system printer
Functions	subroutines, calls
Data types	variables, arrays, structures, tables
String manipulation	string building and parsing, conversions
Numeric variables	integer, floating-point, long
Math	arithmetic, floating-point, random
Data conversion	convert between strings and numerics
Constants	numeric, string
Error management	recover from program errors
Multimedia objects	audio, video, image, animation, MCI

A general-purpose language can be used to write multimedia programs. However, the management of multimedia at the level of a g-p language becomes very complex. Therefore, multimedia authoring languages exist to encapsulate the details of common multimedia functions into a set of still higher-level commands. In order not to lose the flexibility of the g-p language, authoring languages are often written on top of a general language base.

MULTIMEDIA AUTHORING LANGUAGES

A multimedia authoring language is distinguished by having statements that are specific to multimedia objects and structures. For example, any authoring language will have statements for working with audio. Instead of worrying about the details of opening an audio file and passing its data to a player module, with an authoring language you just write a simple statement to identify the file to be played and say "play." Some typical multimedia tasks that are supported by authoring language statements are:

- loading an image from mass storage into memory
- performing a dynamic image transition
- playing an audio file
- playing a video file
- playing an animation
- defining on-screen objects such as windows and controls
- drawing into a window
- displaying text into a window
- receiving user input and assigning action

Any of these tasks would require pages of statements in a general-purpose programming language. In an authoring language, they are often accomplished by a single statement.

Objects

As with an entire authoring interface, an authoring language has a metaphor. Since the language ought to encapsulate a lot of the details of multimedia action into a few powerful statements, it is often appropriate to think of the multimedia items as *objects.* In the programming world, an object is an entity that has associated properties and behavior. (In professional object-oriented programming [OOP], objects have other characteristics, such as polymorphism, inheritance, and en-

AUDIO
OBJECT

PROPERTIES
FILE NAME
START POSITION
CURRENT POSITION
END POSITION
MIX
STATUS

BEHAVIOR
OPEN
PLAY
PAUSE
REWIND
SEEK
CLOSE

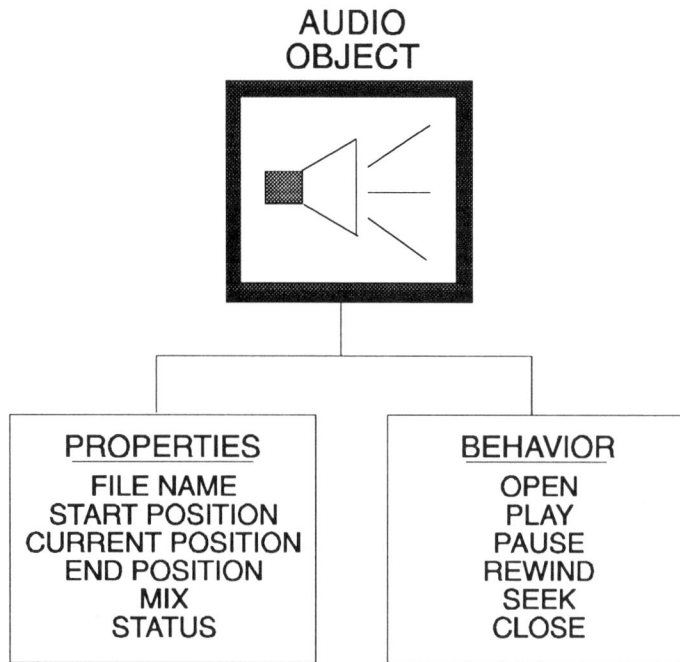

Figure 5.1   A typical multimedia object showing properties and behavior

capsulation. These may not necessarily apply to multimedia objects as they are defined here.) Objects are highly relevant to multimedia items also, and an *object-oriented* concept flows through most authoring languages. Figure 5.1 shows how an object for audio might be characterized by properties and behavior.

The properties of the audio object are the variables that specify what the object is, what it will do when commanded, and what its status is. Thus, the properties include the name of the audio file to be associated with the object, the start and end points in the file to play from and to, the way the object's output should be connected to the speakers (mix), the current play position, and the current play status (paused, playing, or closed). Typically, an audio object will have default values for all its properties except the file name. When an audio object is created by your program, you must deliberately specify any properties that you want to be different from default values.

The behavior items are listed in the form of commands you could issue to control the audio object in real time. Notice that such control implies a multi-tasking environment, because the object is running at the same time your application is sending commands to it. This is an inherent requirement for multimedia objects.

Some multimedia object types are:

- a motion video clip
- a vector drawing
- a bitmap image
- a block of text
- an animation sequence
- a window
- a user-input object
- an audio clip

In the above list, the Window object is somewhat different than the other items, because it can be a *container* for one or more of the other objects. There's nothing wrong with that; in fact, the concept of arranging objects into hierarchies is a very powerful one.

However, the idea of a window goes further than just a container; it provides a metaphor for user interaction. To accomplish this, an on-screen window has the property of being *active* or *inactive*. A window must be active before the user can interact with it. Only one window at a time is active, regardless of how many windows may be visible. In most windowing systems, the active window is high-lighted in a special way. It is placed *on top* of any other windows by a system action that happens automatically when a user clicks a mouse button while the pointer is in any part of a window, or when he touches a window in a touch-driven system. Therefore, the active window is also a channel for user input; in fact, it is the only window that can receive input at a given time.

AUTHORING LANGUAGE EXAMPLES

Although it would be wonderful if there was a universal standard for an authoring language so that everyone's programs would work in all environments, no such thing has been achieved. However, most authoring companies have developed their own standard language, which sometimes applies to a range of products and platforms. In addition, there is an important language subset, which is rapidly becoming standard, known as the MCI (Media Control Interface) language for communicating multimedia commands in Microsoft *Windows* and IBM *OS/2*. Some of the different languages are discussed below.

Language Example—*OpenScript*

Asymetrix *ToolBook* uses an authoring language called *OpenScript*. It is a full-featured programming language, which includes support for all normal computer functions, multimedia functions via DDE and MCI, hypertext features, and some database features. The language is designed to read almost like English text, so you can usually figure out what is going on by reading *OpenScript* scripts. However, this does not necessarily make the language easier to learn and write, because it is not really English, and only *one* choice of the myriad ways you can say something in English actually works for each situation in *OpenScript*. However, it is an important concept, and several other languages have taken similar approaches. The following list gives a summary of the most important *OpenScript* language key words.

Category	Commands
Program control	do-until, if-then-else, conditions-when-else, while, execute, go
Windows	activate, add, check, clear, hide, magnify, move, remove
User input	ask, beep, request
Graphics	draw, importGraphic
File I/O	openFile, closeFile, readFile, writeFile, save as, createFile
Copy, cut, paste	
DDE, OLE	getRemote, setRemote, executeRemote, closeRemote
Printer access	print, printeject
Functions	to get, return, to handle, end, to set
Data types	local, system, properties
String manipulation	ansiToChar, charToAnsi, search
Numeric variables	get, set
Math	abs, cos, sin, tan, exp, log, random, sqrt
Data conversion	
Constants	
Error management	sysError, sysSuspend
Multimedia objects	tbkBitmap, tbkMCI, tbkMM, tbkTimer

There are a total of 750 keywords, constants, etc., in *OpenScript*. This attests to the language's richness and power. But, it is a lot to learn. Below is an example of some *OpenScript* code. You can see that it is quite readable.

```
to handle buttonup
  request "Save Book First?" with "Yes" or "No" or
   "Cancel"
  conditions
  when it is "Yes"
```

```
   send save
 when it is "Cancel"
   break to system
 end conditions
 export "temp.dat" as delimited using "!"
end buttonup
```

Language Example—MCI

MCI is a language *subset* because it applies only to multimedia objects; it does not support the nonmultimedia functions of the system. Nevertheless, it is still important because it applies to a wide range of hardware and software products, and it will be extended to more products in the future. There are two forms of the MCI interface as far as the operating system is concerned—the command-message interface and the command-string interface. The command-message interface is a direct call to the MCI *dynamic link library* (DLL), and it is most relevant to use with general-purpose programming languages. In a DLL interface, you must first intialize the desired DLL, meaning that you make sure it is loaded into memory. Then you call a DLL function by giving its name followed by a list of mandatory or optional arguments. Some authoring assembly products support a general DLL interface, but you definitely have to know programming to use it. The command-string interface is much easier to use because it is based on an ASCII text syntax using an English-like language. Most authoring assembly products support the processing of MCI command strings.

The MCI command-string syntax will be important to you even if you are using a graphical interface authoring assembly system and you are not a programmer. In such an environment, there usually will be a mode where you can write an MCI command string, and the assembly system will pass it on to the *Windows* or *OS/2* system. This is the way that the assembly program can support all MCI devices including ones that did not exist when the assembly program was written. If you know the MCI command-string syntax and you can write MCI commands for your system to pass through this way, you can author any device that has an MCI driver. You are not limited to just those devices for which your authoring system has built-in support. It is open-ended for future new devices.

With MCI, a device is identified by a type name. The next list gives the present MCI device types. Others will be added in the future.

Device Type	Description
cdaudio	CD audio player
dat	Digital audio tape player
digitalvideo	Digital video in a window

mmmovie	Multimedia movie (animation) player
overlay	Analog video in a window
scanner	Image scanner
sequencer	MIDI audio sequencer
vcr	Video cassette recorder/player
videodisc	Videodisc player
waveaudio	WAVE audio player
other	Undefined MCI device

Any new device that you add to your environment will be identified by one of these names when you install its MCI driver software. In subsequent MCI command strings you will use the same name to identify the device. AN MCI command string has three parts: *command, device_name,* and *arguments.* The command is a keyword that specifies the action desired, the device_name is the logical name of an installed device, and the arguments are any parameters required by or optional for the specified command and device. Commands fall into four categories:

1. system commands—These are commands that are provided by the operating system directly. They are: break, which specifies a key that will interrupt an MCI device; sound, which plays system sounds; and sysinfo, which returns information about MCI devices.

2. required commands—These are commands that must be supported by each device. They are: capability, which returns the capabilities of a device; open, which initializes the device; close, which closes the device; info, which returns text information about a device; and status, which returns status information from the device.

3. basic commands—These are the basic commands for operating a device. Their use is optional by the device, but most devices use the ones that apply. They are: load, pause, play, record, resume, save, seek, set, status, and stop.

4. extended commands—These are additional commands or extended definitions of the basic commands that take the device capability beyond the basic commands. Because this is open-ended, there are no specific definitions for extended commands. If you are working with a device that has extended commands, you must obtain the command syntax from the documentation for the device.

The *device_name* is usually the same as the device type names listed previously; but if there is more than one device installed of the same type, the names beyond the first will have integer numbers appended to them.

The objective here is not to teach you MCI commands, but only to show you how simple and easy they are. Here is an example of a command sequence that plays some audio from a CD audio player:

```
open cdaudio1
play cdaudio from 6000 to 12000 wait
close cdaudio
```

Notice that the play command used the optional parameters *from* and *to* to specify the start and end times on the disc to play, and it used the flag *wait* to tell the system to wait until the playback is finished before continuing.

If your authoring assembly tool has CD audio playback already built in, you would not have to use MCI commands for that, because the assembly tool would have its own interface for authoring CD audio. However, for any new device that your assembly tool does not know about, you can author for it by finding the MCI syntax from the device documentation and telling your assembly tool that you want to send bare MCI command strings.

Language Example—*Visual Basic*

Although *Visual Basic* (VB) is a general-purpose programming language, you can use it for multimedia. As explained in the previous chapter, VB has an excellent interface for creating and manipulating windows, and the language is used only to attach actions to events occurring in windows. The language is similar to the old BASIC, which was provided with early PCs, but it has many extensions to increase its power and to make it a true professional structured programming environment. The next list gives a summary of the most important language keywords.

Category	Commands
Program control	do-loop, for-next, gosub-return, goto, if-then-else
Windows	show, hide, load, unload, move, drag, refresh
User input	inputbox$
Graphics	line, circle, point, pset, load picture, print, scale, cls
File I/O	open, close, print#, put, write#, seek, close
Copy, cut, paste	clear, getdata, getformat, gettext, settext, setdata
DDE, OLE	linksend, linkexecute, linkpoke, linkrequest
Printer access	print, printform, enddoc, newpage, scale, tab
Functions	function, sub, call, declare, exit function, exit sub
Data types	integer, long, single, double, currency, string, user-defined
String manipulation	format$, space$, string$, chr$, instr, left$, mid$,

	right$, len
Numeric variables	dim, global, static
Math	exp, log, sqr, atn, cos, sin, tan, abs, sgn, rnd
Data conversion	fix, int, asc, str$, val, hex$
Constants	const
Error management	on error, resume, err, erl, error$, error
Multimedia objects	none

This keyword list is typical for a general-purpose language; there are more than 100 commands, and yet multimedia is not specifically supported. Figure 5.2 shows a code example for *VB*.

This example is from a simple application that draws boxes of color when you click a button labelled Draw. The code shown runs every time you click the Draw button. It initializes currentx to start the drawing at the left side of the target window, and then draws 11 rectangles in a line across the window. It then moves the drawing position down to a new line, revises the draw color, and waits for the user to click the button again. The value of the red color is decremented by 25 each time, and when it reaches zero, the window is cleared and drawing will resume from the top of the window. Except for some global code that initialized the variables and a one-line procedure for another button called Quit, the procedure shown is the entire application. All the code to create the window and to manage user input to the buttons is generated automatically by *VB*'s graphical authoring interface.

Language Example—*MEDIAscript*

The *MEDIAscript* authoring language was designed from the ground up as an authoring language, but at the same time it includes features to make it a general-purpose language as well. There are actually two similar *MEDIAscript* languages or dialects; one is used in the DOS product, which has a language-only authoring interface, and the other is used in *MEDIAscript OS/2*, which has a graphical interface as well as a language interface. (The language interface is accessible only in the Professional version of the product.) The next list shows the *MEDIAscript OS/2 Professional Version* command list.

Category	Commands
Program control	execute, goto, if...endif, quit, rest, run, wait
Windows	window, alert, button, entry, list, scroll
User input	input, entry
Graphics	line, [f]rect, [f]poly, [f]ellipse, clear, draw, font, text
File I/O	assign, cd, copy, delete, dir

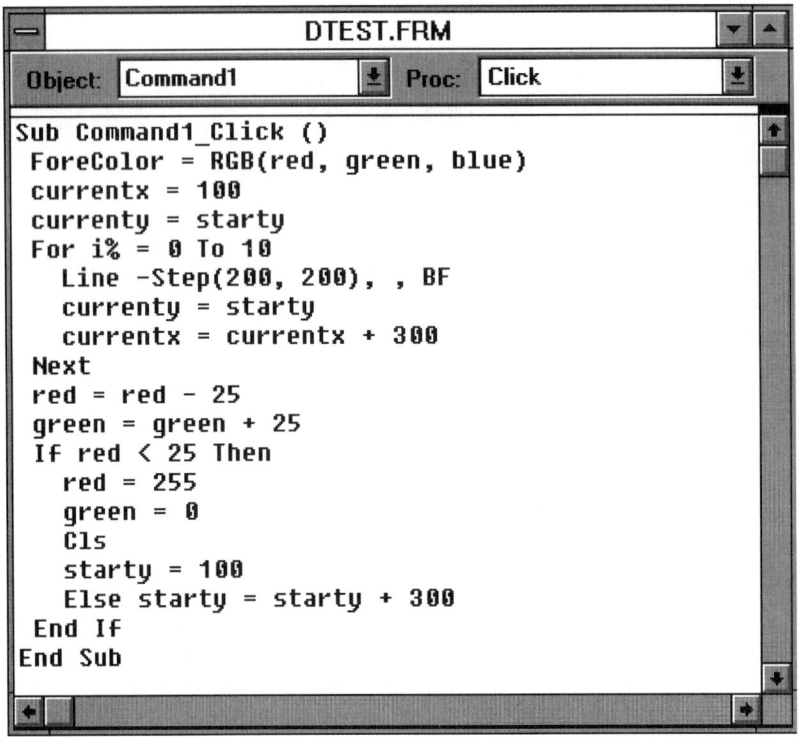

```
┌─────────────────────────────────────────────────────────┐
│ ─                       DTEST.FRM                    ▼ ▲ │
├─────────────────────────────────────────────────────────┤
│ Object: │Command1         │ ±  Proc:  │Click         │ ± │
├─────────────────────────────────────────────────────────┤
│ Sub Command1_Click ()                                 ↑ │
│  ForeColor = RGB(red, green, blue)                      │
│  currentx = 100                                         │
│  currenty = starty                                      │
│  For i% = 0 To 10                                       │
│    Line -Step(200, 200), , BF                           │
│    currenty = starty                                    │
│    currentx = currentx + 300                            │
│  Next                                                   │
│  red = red - 25                                         │
│  green = green + 25                                     │
│  If red < 25 Then                                       │
│    red = 255                                            │
│    green = 0                                            │
│    Cls                                                  │
│    starty = 100                                         │
│    Else starty = starty + 300                           │
│  End If                                                 │
│ End Sub                                                 │
│                                                       ↓ │
├─────────────────────────────────────────────────────────┤
│ ◄ │                                                 │ ► │
└─────────────────────────────────────────────────────────┘
```

Figure 5.2 The *Visual Basic* code window showing the procedure for the main action of the dtest program

Copy, cut, paste	
DDE, OLE, comm	com, DDE
Printer access	print
Functions	script
Data types	long integer, string, rectangle, color
String manipulation	search, str(), set, concatenation, substring
Numeric variables	query, set, rand
Math	+, −, *, /
Data conversion	integer-string, string-integer
Constants	
Error management	echo, error
Multimedia objects	audio, color(), icopy, image, sequence, transition, video

Notice that the *MEDIAscript* syntax appears simpler than some of the other languages. This is not entirely the case; although there are fewer keywords to learn in *MEDIAscript*, they accomplish their power by having many options or

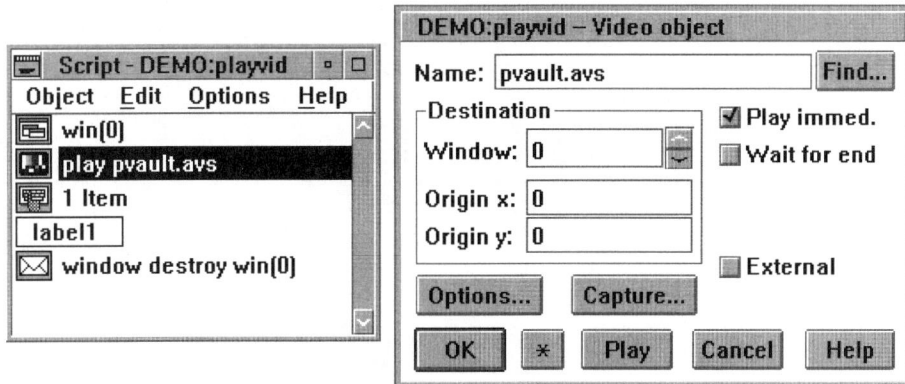

Figure 5.3 A *MEDIAscript* script (left) that plays video in a window. The video object's dialog is open at the right.

arguments attached. This is one way to go in authoring languages—make each command higher level, but support a lot of options.

Most authoring in *MEDIAscript OS/2* is not done with the language because there is an excellent graphical interface. All authoring with the graphical interface results in a language script. In the *Professional Edition*, tools are provided for working at the language level as well as the graphical interface. This is particularly useful when extensions are required that might be impossible or at least difficult to achieve through the graphical interface.

An example of a *MEDIAscript* script that was authored graphically follows (command keywords are in bold):

```
set link="_playvid_end"
window win(0) (5184) (3600) (4016) (2560)  /t:"" /st /f
/v:(0) /i /a
  button push win(0).control(0) (2816) (2128) (800)
  (304) /t:"Exit"
video play "pvault.avs" /d:win(0)
:ip1:input /c:win(0),0
  if (win(0).ctrl&(1<0)):goto label1:endif:* Exit
goto ip1
:label1
window destroy win(0)
```

This script plays the video file pvault.avs in a window. The window is created at the start of the script by the window command, and it is destroyed when the user clicks a pushbutton labelled Exit, created by the button statement. The video statement starts the video playing and the input statement waits for user interaction. If the user clicks the pushbutton, the input command stops waiting, and the if statement checks what he did and passes control to the label: label1, where the window is destroyed and the script ends. The set command at the start of the script simply names the script for use in the *MEDIAscript* Organizer. In the graphical authoring environment, this script appears as shown in Figure 5.3. The script consists of just five objects; each has an authoring dialog associated with it that can be opened by double-clicking the object in the script. The dialog for the video object is open at the right in the figure.

AUTHORING LANGUAGE STANDARDS

Standards are what you define them to be. Part of the definition of a standard is its scope—in what arena do you expect the standard to apply? For example, each of the languages discussed in this chapter is a standard as far as its manufacturer is concerned. Within its software environment, its language is standard. However, the languages are all different, so if we enlarge the arena to include all IBM-compatible PCs (for example) then the languages are no longer standard. Further, we can enlarge the arena to include other platforms than the IBM-compatibles— Apple Macintosh, Sony MMCD, Commodore Amiga, or others. We find a still larger proliferation of incompatible "standards."

The ultimate goal for an authoring language is that code written with the language should run on *any* platform. If you are authoring for your own use or for a small community of users whom you can control, that may not seem important. But if you are writing commercial applications for the widest possible audience, a cross-platform standard will broaden your market. You need write your application only once to target all platforms. That is the goal of Kaleida's *ScriptX* universal scripting language.

Kaleida Labs is a joint venture of Apple Computer and IBM for development of multimedia technologies. *ScriptX* is one of their major projects—to create a universal language that will allow multiple digital platforms to play the same digital file without modification. Kaleida plans to support developers, toolmakers, and hardware vendors to accomplish this through innovative software. Each different platform has to have its own *ScriptX* runtime environment that becomes a part of the hardware package—either stored in ROM or as part of the operating system. Kaleida will work with hardware vendors to accomplish this.

Because different platforms have different features and capabilities, the *ScriptX* runtime environment includes *dynamic adaptation* that allows an application to query the environment of the current platform and decide in real time how it can best present itself. *ScriptX* is fully object-oriented, with the capability for the user to combine objects at runtime. For example, a *ScriptX* model of a fish could have subclasses that show its internal organs or skeleton. A viewer object could have subclasses that provide a magnifier or an x-ray viewer. Combining these objects at runtime would allow the user to zoom in using the magnifier or examine the internals of the fish using the x-ray viewer.

Probably only professional programmers would write in the *ScriptX* language itself. For that reason, a syntax list is not included here. However, the capabilities of *ScriptX* will eventually be available to anyone by providing it as an output format in graphical-interface authoring tools. For example, when you are saving a project from your authoring tool, you could have the option to "save as *ScriptX*." The output you created that way could then run on any *ScriptX* platform. That is the reason Kaleida plans to work with tool vendors.

SUMMARY

Although most assembly products use a lot of graphical authoring, authoring languages are still needed to achieve the most flexible authoring. Compared to general-purpose programming languages, authoring languages tend to have higher-level support for multimedia concepts such as windows, graphics, images, audio, video, and animation. Most authoring languages are also object-oriented. The MCI multimedia control language is becoming an industry standard for device-independent control of multimedia devices.

6

 **Still Images**

Because still images take relatively modest amounts of storage and they are easy to work with, they are probably the best value you can find in multimedia. There's nothing like using photographs or other realistic images to beef up a presentation. You do need some special hardware and software to add high-quality stills to your environment, and this chapter discusses the hardware requirements, the software requirements, and some of the considerations of preparing and manipulating still images in your multimedia applications. Most realistic images are digitized as bitmaps, and that is the primary thrust of this chapter. Vector (drawn) images are a valid alternative in many cases, and some of the principles discussed for bitmaps also apply to vector images; these are covered in detail in the next chapter.

THE NUMBERS FOR VIDEO DISPLAY

Some of the basic attributes of video display, such as pixels, resolution, bits per pixel (bpp), etc., were discussed in Chapter 4. As explained there, a resolution of 640×480 pixels is usually enough for multimedia applications, but 4 bpp (16 colors) is not. To effectively reproduce photographs or other real images, you need at least 16 bpp (32,767 colors) or more. When you consider the amount of memory required to store an image, there is a tradeoff between resolution and bpp, as shown in Table 6.1.

Table 6.1 The amount of space needed to store a single image of various resolutions and colors.

Resolution	4 bpp 16 Colors	8 bpp 256 Colors	16 bpp 65 K Colors	24 bpp 16 M Colors
640 × 480	153,600	307,200	614,400	921,600
800 × 600	240,000	480,000	960,000	1,440,000
1024 × 768	393,216	786,432	1,572,864	2,369,296
1280 × 960	665,360	1,310,720	2,621,440	3,932,160

The storage requirements shown in the table apply in at least four different ways. First, the display memory of the video adaptor must be large enough to hold one image. Second, any off-screen storage of images in system RAM will need the same amount of space. (Off-screen storage is necessary when images are displayed with dynamic transitions or when they are held in RAM for fast response display.) The third requirement is for permanent storage of images on hard disk or other mass storage. The fourth case is for communicating images over a network—the numbers above represent the amount of data that must be sent for each full-screen image. In the latter two cases, you can consider the possibility of *image compression*; the other two situations cannot use compressed images because decompression would slow the operation too much. Image compression is important, in the cases where it can be used, because it reduces the image data size by as much as 20 :1. Notice that vector images are inherently compressed when compared to the bitmaps that they generate; in fact, compression factors can be much greater than 20:1 for vector images.

Video display boards typically have 1 or 2 megabytes of display memory. From Table 6.1, a 1 MB board can do 24 bpp at 640 × 480, 16 bpp at 800 × 600, and 8 bpp at 1024 × 768. With 2 MB of display memory, you can go to 800 × 600 at 24 bpp, 1024 × 768 at 16 bpp, and 1280 × 960 at 8 bpp.

The other consideration that depends on the image data sizes above is speed. Everything else being the same, images will load slower from disk, process slower, and display slower as the image data size increases. Of course, you can offset this by using faster CPUs, faster disk systems, local buses, and video accelerators. Those devices are effective, but they add cost. The bottom line is that higher resolution and higher colors are going to cost more. You have to decide how much it is worth to you to have the ultimate in resolution and color reproduction.

SELECTING VIDEO DISPLAY HARDWARE

The discussion of video display in Chapter 3 and the preceding section provide the necessary input regarding the technical considerations of video display. Now you have to decide what kind of system you need or want. To summarize that information, I will repeat my recommendations here and discuss some of the implications.

First, if you are selecting hardware for authoring, you will benefit greatly by going to higher-than-VGA resolution because it gives you more room on the screen for the many windows used in authoring. That was shown in Figure 3.2. Also, you should have high-color (16 bpp) or true-color (24 bpp) capability so you can reproduce realistic images, even if you will be authoring for standard VGA screens, because it greatly enhances your ability to work with images, and it also makes you ready for the time (which will come) when your target systems also go to high color. Putting all that together, you need a video display adaptor with at least 1 megabyte of RAM and with an accelerator chip onboard. The accelerator is essential to get adequate system response in the high-resolution and high-color modes. Boards fitting these requirements are currently running at street prices below $300. There are several to choose from, and these prices will probably continue to drop as volume builds for these boards.

Another consideration enters if you also want to do image or video capture from analog inputs. First, the price of equivalent boards with capture capability goes up two or three times or more compared to display-only boards. This is mostly a sign of the lower production volume for capture capability. There are also fewer choices.

The high-resolution system will also require a larger monitor—17" or larger. You have to get too close to small monitors at high resolution to see everything that's there, and it quickly becomes uncomfortable. Because monitor prices rise astronomically beyond 17", you may settle for that size. Even so, you will be paying around twice the price of a good 14" VGA screen. In any case, before purchasing, you should see your proposed display board and monitor demonstrated together operating in the modes you plan to use.

Now, if you will be authoring and presenting on the same system, your selection is finished. However, if you are also choosing display hardware for an end-user target system, there are some other considerations. Of course, it would be great if all your users had the same kind of system you use for authoring. That is expensive, and you probably don't need it just for multimedia delivery. If your users are running multimedia on the desktop, a high-color VGA adaptor and a good 14" monitor will be fine, and it will reduce the demands on your authored applications. On the other hand, if you will be playing to large audiences, you may have to consider large screens or even projection displays. The prices will be much higher for these, and still higher if you depart from VGA resolution levels. Again, for multimedia display by itself, standard VGA resolution (640 × 480) is good enough.

When choosing a video monitor, you must make sure that the monitor supports the horizontal and vertical scan frequencies required by the display modes you will be using. The least expensive monitors usually only support the scan frequencies for standard VGA, which are 60 Hz vertical and 31.5 kHz horizontal. However, if you are planning to use super VGA, your monitor will need higher scan frequencies. You can get the exact numbers by looking at the specifications for the super VGA display board you will use and comparing those numbers with the range of scan frequencies supported by the monitor you are considering. Make sure the monitor will go at least as high as the board will require.

IMAGE AUTHORING CONSIDERATIONS

Of course, the most important image authoring consideration is where to get images in the first place. You can either create your own images by capturing or drawing them, or you can acquire them from an image or clip art library. The processes of acquisiton and creation require special tools, which are discussed later in this chapter. Right now, let's consider images from the point of view of assembling an application. The task of integrating still images into a multimedia application is the work of an assembly tool. There are quite a few image features that an assembly tool should provide, as explained below. These are approximately in order of descending importance.

Image Selection

You must choose the file name of the image you are going to work with; you should be able to retrieve images from anywhere in your mass storage. Once you choose an image to use, you should have the choice of copying it into the application's local storage or continuing to read it from wherever it is. Another feature, when you leave the image where it is, is to have means at a later time to identify all of the images (and other assets) used by the application and to build a new directory that contains only the files used by the one application. This is important when you are preparing an application for distribution. These features all sound simple, but you would be surprised at how big a mess you can generate after you have authored ten applications and their contents are scattered all over your mass storage system.

Positioning

Images ordinarily are treated as rectangles, and you should be able to place an image rectangle anywhere in the display area you are working with—either the whole screen, or just within a window. Of course, if you are using windows, you also must specify which window each image goes into. If you need shapes other than rectangles, see the discussion below about transparency.

Cropping

Sometimes a source image contains more information than you want to display. You should be able to select an arbitrary rectangle from a source image and display only that rectangle. This is called *cropping*. Figure 6.1 shows an example of cropping. You can use an image processing tool to do cropping, but it is such a simple feature that most assembly tools also will do it. When you are doing a large amount of cropping (meaning that you are displaying only a small portion of the source image), it usually is advantageous to make a separate cropped image before you are finished authoring, just because it will save storage and speed up loading in the final application. An important application of cropping, which must be handled by cropping in the assembly tool, is using a single image as a

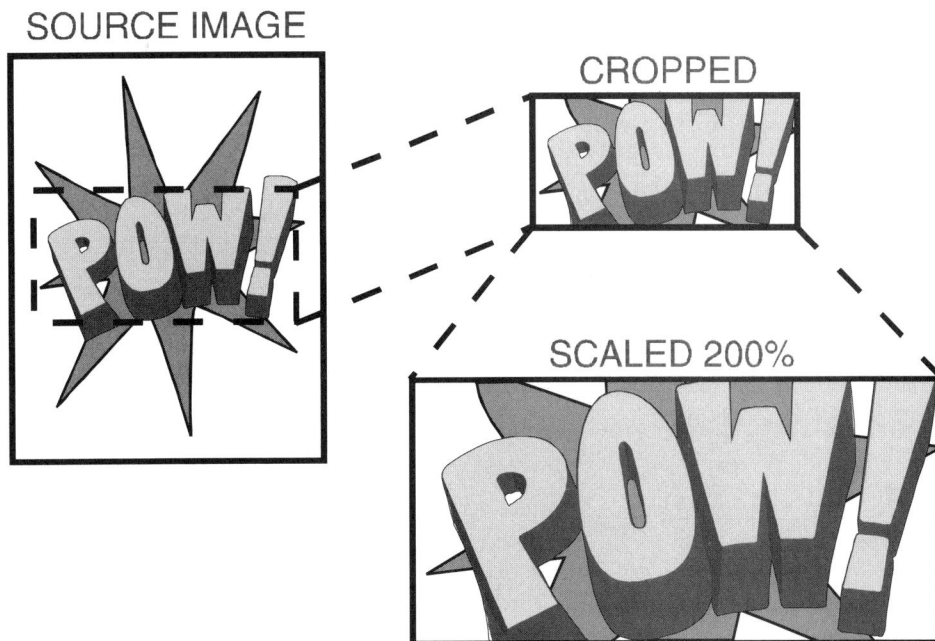

Figure 6.1 Cropping and scaling an image

kind of library containing a multiplicity of small images that are used by the application. That technique is advantageous because it simplifies file management and may also speed up the application because you have to tolerate the delay of image loading only once. In this case, you cannot avoid cropping in real time as the application runs.

Scaling

Sometimes the source image is not the right size to fit your display space. In this case, you need to *scale* the image to fit a display rectangle, as shown in Figure 6.1. It is desirable for an assembly tool to provide a way to scale an image as it is being loaded. Scaling is an additional process that must be performed by the CPU or a video accelerator; it will take time. If scaling takes too long in your application, then you should probably scale the source image during authoring and make a copy of it in the correct size. Sometimes you will display an image in a window so that your end user can adjust its size. In that case, you may want the contents of the window to automatically scale to fit whatever size window the user makes. Some assembly tools offer an option for doing that automatically.

Transitions

If you simply load an image from mass storage into a display area, you usually will get some kind of halting vertical wipe transition as blocks of the image are progressively read from storage by the file system. If you want a prettier, or different, transition than that, the image must first be loaded from mass storage into off-screen RAM, and then a transition must be applied as a separate process. Most assembly tools provide one or more (often many) ways to do that automatically. Transitions by dissolving, random blocking, wiping, shearing, or sliding, are some of the choices. Usually the direction and speed of transitions can also be specified. Figure 6.2 shows some image transition types.

Holding

Sometimes you want to load an image from mass storage and not display it immediately, or hold the image after you have displayed it once so that you can quickly display it again. The example given above, where a single source image holds several blocks that are displayed separately, is a case that requires the ability to keep an image in memory.

| Edges In Vertical | Edges In Horizontal | Edges Out Vertical | Edges Out Horizontal | Random Columns | Random Rows | Square In |
| Square Out | Wipe Left | Wipe Right | Wipe Up | Wipe Down | Checker Board | Random Blocks |

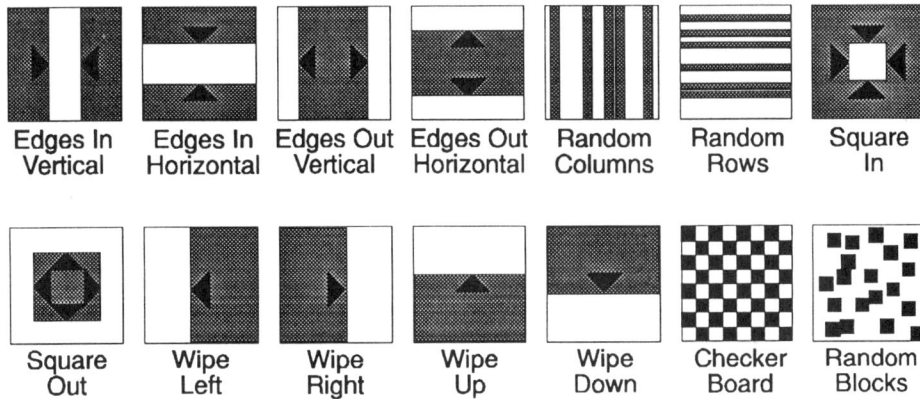

Figure 6.2 Dynamic image transitions

Another case where you want to hold an image is in an interactive application where you want an image to display *immediately* when the user does something. Waiting the several seconds required for it to load from disk is too much delay; you want to load the image ahead of time, so it is ready when the user clicks a button. Not all assembly tools provide these features.

When you do hold images, you have to be sure that there is a way to release the hold; otherwise, you can get all of your memory tied up holding images. One approach to image holding is to simply load an image into a window that is not displayed. Then you can display the image on cue either by making its window visible or by transitioning it from the invisible window to another window that is already visible. When you are finished with the held image, you simply destroy its window.

Transparency

You may want to display images that are not rectangles. That is easily accomplished if the system supports a color in the image that is *transparent*. When the image is being loaded, copied, or transitioned to the screen, any pixels of the transparent color will not be copied, meaning that their location on the screen will remain as it was before the transition. So, if you have an image of a person against a background of the transparent color, you can place that person on a different background by loading the new background first, and then doing a transparent transition of the person's image on top of the background.

In broadcast television, this process is known as *chroma keying*, and it is widely used, for example, to place the weather reporter in front of the weather map. In

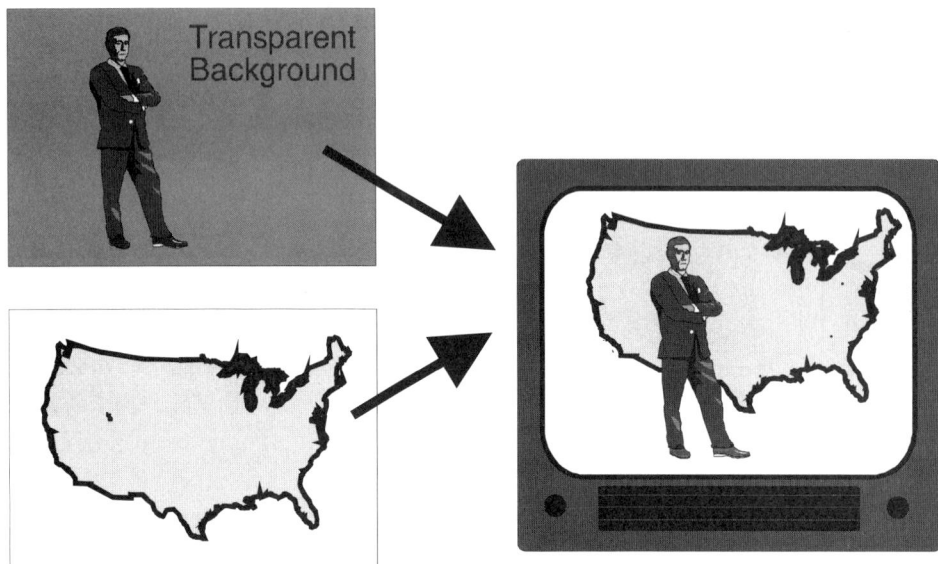

Figure 6.3 Transparency used to place a foreground image on a background image

that case, the weather reporter stands in front of a blue background, and the blue color in the image from the camera looking at him is made transparent. The weather reporter's image is transparently copied frame by frame on top of a fixed image of the weather map background. Figure 6.3 shows this.

IMAGE COMPRESSION

Table 6.1 showed that bitmapped images take a lot of data. This uses up storage and takes time to load or communicate. Therefore, it is highly desirable to use *image compression* to reduce image data size. Many techniques for image compression have been developed over the years, leading to a tremendous confusion of image data formats. This is so bad that you will probably need to have at least one tool for image format conversion so that you can deal with all the different kinds of images you will get. Some of the formats are compressed, and some are not. However, for compressed images, the field is rapidly narrowing to one type of compression which has become a standard — this is called the *JPEG* format. JPEG (pronounced *jay-peg*) stands for *Joint Photographic Expert Group*, which is a body sponsored by the International Standardizing Organization (ISO) and the

International Electrotechnical Commission (IEC) specifically to standardize compression of digital images. The JPEG standard actually is several different standards, but they are combined into a *parameterized* structure so that a JPEG image file always contains the information needed to identify the process required to decompress it. I will not go into a lot of detail of how image compression works, but there are some technical things you should know about image compression in order to help you select authoring hardware and software.

Lossy and Lossless

Some digital compression techniques are *lossless*, meaning that the result of compression-decompression is *exactly* the same as the original data. General-purpose data compression programs such as pkzip.exe do lossless compression. These programs will compress any kind of data, including images, and typically yield about 2:1 compression. For images, the degree of compression depends on how complex the image is. If the image is a bitmap of a graphic containing large areas of identical colors, you will get more than 2:1 compression; if the image is a digitized photograph of a complex scene, the degree of compression is often less than 2:1, sometimes none at all. Specially designed lossless image compression programs don't do much better either.

In order to get more out of image compression, you have to go to *lossy* compression. Lossy means that the output is not the same as the input—something has been lost. In computer terms, this means that there are *errors*. However, because there is a lot of redundant data in a typical image, it is possible to compress so that any errors will be very difficult for a viewer to see in the final reproduction of the image. Much research has been done on this, and excellent lossy compression techniques can deliver compression in the range of 10:1 to 20:1 with virtually invisible artifacts.

JPEG compression provides both lossless and lossy modes of compression. You make this choice when you first compress an image. If you choose lossy, you also can make a tradeoff between the degree of compression and the resulting image quality. Most JPEG compression tools let you play with these parameters and view the resulting reproduced image. Simple images can tolerate more compression than complex images; if you want to achieve the most compression all the time, you would need to experiment with every image. But, that proves tedious if you are doing a lot of images, so most people choose one or two basic levels of compression and go with them.

Compression and Decompression Software

Image compression methods (called *algorithms*) can be implemented entirely in software, because compression is just the transformation of a set of digital data into another set of digital data. However, many algorithms, including JPEG, are extremely computation intensive and can drag down even the fastest PC system for several seconds or more while processing one image. This depends on the resolution and numbers of colors, the same as the file size does. Larger image files take longer to compress or decompress.

The time it takes for compression is not usually much of a problem because compression is done only once during authoring, and five or ten seconds per image can be accommodated. However, decompression takes place every time you access an image, and the user often is waiting for the result. Thus, decompression time is very important. To some extent there is a tradeoff in loading compressed images: The fact that the image is compressed reduces the time to load the image from disk into memory, so you save time there but you lose it later because the image still has to be decompressed. With present CPU power, you will probably not be satisfied with the decompression times for JPEG images running with software alone. Of course, this situation will improve as CPUs become faster in the future.

Dedicated Hardware for Compression and Decompression

Since JPEG compression is a standard and everyone is using it, it makes sense for the chip suppliers to develop custom silicon that does it. This is happening, and a number of video boards have hardware support for JPEG compression and decompression. This reduces compression times to a fraction of a second, and it is definitely the right approach. We will see more of this in the future as multimedia grows. Motion video compression using JPEG hardware has been done at several frames per second; however, there are better algorithms for motion video compression, as you will see in Chapter 8.

CREATING BITMAPPED IMAGES

There are two basic ways to create your own bitmapped images: Capture them from an analog video source such as a camera or VCR, or use a digital image scanner to digitize from hard copy. Both cases involve special equipment and software.

Capturing from Analog Video

To capture from an analog video input, you must have an analog video source such as a camera or a VCR and a digitizing video board. Digitizing is available as an option on some video display adaptors, which have an input for analog video. There are several analog video formats, and these boards accept one or more formats as listed here:

NTSC or PAL (composite video)—This is a standard television video signal; NTSC is the North American standard, PAL is the standard used in western Europe. All VCRs deliver one of these signals because they are the formats used to feed a standard TV monitor. The signal is *encoded* into a *composite* format, meaning that the information has been combined so that it is all on a single cable. The encoding involves some tradeoffs, and does not deliver the highest possible quality, although we are generally satisfied with it for television viewing.

RGB (component video)—This is a three-signal format (three cables), which is available as an output from some video cameras. RGB gives the best possible video quality because there is no encoding to cause loss of quality. However, RGB equipment is more expensive, primarily because it is not so widely used as composite video equipment.

S-video—This is a two-signal format, which is used in some camcorders and VCRs. It is intermediate in quality between NTSC and RGB. It is not as widely available as either of the other formats.

The other hardware you need is an analog video source, either a video camera or VCR. Most inexpensive consumer equipment (camera, VCR, or camcorder) operates only with composite video and delivers disappointing performance when used for still images. Although the performance may look OK when playing motion video, capturing still frames from these sources shows a lot of artifacts that are not so obvious when a succession of frames is being displayed. To get adequate performance for still images, you have to go to semiprofessional or professional equipment, which is two or three times more expensive. However, this equipment usually has RGB output as well, which further contributes to better results. The bottom line is, when you are buying camera equipment for still images, look at the best equipment you can afford, and, by all means, try it out by actually capturing digital still images with it before you commit to a purchase. Simply watching still pictures on a monitor is not a good enough test—you must go through the digitizing process and evaluate the digital image. The reason for this is, when you are watching a live monitor, you are seeing 30 images per second, but your eye is averaging them so any varying artifacts may cancel out. But when you capture to a digital still image, you take only one image out of the 30-per-second sequence and make it into a still. In that case, there is no opportunity for artifacts to be cancelled, and the image may look much worse than it appears coming live from the camera.

VCR equipment for still video is even more of a problem—you cannot get good still images from a VCR unless you go to broadcast-quality equipment. That equipment is priced in the tens of thousands of dollars and up and is out of range for desktop multimedia unless you have some other reason for spending so much money, such as a need to do professional video production. For most users, the best strategy is to not plan on capturing stills from VCRs at all. If you need to capture stills on the fly, use photography and then digitize from photo prints using a good camera or image scanner.

You might think these problems would be less severe when capturing motion video since some distortions could then be averaged out. However, that may not be the case because variation from frame to frame interferes with most motion video compression processes, which usually depend on adjacent frames being similar. The varying artifacts add additional changes between frames that were not there in the original scene.

Digital Stills from Photographs

If you take a few precautions, a photograph is an excellent input medium for creating digital stills. You can capture a photograph by putting it in front of a video camera and digitizing a single frame from the camera, or you can use an image scanner to digitize the photograph directly. Either way, you will get better results if you take some things into account while doing your photography.

There is a considerable mismatch between the capabilities of the photographic system and the digital imaging system. First, digital images typically have much less resolution than even 35-mm photographs, and it is easy to make photos that are far too detailed to be reproduced effectively as a digital image at 640×480 pixels, more or less. Therefore, you should make sure your photographs are as close up as possible and do not contain more detail than you actually need. Further, if you want to crop a photograph, do it during the capture process, not after. That way, you will not be throwing away any of the resolution capability of the digital system.

The second mismatch between photography and digital imaging is in the way they reproduce colors. Photography creates intense (highly saturated) color by building up layers of dye. This means that the most intense colors are also the darkest colors. Digital imaging builds up intense color by turning on colored light in the phosphors of the display CRT. Therefore, the most intense colors are also the brightest—the opposite of photography. You deal with this discrepancy by choosing photographs that were taken with a lot of light, so all the important areas of the scene will be well illuminated. If you can control the lighting when you are shooting photos for digitizing, make sure that any important shadow areas are well illuminated.

You also should limit the contrast range of a photograph (the ratio between the intensities of the brightest and the darkest areas of the picture). One way to do that is to always digitize from photo *prints* rather than *transparencies*. A photo transparency or slide has the greatest contrast and the darkest, most intense, colors—they look great when projected, but they are murder on a digital system.

The color capability mismatch between photography and digital imaging can also be helped by analog processing in the video camera or digital image processing after digitizing. In particular, a technique called *gamma correction* can reduce the contrast range so the picture looks better on the computer screen. Most image capture or image processing software has this capability, and some analog cameras have it. However, too much gamma correction will bring up noise or other artifacts from the analog system, and you may just be trading one problem for another. The best approach is to do as much as you can to tone down the photos before digitizing, and use gamma correction as little as possible.

IMAGE SCANNERS

A color image scanner is a special piece of hardware that does just one thing—it converts hard copy into digital images. This is done by scanning across the source photo or document with a sensor that directly converts the image into digital pixels. Scanners come as *flatbed* where you place the item to be scanned face down over a window and a mechanism inside does the scanning (Figure 6.4). There are also *handheld* scanners, where the sensor is in a device you hold in your hand and manually move across the item to be digitized. Handheld scanners are inexpensive (a few hundred dollars), but their performance is limited both as to source document size and image quality. For professional work, the flatbed scanners are worth their price, which is in the thousand-dollar range for 8" × 14" color scanning.

Flatbed scanners operate at much higher resolution than video cameras, so their resolution is not normally an issue when digitizing images for screen display. Scanning resolutions are in the range of 300 dots per inch, which means that for any source picture larger than about 2", the scanner can deliver more pixels than you will need on any computer screen. However, the discussion above about resolution in the source image still applies because the limitations of the screen resolution are still present.

Likewise, the color problems discussed above for cameras also apply to scanners. You must be concerned about the contrast range of source pictures the same as if you were using a camera. Scanners also have their own particular artifacts that you need to watch out for. For example, you can sometimes get faint lines in the image resulting from variation in the performance of individual dots in the sensor array in the scanner. Most scanner software compensates for this, and a calibration run normally will take care of the problem. If you still see lines, look for another scanner.

SOFTWARE FOR IMAGE CAPTURE

All image capture hardware (boards, scanners) comes bundled with software drivers, and most also provide a capture application. Capture applications are either stand-alone, meaning they only do capture, or they are combined with an image processing or other authoring application. Capture becomes one of the choices for how you input an image into the authoring application, and a

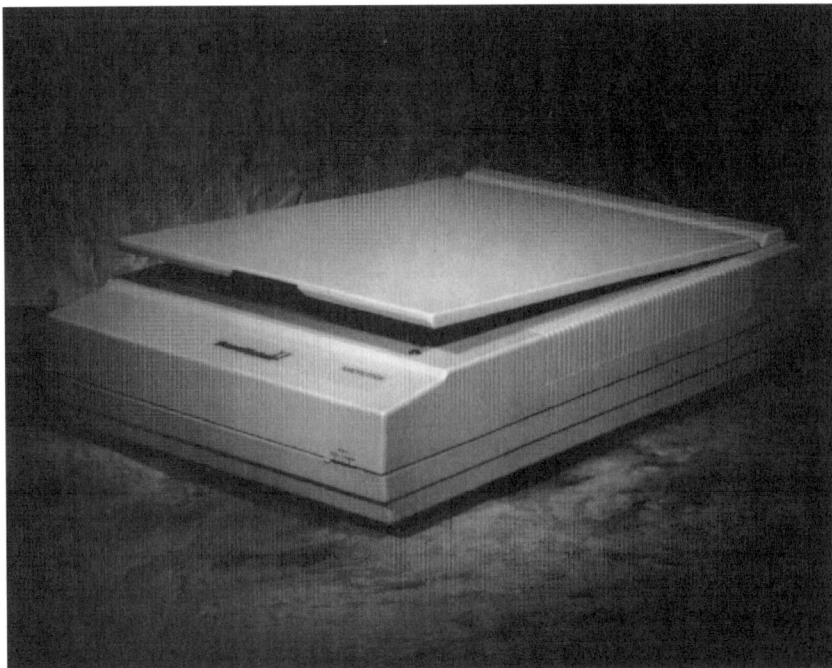

Figure 6.4 A flatbed color image scanner (courtesy of Microtek, Inc.)

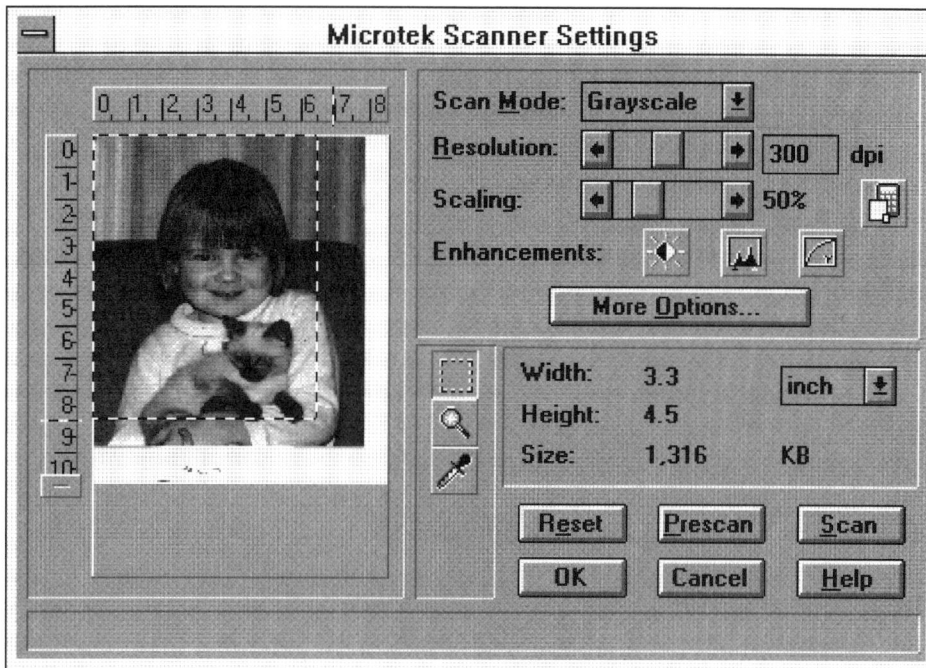

Figure 6.5 Scan dialog from Microtek *Scan Module*

captured image can be treated to any or all of the processing capabilities of the application. A typical image processing with capture application is Aldus's *Photo-Styler*, a full-featured image processor, which also includes software to operate a variety of image scanners. You have to install a driver for the scanner you will use, and then it will appear in the File menu of *PhotoStyler* under the Acquire item. Many scanner drivers support an interface standard called *Twain*, which makes the scanner available to all the Twain-compatible applications in your environment.

Figure 6.5 shows a typical scanner control dialog; this one is from Microtek's *Scan Module*, which is Twain-compatible and is integrated here into *PhotoStyler* under *Windows*.

At the left side of the dialog is a window that represents the active area of the scanner. By running a *prescan*, which is a fast low-resolution scan, you can see the picture you have placed in the scanner. Then, using the controls in the dialog, you can select the exact area of the picture you want to scan, set the resolution and scaling of the image, and using the More Options button, access various image processing steps to apply to the image after it has been scanned. Finally, you click the Scan button to run the final scan. At the end of that process, the scanned image will be in the workspace of *PhotoStyler*, where you can do additional work on it if necessary, and finally save it out in the desired format.

IMAGE PROCESSING TOOLS

Some of the simpler image processing tricks that you can do have already been introduced: cropping and scaling. In addition, there are many other more sophisticated processes available that are extremely useful and important when you need them. Most processes are applied to a *selected* area of an image, rather than the whole image. (Of course, you can select the whole image when you want to process everything.) Therefore, you usually will perform a selection before you do any processing.

One of the powers of an image processing tool is the flexibility it allows in selecting. The rectangular selection is the simplest, but many tools allow a free-form "marquee" selection, where you enclose an area by moving the mouse pointer around its perimeter. Usually the selection outline is indicated by a dotted line. The most powerful selection tools do a selection based on one or more characteristics of the image. For example, with some tools you can select based on colors or color ranges or by following an edge around an object. Thus, you can select any sort of irregular object. Sometimes you can do two selections and either subtract or add them. Some tools can do a "soft edge" selection, meaning that whatever process gets performed within the selection will gradually fade out at the edges. Figure 6.6 shows examples of different types of selections.

Once you have made a selection of the area of the image you want to work on, there are many kinds of processes you can do on or with the selected area. Some of these are listed below. Every tool and effect on this list is included in *PhotoStyler*; examples of many of them are shown in Figure 6.7.

cropping and scaling—These have already been discussed.

copying—The selected area is reproduced at a different location or in a different image.

skew—The selection is sheared horizontally.

masking—Either the selected area or its inverse is blanked out or filled with another image.

flipping—The selected area is reversed left to right or top to bottom.

rotating—The selected area is rotated through any angle.

resizing—The selected area is made smaller or larger.

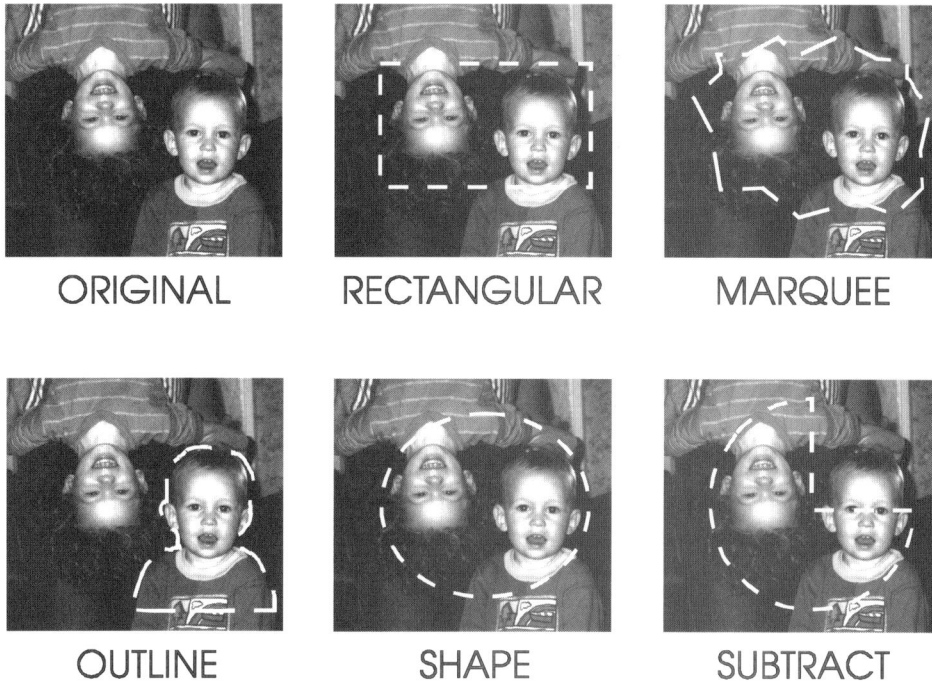

Figure 6.6 Selection techniques

resampling—The number of pixels that reproduces the image is made smaller or larger.

changing perspective—A trapezoidal modification of the image geometry is made to simulate perspective.

distorting—The shape of the selected image is modified to another shape.

shifting—The selected area is moved to another location in the image.

painting—New information is added to the image by painting with colors or patterns.

retouching—Changes are made to the image in ways that still look natural.

airbrushing—Color pixels are "sprayed" on the image in a defined area, but so as to blend with the existing pixels.

erasing—An area of the image is cleared to a background color or pattern.

enhancing—Features of an image such as edges or fine detail are made more visible or less visible.

filling—The selected area is replaced by a color or pattern.

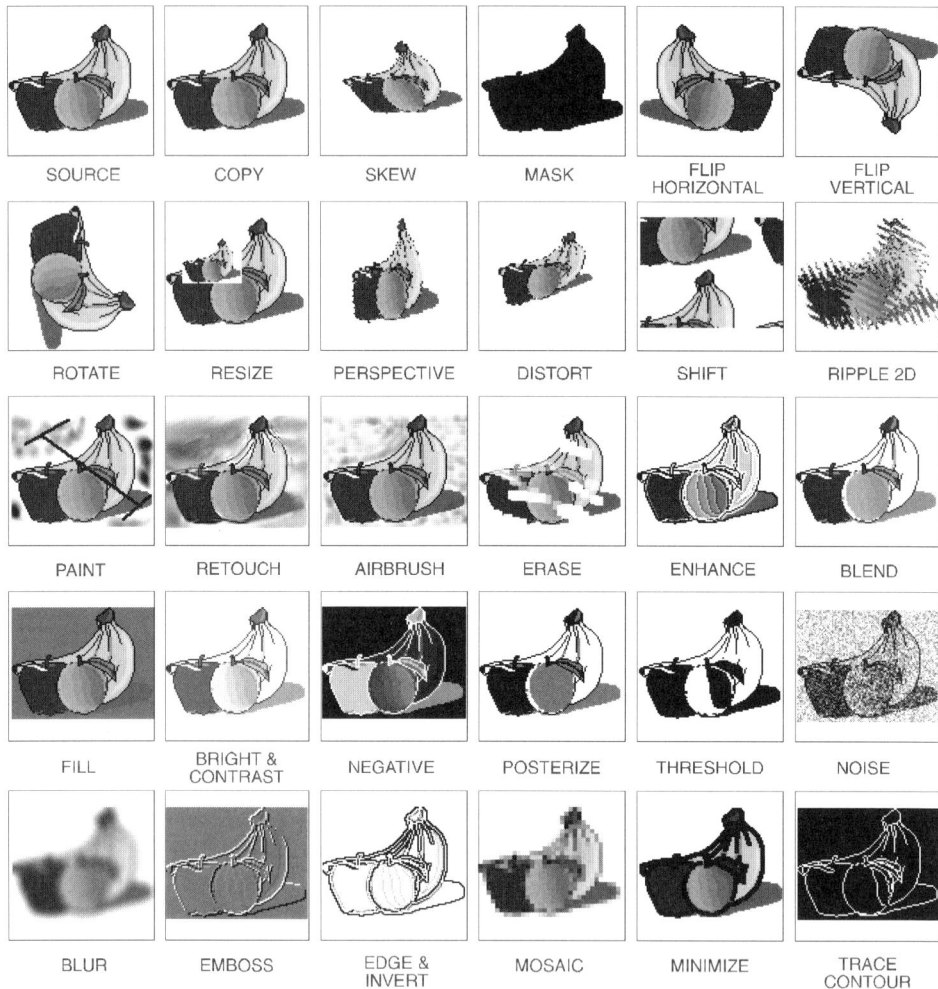

Figure 6.7 Image processing examples **(done with Aldus PhotoStyler.)**

adjusting brightness and contrast—The monochrome brightness and contrast of the selected area are increased or decreased.

adjusting hue and saturation—The color hue (tint) or saturation of the selected area is modified.

equalizing—The grayscale range of the image or selection is redistributed to cover the full grayscale range of the system.

inverting grayscale—The grayscale is reversed; white becomes black, etc.

posterizing—The number of grayscale levels or colors is reduced to give the image a cartoon-like appearance.

thresholding—The image is changed to a silhouette, either black or white; the gray level can be adjusted where black changes to white (the *threshold*).

filtering—Any of a wide range of effects for smoothing, averaging, blurring, despeckling, sharpening, tracing, or adding noise can be applied either to the image or a selection.

applying 2-D and 3-D effects—Any of a wide range of spatial modifications can be applied to the image or a selection.

differencing—The difference between two images can be produced on a pixel-by-pixel basis.

blending—Two images can be combined by a dissolve or blend effect.

correcting gamma—The middle levels of grayscale can be adjusted lighter or darker.

As you can see, there is an overwhelming array of possibilities for digital image processing. You would think that you could fix just about any kind of image problem or create any kind of effect, and this may be true, while it takes a lot of expertise to apply these powers. Unless you are a professional artist, you will probably not be interested in, or have time enough for, applying most of the power in a good image processing tool. However, for the special times when you need one or more of these things, you may want to have such a tool anyway. If you purchase a capture board or a scanner, you may find one of these tools bundled with it.

IMAGE FORMAT CONVERSION TOOLS

The list of image processing tools and effects in the preceding section is almost matched by the list of types of image file formats. Not all are covered here, just the ten or so most important ones. Each is listed below — first giving its name, then the file name extension usually used with it, and then a discussion of its characteristics and use.

Tagged image file format (.tif)—TIFF is one of the most popular and most flexible bitmapped image file formats. Nearly all applications support it. However, it has many variations, and few applications support them all. For this reason many programs ask you to specify the target application when saving an image, to make sure you will get a variation that the target application can handle.

Targa format (.tga, .win)—This bitmapped format was originally developed by Truevision, Inc. for use with its TARGA true color family of boards. Because it was one of the first true color formats for the PC, it is still widely used for 16-bpp, 24-bpp, and 32-bpp bitmapped images.

Bitmapped formats (.bmp)—Both *OS/2* and *Windows* have .bmp formats, but they are not the same. For either 4-bpp or 8-bpp formats, the image can be compressed or uncompressed; it also handles up to 24-bpp images uncompressed only.

PC Paintbrush format (.pcx)—This bitmapped format was developed by Z-Soft Corporation for their PC paint programs (*PC Paintbrush*, etc.). It is widely used and supports most bpp values, with or without palettes.

Windows metafile format (.wmf)—A *metafile* format combines both vector and bitmapped components in an image. WMF is used by many *Windows* draw programs.

Encapsulated PostScript format (.eps)—The *PostScript* language was originally developed for use with laser printers. It is a metafile format, having both bitmapped and vector components.

Graphics Interchange Format (.gif)—This format is CompuServe's standard for bitmapped images. It supports 4-bpp and 8-bpp images with palettes.

Device-Independent Bitmap (.dib)—This is a format developed by Microsoft for display on a variety of display systems (devices).

Computer Graphics Metafile (.cgm)—This is a metafile standard supported by the *American National Standards Institute* (ANSI). It is widely used in the publishing, CAD, and graphics markets.

DVI formats (.a9, .a16, .avs)—DVI Technology has several formats that embody its unique compression methods. The a9 format (sometimes called im9 or cm9) is for images that are in DVI Technology's unique "9-bpp" compressed format. Similarly, a16 (or c16 and i16) is for 16-bpp images, compressed or uncompressed. The .avs format is a general format for DVI video data that can contain any combination of still images, motion video, and audio in any of the DVI formats.

Nearly all tools that are involved with graphics or images support several image file formats. This is usually handled in menu items called Export and Import, although in some cases it will be in the Save as and Open menus. It will be most convenient for you if the image tools you select support the file types you have to deal with. (The other side of this is to try to control the image file types to match the tools you have.) However, the standards for image files are not very good, and there are sometimes small differences between the same standard implemented by two different tools.

The Ultimedia Tools Series deals with the file interchange problem by requiring all their tools to support (at least) a set of file formats called *Resource Interchange FileFormat* (RIFF), which includes formats for bitmaps, vector drawing, animation, audio, and eventually video. More initiatives like this one should help to narrow down the diversity of file formats in the future.

Another approach to file conversion is to build it into the operating system multimedia functions. This is the case for OS/2 2.x. In this system, you can install file conversion filters that will be automatically called by the system when you display images. However, you should realize that software file conversion often is quite slow, and it may not be something that you want your user to have to wait for whenever an image is displayed. For the fastest response in your final application, you will want the images for the application stored in the optimum format. Still, the automatic conversion feature will be a great advantage during the authoring process.

The proliferation of image formats has created a good market for image file conversion tools. One of these tools is *Hijaak PRO*, which converts between nearly all of the file formats in wide use and includes variations for most of the popular applications.

SUMMARY

Still images are the easiest way to add realism to a multimedia presentation. Reproducing realistic images takes an advanced video display adaptor, and if you want to capture your own images, you need either a video camera and digitizing board or an image scanner.

Digital images are usually stored in their own special file formats, of which there are many. Tools are available for creating image files and for converting between the various types. Image processing tools provide the widest range of image effects, and such a tool belongs in the portfolio of any serious multimedia producer.

7

Graphics and Text

On occasion, the image you want does not exist as a real object or scene that you can capture with a video or photographic camera. Or maybe you need an image that isn't real at all, or you want an image generated by the computer. In all these cases, you will need a *drawn* image. Many tools are available for drawing, ranging from very simple functions built into authoring assembly programs, to full professional artist's tools. Draw tools are based on storing a mathematical representation of the image, rather than a bitmap. This is called a *vector* representation, since the image is often described in terms of a series of lines, or vectors. When a vector image is displayed, the computer will *render* the draw data into a bitmap. There are advantages and disadvantages to vector images, but there are many situations where drawing is the way to go. Typically, the data size of a draw image file will be much smaller than the data size of the bitmap it creates when displayed on the screen—in that sense, drawing is a form of image compression. This chapter discusses all the features of vector images and the tools for creating them.

SKILLS REQUIRED FOR GRAPHICS

You might think that you cannot use draw tools unless you are an artist. Although an artist can accomplish wonders with today's sophisticated draw tools, an unskilled person can also do remarkable things using the powers of vector draw tools and especially utilizing *clip art libraries*. A clip art library is a collection of professionally drawn images specifically designed to be imported into your applications, either as complete drawings or as pieces of a drawing. A major advantage of vector drawing is that you can *select* one or more pieces of a drawing and pull them out or modify them. This takes no drawing skill at all—just click the mouse on the desired object. In this way you can build up the drawing you need by cutting and pasting from the clip art library.

COORDINATE SYSTEMS

A vector image consists of a series of numerical values that describe each object in terms of its type, its size, and its location. Size and location are given in terms of *coordinates*, which are numbers that relate to position on the screen or in the target window. The simplest coordinate system is one that specifies pixel locations, but many draw programs do not do that because it ties the image to a specific screen format. A better approach is to use *abstract coordinates* that will allow the drawing to be rendered onto any screen format or even to a hard copy printer. Usually, abstract coordinate systems use a larger range of values than the numbers of pixels on a typical screen, because that allows rendering in various formats at different resolutions without too much loss of accuracy due to interpolation. For example, the MEDIAscript coordinate system uses a range of $10,240 \times 7680$ to represent a full-screen drawing regardless of actual screen resolution. When the drawing is rendered to a 640×480 screen, all values are divided by 16. When rendering to 1024×768, divide by 10, or divide by 12.8 for 800×600. This will make the image look the same on any screen.

Coordinates are numbers, and there are three ways that you can enter them. All tools let you enter coordinates by dragging objects around the screen or target window. When you stop dragging, the current screen positions are converted to coordinates and stored for the object. This is the easiest way to draw, but sometimes you want more precise positioning than you can get with dragging. There are two solutions. First, if you are laying out a screen and want objects to be located relative to rows and columns, most tools let you specify a *grid* that has evenly spaced points, which are the only coordinate values that the system will accept. Thus, any object you draw will *snap* to a grid location when you release it. The second way to get precise positioning is to allow entry of coordinate numbers from the keyboard. That way you can specify any kind of relationship, without being limited to specific grid locations. Some drawing tools support keyboard entry of coordinates.

The last way to enter coordinates is to specify them as *variables*, which will take on their own values at runtime. This is a powerful technique, especially if you want to make a drawing that depends on user input at runtime, or that contains objects that may be animated or iterated as the drawing is displayed. However, variables are a feature of assembly tools, not draw programs, and drawing with variables is only available for a draw tool that is embedded within an assembly tool. Many assembly tools provide this feature. Of course, variables are a programming concept and their use requires some programming knowledge.

PRIMITIVES

Each object in a drawing has a *type*, selected from a list of *primitives*, which are the fundamental drawing metaphors. The usual list of primitives includes: lines, curves, rectangles, ellipses, polygons, and text. Most draw tools have a tool palette for primitive selection. After selecting a primitive, the tool goes into a mode where everything you do in the draw space relates to that type of primitive. Some tools have more than the above list of types, although you will usually find that the other primitives are special cases of the types listed above. Figure 7.1 shows the line, curve, rectangle, ellipse, and polygon primitives.

ATTRIBUTES

There are many ways that a single primitive, such as a rectangle, can be drawn, and these are called *attributes*. For example, you must choose a color in which to draw, so that is an attribute. A rectangle can be either an outline or filled with a color, and that is another attribute. If the rectangle is an outline, the line has a *thickness* attribute. Figure 7.1 shows some attributes for the basic drawing primitives. The list of attributes goes on, especially for a complex primitive such as text, which is discussed in more detail below. Typically, each object of a drawing is stored with its type, coordinates, and attributes, which means that at a later time you can select an object and change any of its attributes. This is a valuable capability, and it is key to the use of clip art libraries.

GROUPS AND LAYERS

Most draw tools allow you to collect a number of objects by selecting them all at the same time and specifying that you want these objects to become a *group*. Once objects are grouped, they can move together around the screen and maintain the same relative relationships. Similarly, they can be specified to share certain attributes (and not share others).

A *layer* is a special kind of group that is useful when you want to exercise control over how the drawing is to be rendered or output. It is primarily a feature of *computer-aided design* (CAD) tools, but it sometimes appears in multimedia tools

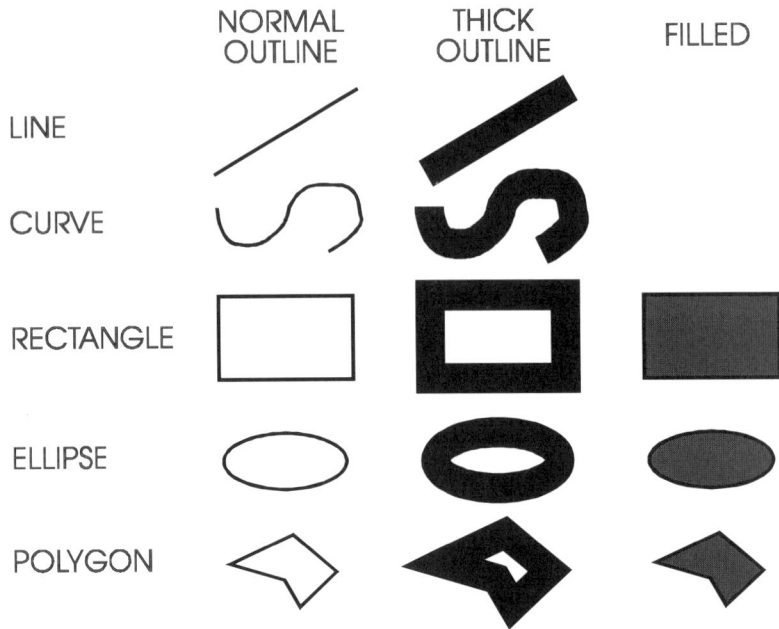

Figure 7.1 Drawing primitives using the attributes of outline, filled, and thickness

that have a CAD heritage. An example of the use of layers is a mechanical drawing that contains views of a part along with dimensions drawn in the usual mechanical drafting way. By placing the dimension information by itself in a separate layer, it is easy to render the drawing either with or without the dimensioning simply by switching on or off display of the dimensioning layer. Layers, however, add unnecessary complexity to drawing for most multimedia purposes.

ORDER OF DRAWING

When objects in a drawing overlap, the appearance of the drawing will depend on the order in which the objects are drawn. Objects drawn last are in front, and the first object drawn is in back. By drawing overlapping primitives, you can easily create shapes that are not possible with a single primitive. For example (Figure 7.2), you can draw a new-moon shape by first drawing a circle in the moon color, and then drawing another circle in the background color slightly displaced to the right. It is important that a drawing tool have means for editing the order of drawing—this is usually called *arranging*.

Figure 7.2 Drawing a new moon shape with two overlapping circles

COLORS

A draw tool must contain the means for the author to choose colors for each object drawn. This is usually done by a *palette* technique, where an array of predetermined colors is provided. Since high-color and true-color display formats are capable of far more colors than can be displayed in a single array, most tools also offer a *color mixing* dialog to create custom colors by manipulating the RGB values for a color. Custom colors can usually be placed into a working palette for repeated selection later. Figure 7.3 shows the color palette and mixing dialog from *Visual Basic*. Notice that the author can either select a color from the spectrum display or type in values for RGB or hue, saturation, and luminance. Colors designed this way can be placed in the custom colors palette below the main palette. Because colors can look differently when shown in larger blocks, or when shown with text, the dialog provides areas to preview the chosen color.

USING CLIP ART

Figure 7.4 shows a typical clip art library—Lotus *SmartPics*. The clip items are held by subject in a series of files that are itemized in the directory list window at the top of the dialog. You first choose a subject from the list, and the individual drawings for that subject then appear in the selection list at the bottom of the dialog. When you make a selection from that window, you can then specify that it be copied to the *Windows* clipboard. At that point you can close or minimize the clip art window and go to your draw or assembly application and bring in the clip art by using paste from the Edit menu. You can then use the draw tools to

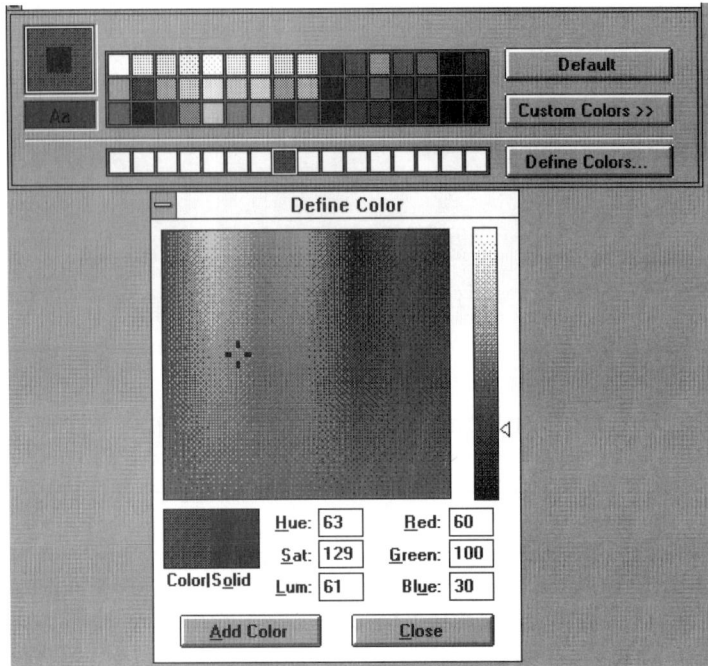

Figure 7.3 Color palette and mixing dialog from *Visual Basic*

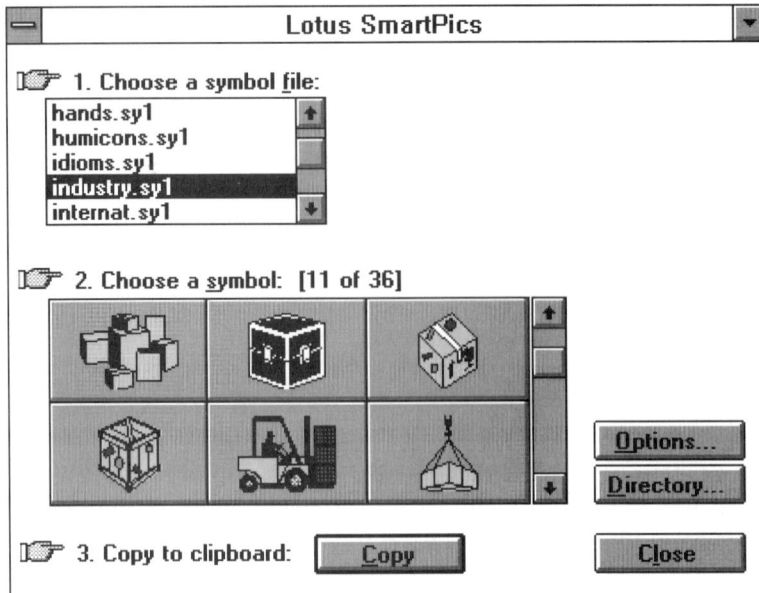

Figure 7.4 Lotus *SmartPics* clip art library

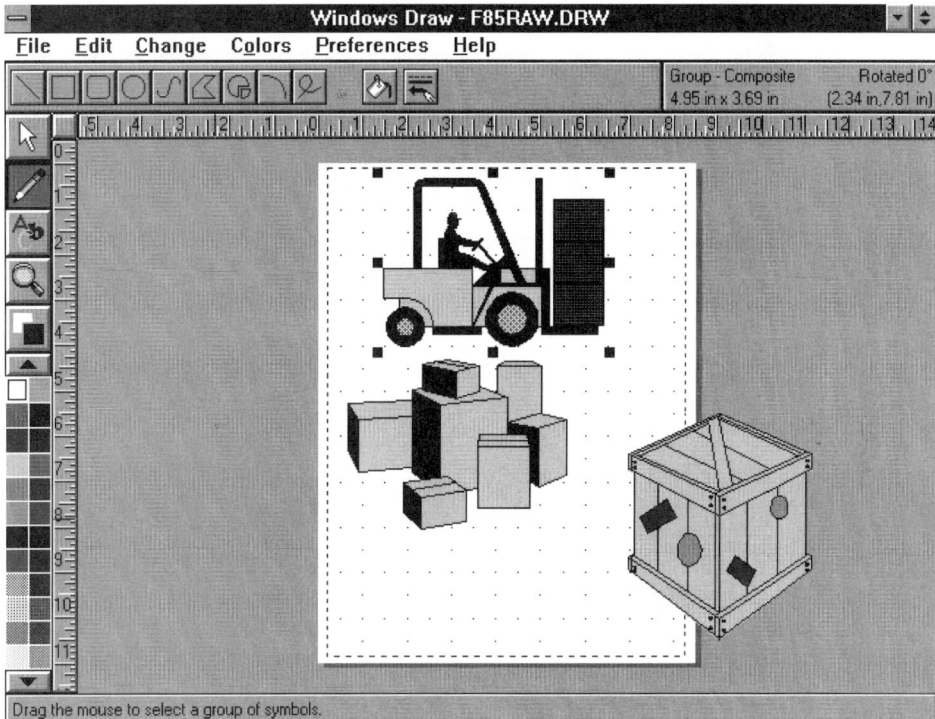

Figure 7.5 A *Windows Draw* screen showing three clip art objects brought over from *SmartPics*

make any changes you need. All clip art libraries work in this way, although some, which are integrated into draw tools, can eliminate the specific copy and paste steps.

As an example of using clip art objects to make your own unique drawing, you can select several of the items shown in Figure 7.4 to create a more comprehensive drawing of a warehouse scene. The steps are to select and copy each of the clip art objects you need, moving them with Paste into a draw program where you will combine and manipulate them. Figure 7.5 shows three of the clip art objects from Figure 7.4 moved into Micrografx *Windows Draw*, ready for use in creating the scene.

Now you can use the tools of the draw program to resize, position, and otherwise modify the clip art objects to make the desired scene. Figure 7.6 shows the final image resulting from that. Notice that the text tools of the draw program were also used to create the sign at the top of the picture.

Figure 7.6 The final image resulting from manipulating the clip art objects in *Windows Draw*

DRAW TOOLS

All drawing tools use at least two windows—one is the target window that holds the drawing, and the second is a tools palette window for selection of the current tool. Sometimes the target window is the full screen, and the tools palette floats on top of it; in other cases, they are two actual windows. The metaphor is generally the same—a tool (primitive) is selected from the tools palette, and you then work with the mouse pointer in the target window. Usually, the mouse pointer or icon changes, depending on the current tool selected, to help you keep track of what you are doing. Beyond that, different programs have their own personalities, and you have to try them out to find one that suits your taste and degree of skill.

Not all drawing tools are true vector tools. Some tools simply use the primitives metaphor to draw a bitmap. The result is that the drawn image cannot be edited by selection of individual objects—once they are drawn they are part of the bitmap and it is not possible to select them. You can select a region of the bitmap to work on, but there is no way to know what kind of primitives may be in that region. These are called *paint* tools, and they are useful when you need drawing effects that are difficult to produce in vector form, such as spray painting or shading. Paint tools are also good for drawing on top of images that are already in bitmap form. Some tools have both paint and vector modes which can be mixed in the

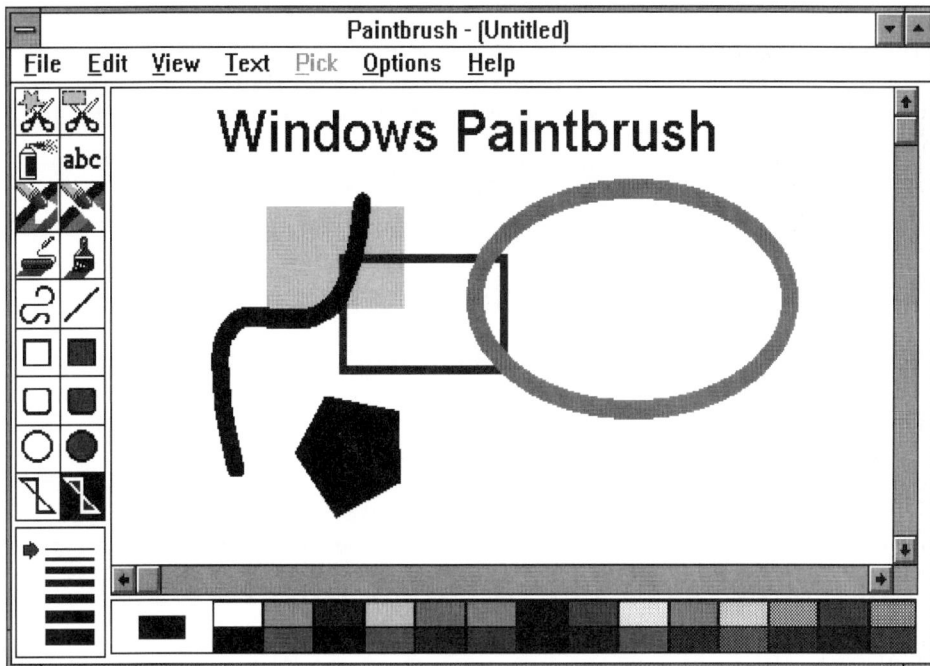

Figure 7.7 The drawing screen of *Windows Paintbrush.*

same image; for these tools, the final output is a bitmapped image, but there may also be means to store the raw data for the vector parts of the image. Note that all vector drawing tools are capable of outputting a drawing as a bitmap, but once you do this, you will lose all the vector data that would allow you to modify the image later. Let's look at a few examples of drawing and painting tools.

Paint Tool—Microsoft *Windows Paintbrush*

This tool is bundled with Microsoft *Windows.* Its screen is shown in Figure 7.7. There is a menu bar at the top of the screen, a tool palette at the left, and a color palette at the bottom. The rest of the screen is the target drawing area. This program is a paint tool; once an item is drawn, it is in bitmapped form and can no longer be edited. The Edit menu does have an Undo feature that allows the most recent action to be reversed. This is accomplished by maintaining a copy of the target bitmap offscreen—an operation can be undone by copying the right part of the off-screen image to the screen, but you can do that only once. With paint tools, it is a good idea to keep a copy of your original image on disk under another file name, so you can revert to an earlier version if needed to undo more than one operation.

The target area of Figure 7.7 shows the result of drawing with the rectangle, ellipse, polygon, text, and curve primitives. Notice that the tool palette provides for choice of outline or filled objects by having two palette items for each primitive that has this attribute. Note also that the bottom of the tool palette provides selection of the thickness attribute for outlines, lines, or curves. Other painting attributes (especially for text) are available in the menu bar.

Draw Tool—Micrografx *Windows Draw*

Windows Draw is a low-priced vector draw tool; its screen was shown in Figure 7.5. The top-level tool palette is at the left, with a color palette below it. When one of the icons of the tool palette is selected, the icon toolbar at the top of the screen changes to provide more detailed selection. For example, selection of the pencil (draw) icon at the left causes the toolbar to show all the draw primitives available. Actual drawing requires a selection from the toolbar. Rulers on the draw window and a status box at the top right of the screen allow you to keep track of dimensions and coordinates while you are drawing.

Draw Module—Microsoft *PowerPoint*

PowerPoint is a presentation authoring package and, like most of those packages, it has a built-in vector draw module. The screen for this is shown in Figure 7.8. A draw tool palette is at the left of the screen, and a toolbar at the top provides additional draw choices, as well as giving access to the other modules of *PowerPoint*. One unique "primitive," called the *shape* is in use. By selecting from the shape menu shown, you can draw the shapes at any size and position. The shape rubber-bands in exactly the same way rectangles or ellipses do. This is a very powerful feature.

One caution about the draw modules of some presentation packages is that they may not be able to output a drawing by itself, but only as part of a proprietary presentation format. Therefore, you could not use a presentation package's draw module to draw pictures for use by another tool. This is not the case with *PowerPoint*, which can output a standard *Windows* metafile that most other *Windows* tools can read. However, *PowerPoint* cannot import a metafile directly— you must use another application to place the picture on the *Windows* clipboard; then you can paste it into *PowerPoint*.

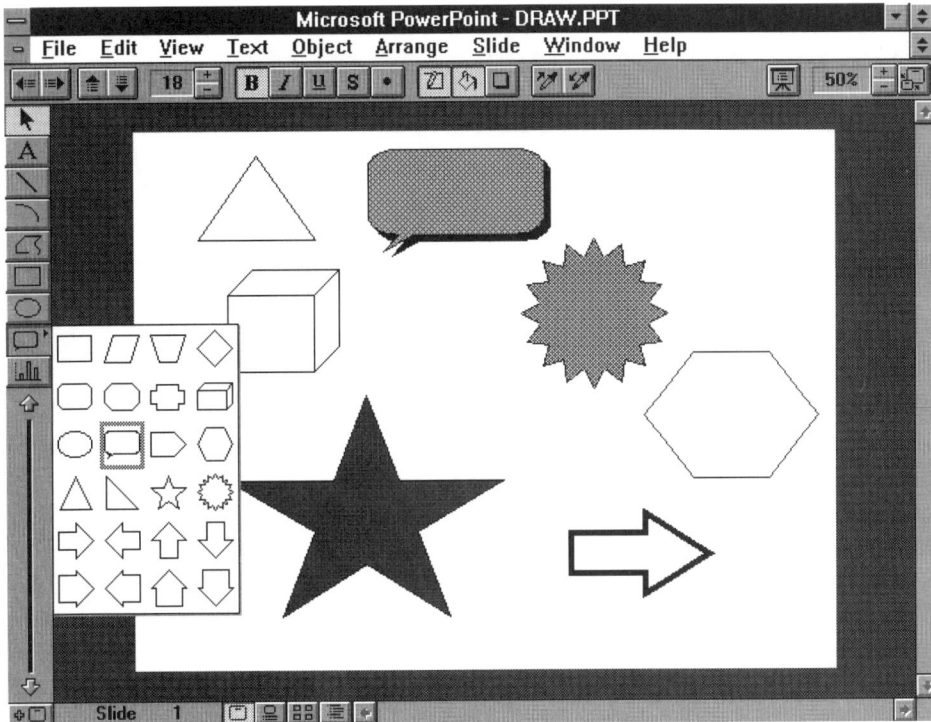

Figure 7.8   The draw module of *PowerPoint*. The shape tool is in use.

Draw Module—Asymetrix *Multimedia ToolBook*

Multimedia *ToolBook* is a multimedia assembly program, and like most of those programs, it has a built-in draw module. The screen is shown in Figure 7.9. The draw window is at the center of the screen, and the tool palette and several selector windows are surrounding it. Each of these items is a separate window that can be placed anywhere on the screen or even hidden.

The draw tool palette is at the left in the figure, and palettes for line thickness, fill patterns, and colors are positioned to the right.

Draw Module — Network Technology *MEDIAscript OS/2*

The draw module of *MEDIAscript OS/2* differs from some of the others discussed here because it provides for either freehand drawing with the mouse or entering and editing coordinate numbers and variable names or expressions from the keyboard. Windows involved in doing this are shown in Figure 7.10. At the top

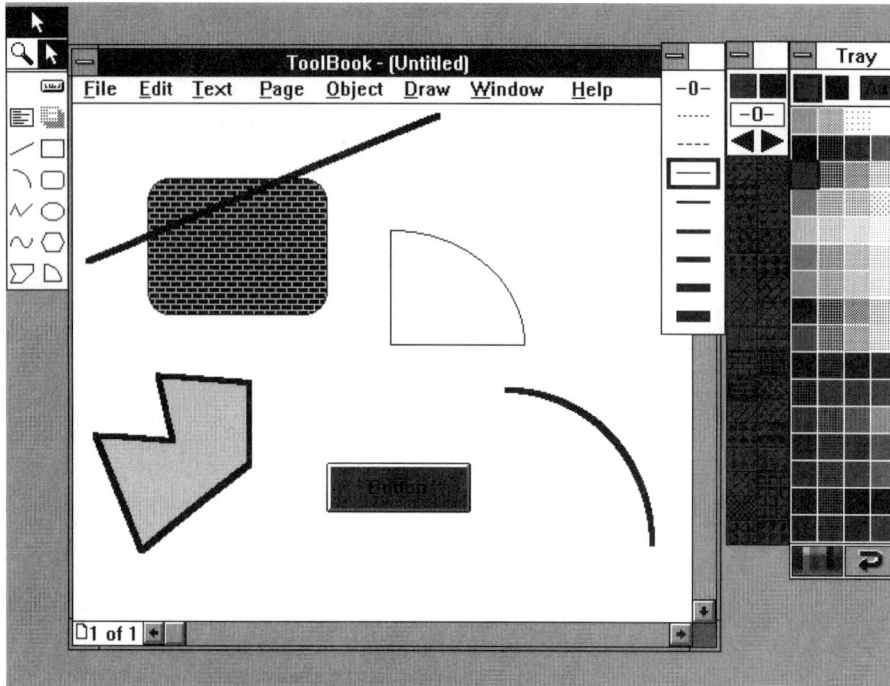

Figure 7.9   The draw module of Asymetrix *Multimedia ToolBook*.

left in the figure is the main Draw dialog and to the right is a target drawing window. When you are drawing text, the window at the bottom left can be called up to select fonts, sizes, and styles. A fourth window for color mixing can be opened; it is shown at the bottom right in the figure.

The tool palette is seen at the center of the main Draw dialog, and entry fields at the bottom of the dialog provide for entry or editing of the parameters of the selected object in the target window. At the top left in the dialog is a selector for choosing which window to draw into—*MEDIAscript* supports a number of simultaneous windows, so you have to specify which one a particular draw object will affect. When you open an existing window for drawing, you will see anything that is already displayed in that window, so you can easily draw in proper relationship to whatever else may be there. A list box at the left of the dialog gives a list of the objects in the order in which they are displayed. This list can be used for moving between objects or for arranging their order of display.

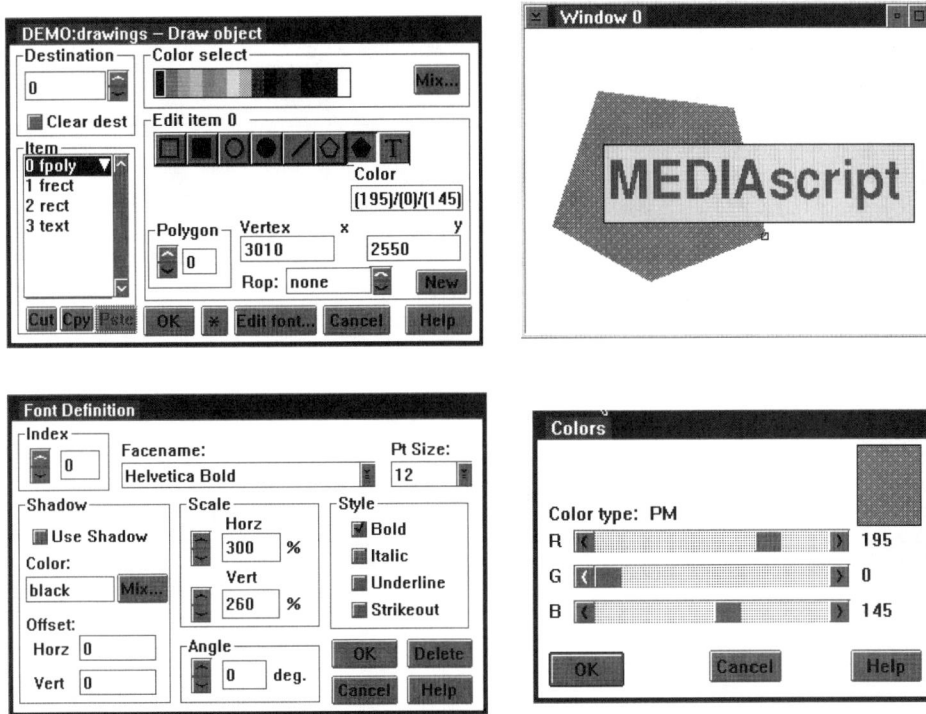

Figure 7.10   *MEDIAscript OS/2* draw dialogs

Draw Tool—*CorelDRAW!*

Moving toward some of the tools of professional graphic artists, *CorelDRAW!* provides an impressive array of capabilities for a mid-priced product. Figure 7.11 shows its drawing screen. The environment appears deceptively simple, with a small tool palette at the left, a color palette at the bottom, and menu and status bars at the top. However, notice the small rectangles that appear like window titles in the status bar (called "Text," "Extrude," and "Fill"); they are *roll-up* dialogs that expose the full powers of the product when activated. Figure 7.12 has the roll-ups in view, showing the selections that created the extruded and shaded text that is selected on the screen.

The roll-up dialogs are selected from the menu bar, and they can be placed anywhere on the screen, so you can position them to be convenient to the work at hand. When not in use, they can either be rolled up — leaving their title bar showing—or they can be closed completely.

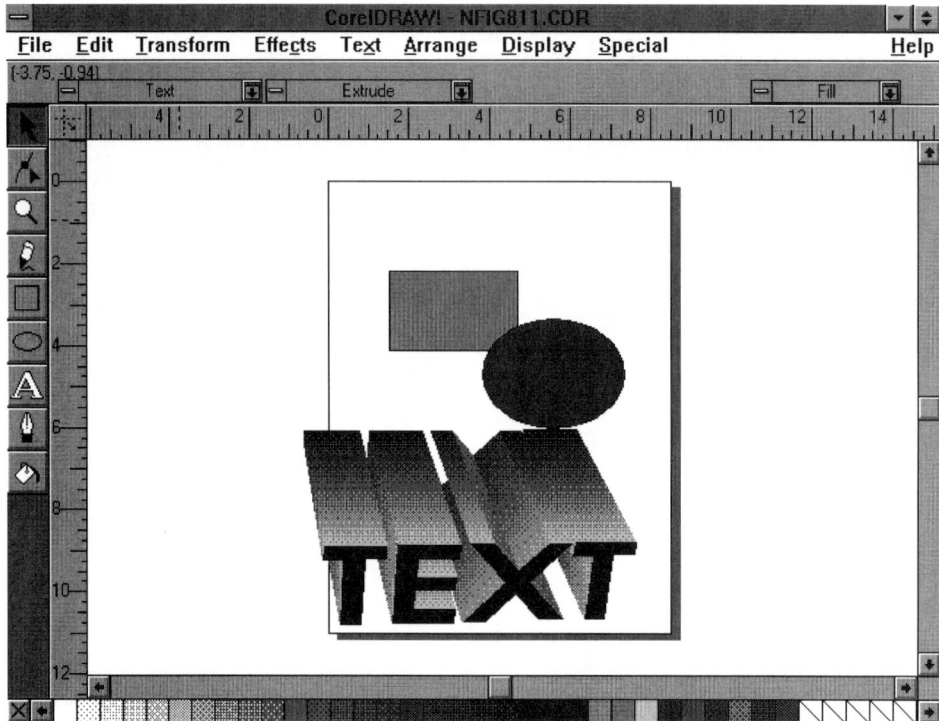

Figure 7.11   The screen of *CorelDRAW!*

You can see from these examples of draw programs that there are many ways to implement the graphics and text primitives metaphor. If you will be doing a lot of drawing, you should take the time to try out the drawing capabilities of the programs you are interested in. While all the programs will do a good job, the bottom line is determined by your personal preferences about how to work and by what kind of capabilities you need and are prepared to learn how to use.

TEXT OBJECTS

Although most draw programs include text as just another primitive in the tool palette, text is actually a different metaphor because of the large number of attributes associated with it. With text, you have to deal with the issues of font selection, text style, and text effects. Most draw programs have separate menu items or palettes to present these choices, each of which is covered below.

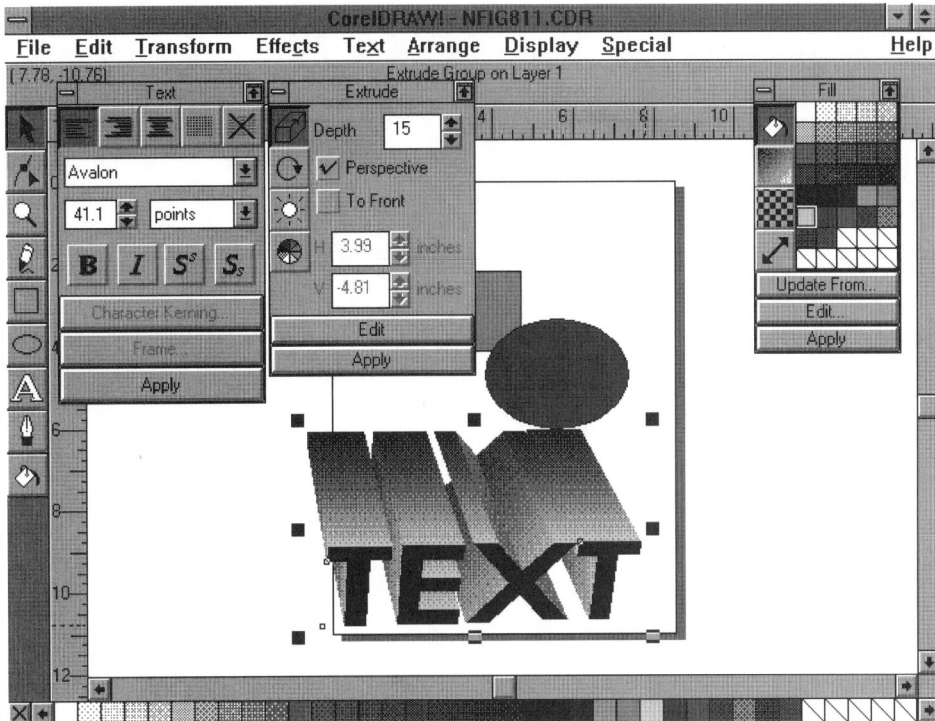

Figure 7.12 The screen of *CorelDRAW!* with some roll-ups in view

Fonts

The exact description of each character of text is determined by its font. Font *files* contain these character descriptions; they can be created as either bitmapped or vector fonts. A bitmapped font contains pixels for each character for a certain size and style of text—you must have a separate bitmapped font for each size and style combination you will use. This is a major disadvantage, but the major advantage of bitmapped fonts is that they render quickly because there are no mathematics involved. However, as CPUs are becoming faster and more power-ful, this advantage is disappearing, and bitmapped fonts are going out of use.

Vector fonts are mathematical descriptions of the characters, which can be rendered in a wide range of sizes and (theoretically) in various styles as well. But, a better job can be done on styles by creating unique vector files for each style combination, and that is the most common approach. Another common font variation is to have separate font files for screen, printer, and plotter output. This is useful because the unique characteristics of each device can be taken into

Prestige *Brush Bold*

Cooper Black Perpetua Bold

Optimum Utopia

Mural Script **Broadway**

Times New Roman

Script Bold

Figure 7.13   Font types from Micrografx *Windows Draw*

account. Microsoft *Windows* has a special font technology, called *TrueType*, that eliminates the need for different font files for each device. With TrueType, your documents look the same rendered on screen or printer.

There are literally thousands of font types, and it is not unusual to have 30 or more different fonts in your system. Figure 7.13 shows examples of typical font types. Various fonts are designed for use in body text, headings, diagrams, or display headlines. Ordinarily, you would choose a small number of fonts for use in any one application, because too many fonts will become distracting. It is important that all authoring tools you use for image or text creation should use the same font types so that all your material will be uniform. Be aware that a large number of fonts can use up a lot of hard disk space and may slow down your system. Install only the fonts you will actually use.

Under *Windows* or *OS/2*, fonts are managed by the operating system and, therefore, all tool programs using that operating system will have access to the same fonts. This is not the case for DOS programs, because DOS has no native font management feature. If you are going to combine DOS, *Windows*, and *OS/2* tools in your environment, you will have to give attention to the font uniformity between the different systems to make sure that the font types you need are available in all the systems.

Times New Roman

Bold   *Italic*

Bold Italic

Outline

Figure 7.14 Text styles from *CorelDraw!*

Text Styles

Text can be presented in different styles, such as italic, bold, underline, outline, etc., which are normally used to create marks of emphasis in the text. Figure 7.14 shows a variety of text styles and combinations, all using the same font name. Text styles are like font types—you can go overboard in using too many of them. However, if your application follows a careful plan for its use of text styles in specific situations, the result is very effective. In *Windows* and *OS/2*, text styles are also part of the operating system's font management features, so most applications will have the same portfolio of styles.

Text Effects

The more sophisticated draw programs provide a dazzling array of text effects, including shadowing, extrusion, textured fills, text-on-a-curve, modulated sizes, etc. Examples of some of these from *CorelDRAW!* are shown in Figure 7.15. Still more effects, particularly those based on shading, can be done with paint programs.

TEXT

TEXT Rotated

TEXT on a curve

Extruded

TEXT Skewed

TEXT Envelope

Figure 7.4 Examples of text effects done with *CorelDRAW!*

SUMMARY

Graphics and text are key multimedia elements. They often carry the meat of an application's message. Therefore, working with them is an important part of authoring. All authoring assembly tools have graphics and text capability to some degree; in addition, there are many specialty tools available that let you do as elaborate a job as you wish.

All authoring of graphics and text uses the primitives metaphor, but there are many different environments for that in the various products. This chapter reviewed some of the key approaches, but the bottom line is that you have to decide for yourself which tools will suit your style, your skill, and your commitment of time to this area of authoring.

8

Audio and Video

Television has shown us the power of electronic audio and video media to inform, teach, and entertain. But we have had to wait until now to be able to include those powers in our computer applications. The promise of multimedia computing is really fulfilled when we use audio and video to enhance the computer's presentation. Motion video is (superficially) an extension of the still image capabilities discussed in the previous chapter—we simply have to display a new still image every thirtieth of a second and we have motion! That's a pretty large challenge in itself, but we have to present audio, too, and we have to make sure the two are synchronized. This chapter explores those problems and discusses hardware and software for digital motion video with audio.

THE NUMERICAL CHALLENGE OF DIGITAL VIDEO

Let's look at some of the numbers characterizing a motion video data stream. Notice that it is called a *stream*, because data must flow continuously the entire time that video (or audio) is playing. Thus, I will talk about bytes *per second*. Motion video is created by displaying new or updated pictures fast enough so that the viewer sees smooth motion. This normally means 30 frames per second—each individual picture in a video stream is called a *frame*. If there is not too much motion, you can sometimes get away with lower rates—maybe down to 15 per second, but anything lower than that becomes jerky.

Since we want our motion video to be realistic, we have to use at least 16 bpp to display realistic colors. At 640 × 480 pixels, that means 614,400 bytes per frame, and at 30 frames per second, 18.4 megabytes per second. Such rates are far beyond the capabilities of the fastest PCs, and, worse still, when we look at storing minutes or hours of video, the numbers become astronomical. For example, a CD-ROM disc (650 megabytes) only stores 35 seconds of such video! Obviously, the brute-force approach of displaying a sequence of still images won't work. Fortunately, there are a lot of techniques we can use to reduce the requirements until they come within the capabilities of today's desktop PC.

Video Compression

Probably the most important thing we can do is apply the same techniques of video compression that we use on still images. We spoke of the redundancy in a still image that can allow up to 10:1 data compression without serious impairment of the reproduction; the redundancy in a still image occurs because adjacent pixels are often similar, and this is called *spatial* redundancy. However, a motion stream has additional redundancy because successive frames are often very similar, and this is called *temporal* redundancy. By exploiting temporal redundancy, we need only send enough information to create each new frame by updating the previous frame; that way we can usually gain another 3:1 of compression. So we have 30:1 compression—now our 650-megabyte CD-ROM disc can store 17.5 minutes of video.

But wait a minute, it's not as simple as that! Compression and decompression take time—a PC cannot come close to performing it at 30 frames per second. As we said for stills, an unaided PC will take several seconds per frame to do JPEG decompression, and we want to do temporal processing as well, so the whole idea still won't work. But we don't have to give up because there are several possibilities left. For one, we can add hardware to the PC to assist the CPU by doing the compression or decompression for it—that is what the DVI Technology boards (ActionMedia II and others) do. However, even those boards have to make another compromise to accomplish the task: They must reduce the resolution for motion video to be less than 640 × 480 pixels.

Reduced resolution for motion video is not as bad as it sounds—DVI Technology uses 256 × 240 pixels for full-screen motion video, and the pictures look surprisingly good. The reason is that the combination of a large number of colors and the motion itself partially compensates for lower resolution. The only thing you have to do is to perform some *pixel interpolation* to make sure that the viewer will not see the individual pixels as blocks of color (this is called *pixellation*). The DVI boards have interpolation built in, so you don't see any pixellation in DVI motion video. The reduced resolution is another factor of 5, which would make the CD-ROM video capacity about 75 minutes.

To finish the DVI compression story, there is one other technique that is used, called *color subsampling*. This technique (which is also used in NTSC and PAL color TV) further reduces the resolution, but only for the color parts of the image. Because the human eye does not see fine detail in colors, reduced color resolution does not visually impair an image. Color subsampling theoretically produces another compression factor of 2.7, and it is the reason that the DVI folks speak of *9 bpp*, which occurs because the color subsampling reproduces a 24-bpp image with an average of 9 bits per pixel. (DVI equipment can also use the 9-bpp technique on still images or graphics, which delivers further compression for those as well.) However, these numbers add up to a little too much—it now looks like we have more compression than DVI technology actually can do. The reason is that the DVI boards do not provide as much basic compression as you can get without time constraints (after all, DVI boards have to do it 30 times per second!); actual CD full-screen video capacity for DVI Technology is 72 minutes.

MPEG

There are many ways to do video compression, which is a situation that calls for standards. One industry initiative for standardising video compression is the *Motion Picture Expert Group* (MPEG) of the IEC. (The IEC is the same group that parented JPEG for still image compression.) The MPEG objectives are very ambitious, providing for a parameterised standard that encompasses different algorithms for different needs. MPEG compression of motion video requires special hardware; it cannot be done in software alone. So far, low-cost MPEG products have not been introduced to the desktop market. However, MPEG is an important potential, and it is likely to be available in the future on software-driven compression/decompression hardware such as the Intel chips that support DVI Technology.

Software-Only Video

The preceding discussion showed what we can do with some additional hardware for motion video. However, we ought to be able to do *something* without extra hardware, so how can we get motion video on our computer using its existing powers? This is what is called *software-only* video, and there are several systems available: IBM's *Ultimotion*, Microsoft's *Video for Windows*, Intel's *Indeo*, and Apple's *QuickTime for Windows*.

It is interesting to relate software-only video requirements to the processing speed of typical CPUs. CPU speed is usually discussed in terms of *Millions of Instructions per Second* (MIPS), which refers to the average rate at which the CPU can execute its instruction set. We have to think of an average, because with a CISC CPU, different instructions take different times to execute. With the fastest 486 CPUs, the speed ratings are in the range of 20 MIPS. Now, for video compression, we can relate this to how many pixels the video system must display per second. For example, the 256×240 video screen used by DVI Technology at

30 frames per second requires 1.8 million displayed pixels per second. Relating that to a CPU speed of 20 MIPS, it means we have, on the average, about 11 instructions per pixel available to do everything to play the video, which would include retrieving from disk, decompressing, and sending decompressed pixels to the display adaptor. Eleven instructions per pixel are not nearly enough to do that!

However, with software video we can make a tradeoff regarding the amount of compression that is used. In the previous example, if you could get data off the disk at 1.8 million pixels per second, no decompression would be needed because we wouldn't have to compress in the first place, and then 11 instructions per pixel might actually work. However, if we are using 16-bit pixels (because we are not going to compress anything), we have to get 3.6 megabytes per second from the mass storage system, which is nearly 10 times faster than most hard disks are today. So that won't work either.

But software video does work today—it is done by using fewer pixels (meaning a smaller window of video), lowering the frame rate (remember we said that 15 frames per second will sometimes work), and lowering the bits per pixel. For example, if we use 160×120 pixels at 8 bpp and 15 frames per second, that takes 288,000 pixels per second, or 288 KB per second data rate, and that works for many hard disks. In fact, that pixel rate gives us about 100 instructions per pixel for our 20-MIPS CPU, which is enough to actually do some compression. Therefore, at 8 bpp and 15 frames/second, a 20-MIPS CPU can probably do more than a 160×120 window of video, or we could have the same window at a higher frame rate.

However, the MIPS rate of CPUs will continue to grow year after year. Some have forecasted that a common CPU in the year 2000 will do 1000 MIPS! That kind of CPU will be able to do software-only motion video with nearly a full-screen window and close to 30 frames/second. However, it will still require some speed improvement of mass storage to make the data available to the CPU fast enough. Mass storage data rates will also improve in the coming years, but not nearly as fast as CPU speed. Thus, the software-only video system of the future will probably be designed to use most of the CPU power for compression and decompression so as to not require too much from the mass storage system.

Microsoft *Video for Windows*

Microsoft has provided an environment for the growth of motion video capability in *Windows*, with its *Video for Windows* (VFW) product. VFW includes drivers, tools, and sample data files to support experimenting and actual development of video and audio clips that will play on many systems. A range of hardware configurations is supported, and the system is extensible for both hardware and software enhancements in the future. The VFW package includes:

- a video capture tool—vidcap
- a video editor tool—videdit
- a media player—media player
- a bitmap editor tool—bitedit
- a color palette tool—paledit
- a converter for Apple *QuickTime* movies—VFW converter
- and a waveform audio editor tool—waveedit

There also is a CD-ROM of sample video and audio data in several formats and a media browser tool for exploring the VFW CD-ROM, which is included in the package.

With VFW, you capture video from an analog source using vidcap (you must have capture hardware for this), and then you can edit and compress one or more video clips using videdit. The present release of VFW supports three compression algorithms: Microsoft RLE (run-length encoding), Microsoft Video 1, and Intel *Indeo*. The environment is set up so that additional algorithms or modifications will be easy to add to the system. Of course, this should be almost an inherent feature of a software-based system. The editor also can import animation files in the Autodesk *Animator* format, and Apple *QuickTime* movies can be imported using the converter tool.

The use of the three compression formats is as follows:

1. Microsoft Video 1—This is the default compressor for VFW. It delivers a fixed data rate that you choose before compressing, and it offers scalable quality depending on the system resources available at play time. It works at 8 bpp, 16 bpp, or 24 bpp.

2. Microsoft RLE—This is the low-end compressor to use when the target system is limited in capability. It operates only at 8 bpp.

3. Intel *Indeo*—This compressor must be used if the video is to be played back using the Intel or IBM *ActionMedia II* board. Files compressed with *Indeo* can also play back at reduced quality on 80486 systems using a software-only version of the *Indeo* algorithm. With the *ActionMedia II* card, *Indeo* provides the highest quality video available.

The output of the VFW editor is in the *audio/video interleaved* (AVI) format, which is a Microsoft standard for audio/video files. The principal feature of AVI is that the audio and video are interleaved on a frame basis, meaning that the audio and video for each frame are stored together. This facilitates the synchronization of audio and video. Interleaving is also a feature of the DVI Technology AVS file format that has been in use since 1987.

Color Palettes for Video

An 8-bpp image reproduction depends on a 256-color palette. On VGA and super VGA displays, the 8-bpp palette can contain up to 256 colors selected from an 18-bpp or 24-bpp gamut of available colors. Video reproduction is very dependent on choosing a palette that contains the colors most widely used in the particular video being shown. This is a problem in several ways, which is the reason that you will not be satisfied with motion video (or reproduction of realistic still images either) until you can get to at least 16 bpp.

But many of today's systems will not go beyond 8 bpp, so we have to face the 8-bpp palette problems. You can do a remarkably good job of reproducing most single images if you have the freedom to tailor a 256-color palette to that one image. In a motion stream, that would mean tailoring the palette for each frame. However, a palette is a nontrivial amount of data—it can be as much as 768 bytes. Thus, most motion video schemes try to use a single palette for an entire video clip, since constant re-loading of palettes would slow down the system. One task of a palette editor is to examine a frame or collection of frames and determine the optimum palette for them. This is tricky, and there are numerous algorithms available for doing it. The more frames involved, the harder it gets. The problem gets even worse when you consider editing of video and video transition effects. You have to either find a palette that will suit all the videos, or you have to decide when in the video sequence you will reload the palette. It is always a compromise.

In a windowed environment, there is another problem—the entire display at any time is sharing the same palette. If you switch palettes for motion video and there are other windows on the screen, their colors can potentially change too. Most of the things on a windowed screen are made up of the window system objects such as window borders, title bars, controls, and backgrounds. One approach in a 256-color system is to make the window system stick to a subset of the color palette, 16 colors for example, and limit the video system to never change those colors. This means that the number of custom colors for displaying video reduces to 236 colors. Most systems work with that limit. However, there will still be a problem if there is more than one window containing video or an image. All this is the reason I keep saying that 8 bpp is a temporary stop along the curve of continuing system improvement. You really need 16 bpp!

The performance of VFW without any hardware assist is pretty limited on any except the fastest platforms—the video windows are small, the frame rate is low, and the color palette is limited to 8 bpp. However, VFW is an environment that will benefit when you add hardware such as the *ActionMedia II* card, and it will grow with other system performance enhancements as well. It is the basis for much wider use of digital video under *Windows* in the future.

DIGITAL AUDIO

Before we go too much further with motion video, we should discuss audio. Video people tend to neglect audio but, in fact, it is an essential part of the motion video system. Just turn down the sound on your TV for a while and see what happens to the TV's effectiveness to inform, teach, or entertain. Most of the message of a TV program comes in the audio—the video simply enhances the experience. You can usually get the gist of a program better by listening to the sound alone than by watching the picture alone. So we should not neglect audio in multimedia computing either.

The computer, of course, already has a video screen even when we don't have any hardware or software for motion video. Therefore, the existing video screen can benefit from an audio message. This is a natural (and easy) first step into multimedia, and it adds immeasurably to your applications. Most computers already have an audio system; however, it is usually a 1-bit driver feeding a tiny speaker that was intended only for delivering the beep sounds that early computers made. Software companies over the years have written some remarkable programs to make this simple hardware deliver voice or music, but the quality limitations are severe. There is no substitute for adding better hardware to support high-quality audio. Fortunately, today, for approximately two hundred dollars, you can get a stereo audio add-in board that will deliver up to CD-quality audio, and it will capture high-quality stereo audio from any audio source you have. (Typical products are the *ProAudio Spectrum 16* by Media Vision or the *Sound Blaster 16* by Creative Labs, Inc.) Many PC manufacturers or marketers are building an audio board into all systems targeted for multimedia use.

Audio Data Requirements

Audio data rates are lower than video, but they are still significant. This is especially true because you cannot compress audio as much as you can compress video. Just like video, you pay for higher quality with higher data rates. Digital audio performance is determined by *sampling rate* and *bits per sample* (bps). This is

Table 8.1 Digital audio algorithms: data rates and performance.

Bits/Sample (bps)	Sampling Rate (Hz)	Bytes per Minute	Audio Bandwidth	Compress	Stereo
4	11,025	331 KB	5 kHz	yes	no
4	22,050	662 KB	10 kHz	yes	no
4	22,050	1.32 MB	10 kHz	yes	yes
4	44,100	1.32 MB	18 kHz	yes	no
4	44,100	2.65 MB	18 kHz	yes	yes
8	22,050	1.32 MB	10 kHz	no	no
8	22,050	2.65 MB	10 kHz	no	yes
16	44,100	5.3 MB	18 kHz	no	no
16	44,100	10.6 MB	18 kHz	no	yes

something like video, where sampling rate equates to resolution and bps equates to bpp. The higher these numbers are, the higher the audio performance. Table 8.1 shows some typical audio algorithms and their quality performance and data rates. (These algorithms are the ones recommended by the Ultimedia Tools Series specifications.)

All of the 4-bps algorithms in the table use compression and decompression; the type is *Adaptive Differential Pulse Code Modulation* (ADPCM). The effect of the ADPCM decompression process is to expand the effective bps to 16, although the process is not perfect. However, the overall performance of the 4-bps ADPCM is usually somewhat better than the 8-bps uncompressed algorithms, but not as good as the 16-bps uncompressed algorithms. Thus, the degree of compression is somewhere between 2:1 and 4:1. Note that using audio compression requires significant processing power; this is normally provided on audio boards that support compressed audio by adding a *Digital Signal Processor* (DSP) chip to the board. That way, the DSP chip runs the audio process without affecting the system CPU and bus except for providing the input data stream from hard disk or CD-ROM.

Note that the audio bandwidth is always a little less than half the sampling rate. This will always be the case because half the sampling rate is the theoretical limit for bandwidth of a sampled system. The lowest sampling rate system (11,025 Hz) is normally used only for speech—although it will reproduce music, the result is not very good because the bandwidth is too low.

Also notice that using stereo always doubles the data rate. The two stereo channels are independent of each other, and they can also be used for purposes other than stereo—for example, to provide a second language track.

CAPTURING AUDIO AND VIDEO

To do your own capture, you must have audio and video sources and audio and video digitizing boards. Then you need capture software to go with the hardware you have selected. Depending on the capabilities of the capture software and your objectives, you also may want audio and video editing software, so you can make changes to material that you have captured. Editing becomes mandatory when you are creating a sequence where it is impossible to record the sequence all at once in real time. Because of different scenes, different camera angles, or multiple audio sources, there may not be any alternative to doing some editing. Essentially, all professionally produced audio and video has been edited.

The process of originally capturing audio, video, or both from live sources is called *production*. All processes that are done after production, whether editing, assembly, or enhancement, are called *postproduction*. For professional audio/video production and postproduction, there is special equipment for each step of the process. This equipment is beyond the scope of this book, and it is beyond the pocketbook of most multimedia producers. However, an amazingly large portion of the professional capability can be achieved on a PC through software, and that's what I will talk about here.

Audio Capture Software

Capture software often comes as a module within another tool, such as an assembly tool or an editing tool. It also comes in stand-alone form; for example, *Windows 3.1* includes an audio capture tool called Sound Recorder. Figure 8.1 shows the control panel for *Sound Recorder*, which operates by capturing audio into system RAM, which means the amount of continuous sound captured is limited to what will fit into RAM at one time, typically only a couple of minutes. Look at the data rates in Table 8.1, and compare them to your system RAM size to get a feel for that, but, remember, there are other things that will use some of your RAM, so it is not all available for audio capture.

The control panel provides the usual file menu capabilities of New, Open, Save, and Save as, so you can not only capture new audio by itself and save it to disk, you can also load an old audio file and preview it or even add newly captured material to it before saving it to disk with a new name. *Sound Recorder* also provides limited sound effects, including echo, volume control, reverse play, and speed control. The important thing to remember is that the maximum length of audio must fit into RAM. *Sound Recorder* does not provide any way to select the audio algorithm; that must be done by directly controlling your audio hardware from another program.

Figure 8.1   The control panel of *Sound Recorder,* the audio capture utility included with *Windows 3.1*

Of course, if you are always going to use the same algorithm, you need make that selection only once. However, most sound hardware comes with its own version of a program like *Sound Recorder,* which will usually include algorithm selection, and it may have other advanced features as well.

Video Capture

As already mentioned, you need some hardware to do video capture. Some video display boards are available with the analog-to-digital (A-D) conversion hardware for capturing. These boards receive an analog video input in one or more formats and display digitized images of the analog signals. They also can send the digitized data to mass storage in the system. However, video capture is a different animal depending on whether you have video compression hardware or not. Without compression hardware, you usually cannot capture motion frames at full frame rate (30 per second). You can get around this by capturing motion frames one at a time, storing each one to hard disk before going on to the next frame. This limitation occurs because the PC system cannot handle the data rate of streaming uncompressed frames in real time, and software-only compression takes too long to be done on the fly.

When dealing with uncompressed motion video streams, you can trade between the size of the image (pixel count), the bits per pixel, and the frame rate to control the resulting stream's data rate. Table 8.2 shows those tradeoffs.

Table 8.2 Image size, bpp, and frame rate versus stream data rate.

Pixels	Bits/Pixel	Frames/Second	Bytes/Second
640×480	24	30	27,648,000
320×240	24	30	6,912,000
320×240	8	15	1,152,000
160×120	8	15	288,000
160×120	8	8	153,000
160×120	8	5	96,000

The first line of the table is a full-screen VGA video at 24 bpp and 30 frames per second—it is the "ultimate" (for today, at least). The data rate is almost 28 megabytes per second, which is astronomical compared to what a PC can do. The succeeding lines of the table show increasing compromises in pixel size, bpp, and frame rate to get the data rate down to the PC range, which is 100,000 to 300,000 bytes/second. This shows clearly why you can only capture a postage stamp-sized window without some kind of in-line video compression.

If you lower the frame rate to reduce data rate, you also gain CPU processing time per frame, which means you have time to do some simple compression inline. For that reason, the tradeoffs in designing a practical software-only capture system are more complex than indicated by Table 8.2, and at low frame rates you may be able to do better than the table indicates.

This difficulty of capturing in real time is a serious limitation. It means that you may not be able to capture image sizes and frame rates that you would be able to play back if you could just get them captured and compressed. One solution to the capture problem is to use a video source that steps a frame at a time and then waits for you to capture, compress, and store the frame before moving to the next one. You can run a low-cost VCR in still frame mode to do that, but the picture quality is severely degraded—to the point that it is not practical for digitizing and compressing. If you have access to broadcast-quality video recorders, some of them can do single-step playback with good results, but that is going to get expensive. A laser video disc will do a good job in single-frame mode, but getting your video onto the laser disc in the first place is expensive and time consuming. With today's desktop PCs, software-only video capture is not a practical medium for anything other than a few demonstration sequences. If you are serious about capturing your own video, you should have some compression hardware.

The best video capture and compression hardware today is the IBM and Intel *ActionMedia II* board; with it you can capture and compress on the fly from live or recorded sources and do direct-to-disk recording of simultaneous motion video and audio. The video has 24-bit color quality and can be up to full screen

Figure 8.2   Window of the Microsoft *vidcap* video and audio capture tool

in size. You also can capture in a format that can be played back (at reduced quality) with software-only players. This is a key feature of Intel *Indeo* compressed video.

Software for Video Capture

Software-only capture and compression can be done with the Microsoft *Video for Windows vidcap* tool, whose windows are shown in Figure 8.2. This tool works with several different video capture boards, with or without compression hardware, including the *ActionMedia II* board. *Vidcap* will support real-time or step-frame capture. In real-time capture, when you don't have compression hardware, you can set up the system so that it will capture frames as fast as it can. This will usually mean a low frame rate because of the time it takes to store each frame.

Figure 8.3 *MEDIAscript OS/2* video capture tools

MEDIAscript Video Capture Tools

The *MEDIAscript OS/2* authoring products have built-in video capture tools using the *ActionMedia II* hardware. There are two versions of the capture tool: one uses a conventional OS/2 dialog box for control, and the other uses a custom control dialog that looks like a VCR. Figure 8.3 shows both forms.

MEDIAscript uses the DVI Technology RTV video compression algorithm, which provides options for capture resolution, frame rate, reference frame count, audio parameters, and degree of video compression. The dialogs offer several combinations of the RTV parameters, but through the *MEDIAscript* language an author can access the full range of parameters to create her own preference. During capture, the dialog box shows dynamically the byte size of the video file

Figure 8.4 The main editing window of Microsoft *VidEdit*

as it grows. After capture, the video can be reviewed by playing it back using the video browse tools in *MEDIAscript*.

Video Editing Software—Microsoft *VidEdit*

It is seldom that you can capture video exactly the way you want it for your application. You almost always will need to do some *editing*. With editing, you can select exactly the cuts you want to use, combine several cuts into one sequence, adjust the audio separately from the video, and add video transition effects. A motion video editor tool called *VidEdit* is included with Microsoft *Video for Windows*. The main window of *VidEdit* is shown in Figure 8.4.

VidEdit works with one video file at a time, in either compressed or uncompressed form. When you are finished editing, you can create a new compressed file output. Often you will need to combine contents from several video files, captured at different times, into a single output sequence. You do that with *VidEdit* by opening the file containing the first cut, selecting the exact frames for the cut and copying them to the *Windows* clipboard. Then you start the new file and paste the frames for the first cut into it from the clipboard. To add the other cuts, you repeat the open-copy-open-paste process. Finally, you can save the new file to hard disk. At any point in this process, you can review the new file by playing it or single-stepping it frame by frame.

Because *VidEdit* has only one file open at a time, if you want to make a change in the sequence, you have to go back through the copy-paste process to make the change. However, you can have more than one instance of *VidEdit* open at a time, so you can simply jump between two or more *VidEdit* windows to perform the process; each instance of *VidEdit* has one of the source files. *VidEdit* provides various options for formatting and compressing the new file, and it also can import movie files in Autodesk *Animator* format or in several Microsoft formats. The final file is normally output in *Video for Windows* audio/video interleaved (AVI) format.

VidEdit is a fully functional editor, but it is a simple one. Although it does most of the basic tasks of audio or video editing, the procedures often get tedious, and there is nothing to help you keep track of your material or create command lists so that edit tasks could be revisited at a later time. It also does not provide anything except cut transitions. If you plan some serious editing, you need more.

Video Editing Software—TouchVision's *D/Vision Pro*

True professional-style video (or audio) editing provides an environment where each of the source videos is available in its own window. The editor can roll each of the videos in "shuttle" mode, where she can smoothly move forward or backward through the video at variable speeds from single step to high speed to select edit cut points. As a series of cuts are defined this way, an *edit decision list* (EDL) is built, from which the final video can be constructed. The final video is previewed by playing it from the EDL, also in shuttle mode. This kind of editing is called *nonlinear*, to distinguish it from conventional videotape editing where one must record a new tape before the edited sequence can be viewed. In nonlinear editing, the playback mechanism (your hard disk) is random access, so the EDL can be readily played in real time for previewing. TouchVision Systems offers *D/Vision Pro*, which does all that—and more. It is a PC-based professional nonlinear video editor that runs under DOS.

D/Vision Pro requires the *ActionMedia II* board, and it works with video and audio in the DVI Technology RTV formats. If you use VCR source material that contains a time code track, you can perform a final full-quality assembly of your video by using the EDL created by *D/Vision Pro* to control a VCR editing system. Alternatively, you can assemble a final cut on your PC in the RTV format, which will be playable on any *ActionMedia II* equipped system. The third output possibility is what TouchVision calls *SupeRTV*, a high-data rate RTV format, which can be played on the authoring system to output NTSC video from the *ActionMedia II* card to a VCR. This way you can make a high-quality analog video tape right from your PC.

D/Vision Pro is a complete editing environment. It provides an excellent RTV capture tool so you can digitize and compress your source video into the PC from any video source. If the video source has time code, that is retained by the computer and is used for constructing the EDL. *D/Vision Pro* uses two display monitors: One shows one or more windows of DVI video, and the other shows a command screen display. Both monitors are controlled by a mouse or trackball cursor (TouchVision recommends a trackball). You move between the monitors by moving the cursor off the edge of the screen toward the other monitor. The screen displays for capture are shown in Figure 8.5.

The capture setup dialogs provide for control of a source VCR, when you are using that type of source, and it helps you keep track of your RTV files (called "reels"), with long file names, and manual or automatic logging of key points in the video. You can create new reels, or you can add onto an existing reel. During capture, the source video is displayed on the DVI monitor, and the control monitor shows a status display, as shown at the bottom of Figure 8.5. During capture, the mouse is disabled so you must use the keyboard function keys for control of record, pause, and quit..

Once all your source material is captured into one or more source reels, you can go into the editing process. Figure 8.6 shows the basic editing screen setup for the two displays. The DVI monitor has several formats, showing either one video full screen, two videos side by side in windows, or up to twelve videos in smaller windows. One video window can show the current position in the edited stream being created, and the other windows can show multiple points in the source material.

The control monitor shows two VCR controllers at the top of the screen, one for the current source video and one for the output video. The output video controller has a "record" button; when it is clicked (it turns red), everything you do in the current source video is "copied" to the output video. The word "copied" is in quotes because no copy actually occurs; what happens is that the frames being recorded are placed into the EDL at the right place, so they will be called up when the EDL is played. *D/Vision Pro* plays your edited scene by having the hard disk go back to the source files and pick out the frames you selected and present them in the order you indicated. The hard disk is fast enough that this happens without any interruptions or delays in the video.

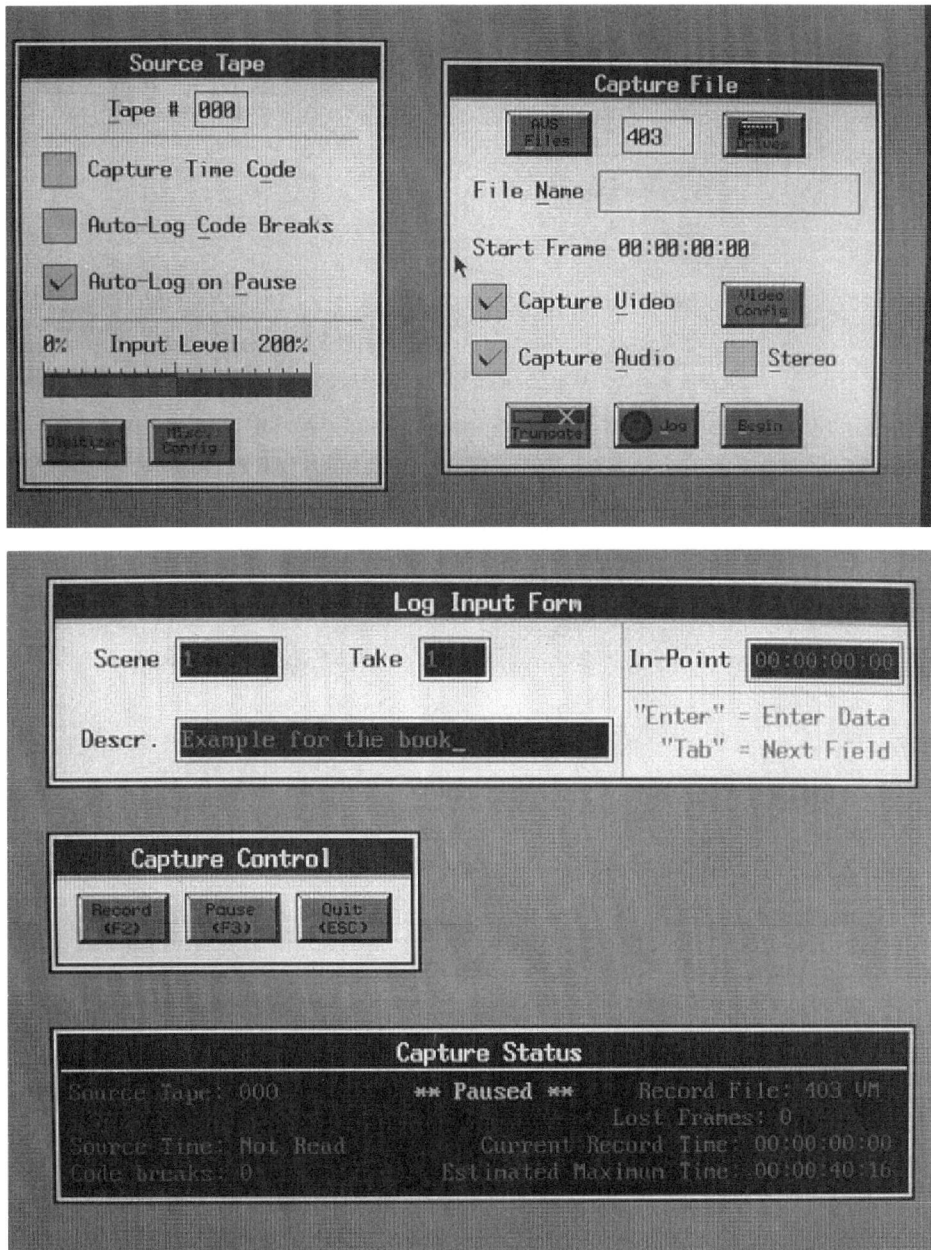

Figure 8.5 *D/Vision Pro* capture screens—setup screen (top), capture control screen (bottom)

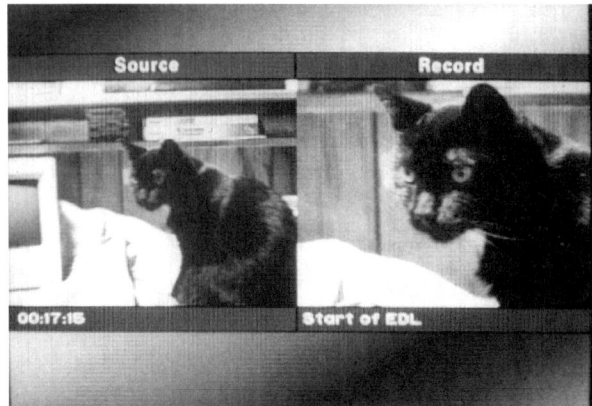

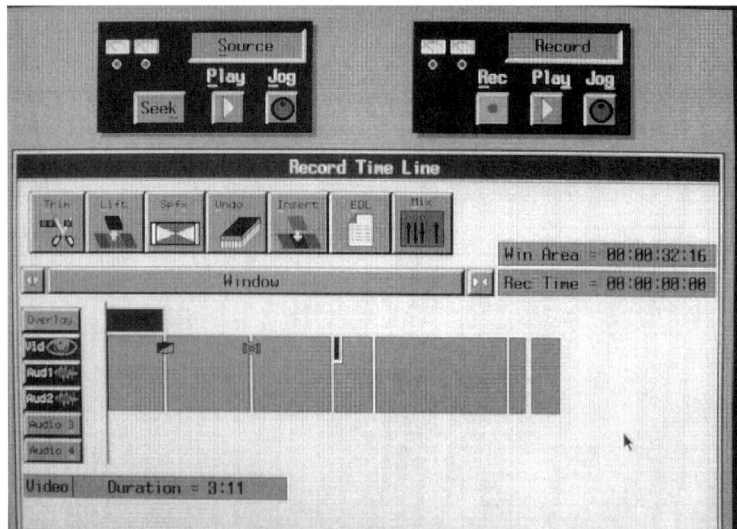

Figure 8.6 *D/Vision Pro* editing screens—video screen (top), control screen (bottom)

D/Vision Pro also can add dynamic transitions between your cuts—wipes, dissolves, or fades. Transitions are very smooth, and there is a choice of 10 different wipes in either of two directions. The results are very professional.

TouchVision Systems has two versions of *D/Vision*—the Pro version, which was described, and a standard version. The standard version is medium priced, but it uses a single-monitor interface, and it does not do supeRTV, importing of other graphics or animation formats, output of the EDL for external use, or time code support. In addition, the Pro version provides for editing of up to six audio tracks.

If you have sophisticated needs, the higher price of the Pro version is definitely worth it.

SUMMARY

Digital motion video has been a challenge in low-priced PC systems. However, with today's tools, producing your own motion video and audio is definitely practical on a desktop PC. Tools and hardware at several price levels let you do video capture, compression, and editing. Whatever sophistication you may require is now available on the desktop.

9

 **Animation**

Motion is an important attribute that contributes to the effectiveness of your computer screens to convey their messages. I have already discussed motion video, which is relatively easy to produce with a video camera, but it is extremely demanding of the computer resources for processing power and storage. Animation is another way to achieve motion—it makes much more modest demands on storage and processing power, but it is typically more difficult to produce. This chapter discusses animation and the tools that are needed to create it.

WHAT IS ANIMATION?

You surely are familiar with cartoon animation as it is used in the movies and on television. You also probably know something about the process for creating animation where artists meticulously draw each frame of a scene and then capture them frame by frame with a movie camera. Thus, an animation is just a series of frames, which are presented in a rapid sequence to create the illusion of motion. In the movies, frames are displayed at 24 per second; in television the rate is 30 per second. In each case, the animation creation process results in a film or video tape containing a series of complete frames that are simply played through a projector or VCR to show the animation. Figure 9.1 shows some of the frames for a simple animation of a bouncing ball.

Computer animation is exactly the same—a series of frames is displayed in rapid sequence, but the difference is that the computer can manipulate each frame so a complete representation of every frame does not have to be stored. Instead, a computer animation file stores only the raw materials for the frames, along with instructions for how the computer will assemble each frame at runtime. In the bouncing ball example of Figure 9.1, the computer stores

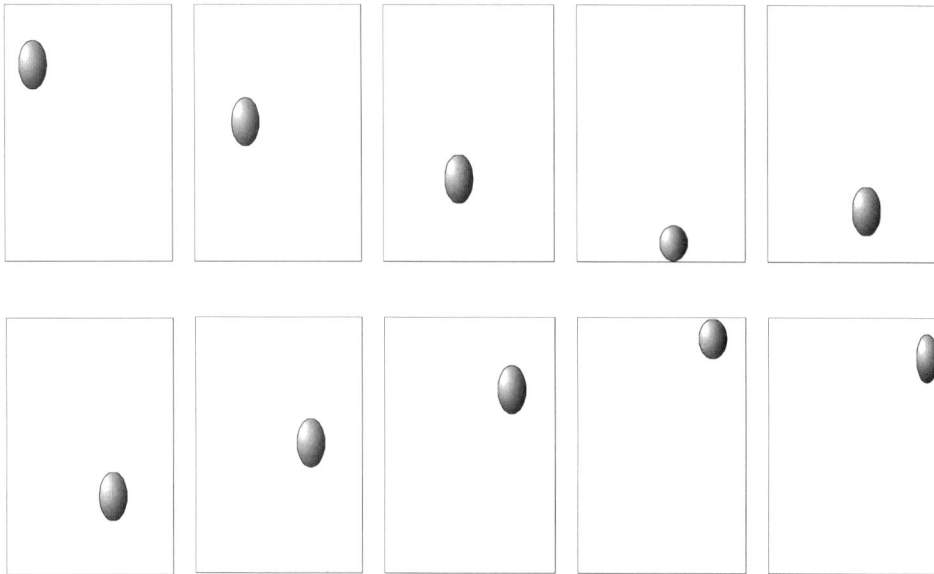

Figure 9.1   Frames for the animation of a bouncing ball

instructions for drawing the ball only once and then stores coordinates in each frame for drawing the ball as it moves. The flattening of the ball at the bounce point is accomplished by modifying the ball drawing instructions for the frames at the bounce point.

Furthermore, the computer can also assist in the creation process, giving to the animator in a few keystrokes, powers that formerly required teams of skilled artists working for many hours. The computer can handle complex drawing tasks and can be told how to modify each frame to accomplish the desired motion effects. Scenes can be built up from a number of objects, where each object has its own unique instructions for how it will behave from one frame to the next.

ADVANTAGES/DISADVANTAGES OF ANIMATION

Because an animation file stores only the instructions for drawing each frame, not the entire frame itself, animation files can be many times smaller than motion video files. At runtime the computer creates or *renders* each frame just before it is displayed. No special hardware is needed to display animations, but rendering a complex animation in real time may require a very powerful CPU. On a typical multimedia delivery PC having a 386 CPU, you will not be able to smoothly animate large objects. However, you can have small objects move around the full screen, because the CPU has to manipulate only the pixels involved in the animated object. Pixels on the screen that are not involved in moving the object or objects do not have to be touched and do not use any CPU power.

If you attempt to display animation that is too complex to be handled by the CPU of the delivery system, the frame rate simply slows down, causing the animation to become jerky. The computer renders the frames of the animation as fast as it can. Most animation drivers will automatically skip frames in the animation to keep the overall playing time approximately correct.

You can smoothly control the speed of animation up to the maximum rate achievable by the system. This capability for variable speed can be an advantage when it is necessary to synchronize animation with another concurrent object, such as audio. You probably cannot adjust the speed of audio playback, so the controllability of the video part of animation accomplishes the synchronization.

CREATING ANIMATION WITH A COMPUTER

There are several approaches to creating animation with a computer. Depending on the objectives for the animation, all the approaches require a degree of skill from the author. If you intend to create elaborate animations with many realistic objects moving at once in many dimensions, you will not only require a powerful PC system and an expensive animation software tool, but you will need some artistic skill and a substantial commitment of time to learn how to use your animation tools. Animation at that level is not something that you can be successful at unless you do a lot of it and develop the experience needed. At the other end of the scale, if you only want to have one or two simple objects moving about the screen, you can get simple tools with which you can quickly create such animations. A number of authoring assembly tools have simple animation functions built in, and stand-alone animation tools are available at all levels of sophistication.

There are clip libraries for animation too, just like for audio and images. Sometimes you can find the animation you need in a library, or you can start with a library animation and modify it for your purpose. As with audio, video, or images, the right clip libraries for animation can be valuable resources.

Animation along a Path

The simplest form of animation is to move an object along a path on the screen. The object could be a single graphic primitive, like a circle (the ball in Figure

9.1), or it could be a complete drawing, such as a bird, for example. In the movies, such an object for animation is called a *cel*, which is an abbreviation for "celluloid." This name originated in film, because animation objects were originally drawn on sheets of celluloid, which were positioned in front of background scenes and photographed a frame at a time as they were manually moved. A computer can do the same process; it's much easier, and it can be in real time. The computer begins playing an animation by drawing the object in its position at the start of the path. Then it immediately draws the next frame offscreen (in memory) with the object in its new position, waits until it is time to display the next frame, and displays the next frame by a simple memory move. This process repeats for successive frames until the object has moved to the end of the path.

This simple action is the basis for most animation tools. You draw the cel to animate or select it from a library; define a path with line, curve, polygon, or freehand drawing tools; and specify frame rate and how many frames to use to cover the path. That's all there is to it—so far, it takes very little skill. Actual animation tools allow you to have multiple objects animating simultaneously this way. Each object moves at its own speed along its own path. That is a little more interesting.

Animated Cels

The animation described so far is not very realistic, because each cel is drawn exactly the same way in each frame. A much better effect is created if you modify the cel in successive frames; for example, you make the bird's wings flap, or the man's arms and legs move as he walks. For cyclical motions like flying or walking, you create a group of cels, which are presented in sequence on successive frames. Such a cyclical group of cels is often called an *actor* or an *animated cel*. For walking or flying, the animation becomes surprisingly realistic with even a small number of cels in the actor—anywhere from four to eight will do it. Figure 9.2 shows the cels for a walking man actor.

But now some skill becomes necessary, because it is quite an art to draw an actor that will display smooth and realistic motion. Also, there needs to be some coordination between the rate the actor moves along the path and the rate with which the actor cycles through his cels. This is an opportunity for another clip library—you can acquire (or build your own) library of actors, which you can use in different combinations to produce many animations.

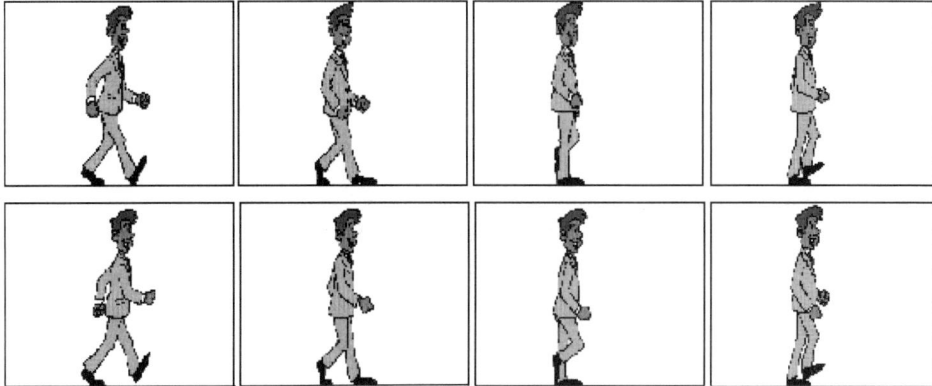

Figure 9.2   An eight-cel actor for a man walking (from *Animation Works Interactive*)

Backgrounds

The animation process I have been describing can be performed on top of any background. You can have a window of a solid color, shaded colors, a drawing, or a realistic image. Alternatively, you could perform the animation over anything that was on the screen at the time (not all tools will do this). Once the background is something other than a solid color, you can also add more realism by moving the backgound along a path during the animation. Then you could have a bird actor flying while the background (sky) scrolls in the opposite direction, giving the illusion that the bird is covering distance relative to the background. Thus, another dimension is added to the animation, but it takes a little more skill to know exactly how to use it.

3-D Animation

An element of three dimensions can be created in animations using the techniques described, but only by the way you draw the actors. For example, you might make an actor of a dancing person who turns while he dances along a path. However, it is still a 2-D animation because the path is in two dimensions. To get to real 3-D, there must be 3-D paths. Some tools support that, including the capability to adjust the size of an actor according to a perspective algorithm based on location in the 3-D scene. This adds more realism; but at the same time, it calls for more processing power in the computer and more skill from the author of the animation.

Tweening and Morphing

With the most advanced animation tools, you don't have to actually draw every frame of a sequence or an actor—you can just draw some key frames, and then have the computer automatically create intermediate frames that will smooth out the motion. This process is called *tweening*—creating the frames in between. Tweening is a complex task that takes a lot of processing, maybe several seconds or more per frame, so it is usually only done during authoring; the in-between frames are then stored just like the other frames in the actors.

One of the more advanced techniques for tweening is called *morphing*, or *polymorphic tweening*, which is a transformation from one shape to another. The famous drawing by M. C. Escher where fish transform into birds, etc., is an example of morphing. Advanced animation tools can do morphing during authoring to create some very interesting transition effects. Figure 9.3 is an example of polymorphic tweening, where an oval is transformed into a star in eight frames.

There are many other transformations that can be performed in animation. The more sophisticated animation tools have a dazzling array of capabilities, many of which can even be combined in a single effect. This vast portfolio of effects takes a lot of skill to use; you will need a real commitment to animation to get into the more advanced tools.

ANIMATION TOOL—*Animation Works Interactive*

Gold Disk, Inc. offers *Animation Works Interactive* (AWI), which is a package of easy-to-use animation tools in the medium price range, running under *Windows*. The principal tools are the *Movie Editor*, which performs assembly of complete animations; the *Cel Editor*, where you build cels and actors; and the *Background Editor*, which is a paint tool for building backgrounds. Although these tools are separate applications, you can run them all at the same time and move freely between them, creating an integrated working environment. AWI supports cels, actors, many kinds of paths, backgrounds with scrolling, sound, interactivity, actor libraries, and more. It is a very good value for the price and can readily be learned even by a casual animator.

Figure 9.4 shows the main screen of the *Movie Editor*. The client area of the *Movie Editor* screen shows the current frame from the animation being edited. Each of the fish shown is an actor (some are duplicates of the same actor). The dotted line shows the path of one fish that has been selected. At the bottom right is a player control panel for previewing the animation; it provides start-stop, single-step, and forward/backward control. At the upper right is the Actor

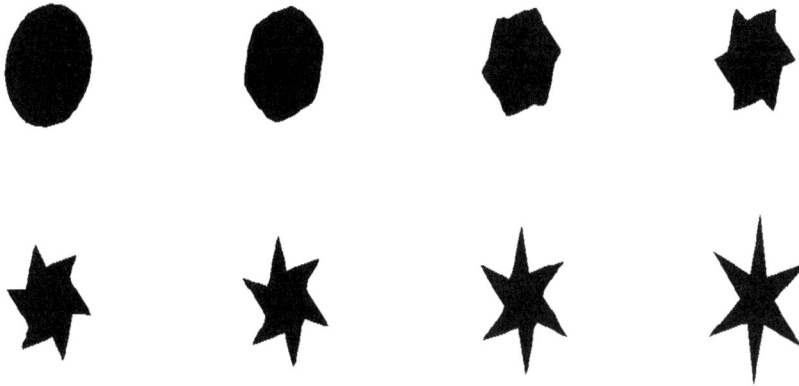

Figure 9.3 An example of polymorphic tweening using Autodesk *Animator*

window; it has a list box at the top showing all the actors in the current animation file. The selected actor is shown, and its behavior can be previewed by clicking on the icon at the lower right of the Actor window. The disk icon at the lower left of the actor window gives access to the library of actors; additional actors can be brought into the current animation if needed.

The tool palette is at the left of the screen; this is the default location, but it can be placed anywhere. Tools for selection, text, and a variety of path formats can be chosen from the palette. The menu bar at the top of the screen provides additional controls for background effects, sound, interactivity, file management, text attributes, nesting one animation within another, and many other special effects and events. The *Movie Editor* contains many features for control of other applications from within an animation, using MCI, DDE, or OLE—features that you expect in an authoring assembly package. Therefore, you could use AWI to create certain types of complete applications, particularly those that were primarily animation-based. However, AWI competes with broader-based assembly packages only on the basis of its animation strength, which is substantial. I heartily recommend AWI for animation; but for general authoring assembly, you should probably look at tools that specialize in assembly.

The AWI *Cel Editor* is used to create and modify cels and actors; its screen is shown in Figure 9.5. The *Cel Editor* is basically a paint tool with special features to handle the unique needs of drawing a series of cels and packaging them as an actor. AWI has a special file format for actors with the .act name extension; the *Cel Editor* works with those files. AWI cels are bitmaps, so you use bitmapped painting tools on them. The tool palette is at the left of Figure 9.5. Since an actor

Figure 9.4 *Movie Editor* screen from *Animation Works Interactive*

can itself be an animation, a control panel window at the lower right of the screen gives frame selection or playback control to view the animation of the actor being edited. The menu bar at the top of the screen gives access to file management and many other capabilities.

The *Background Editor* is a paint tool for working with bitmap images for backgrounds. Its screen is similar to the *Cel Editor* except it does not need any control panel. The *Background Editor* can input images in several formats for use as animation backgrounds.

AWI is a good tool for the beginning animator; you will find its tools easy to learn and you can use it to create very effective animations.

ANIMATION TOOL—*Animator Pro*

Autodesk *Animator Pro* is a high-end professional animation package that has the advanced features an animation specialist needs to create animations day in and day out. Its interface focuses much more on power than on ease of use, so it is a

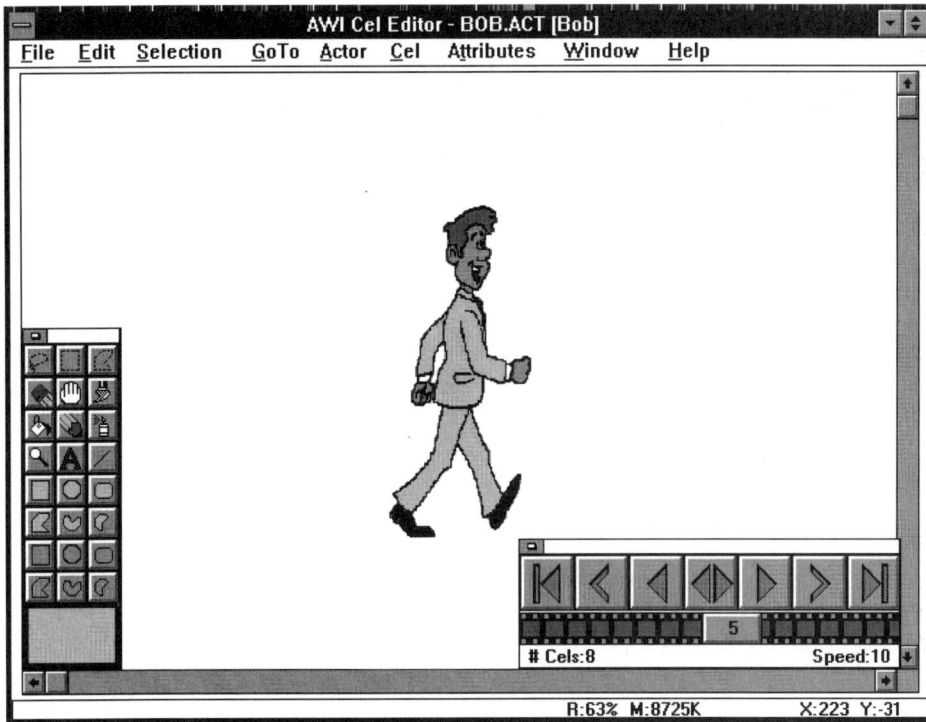

Figure 9.5 The AWI *Cel Editor* screen

little more difficult to learn, but there are depths of power that the most experienced animator will appreciate.

Animator Pro operates with a minimum of 256 screen colors. If you have a standard VGA, it will use 320×240 resolution, which is the only VGA resolution mode having 256 colors. If you have a super VGA and an appropriate driver, you can use higher-resolution modes. When you are playing back animations using the *Animator Windows Player,* the 320×240 animation will play in a window on higher-resolution screens. However, if the screen has only 16 colors, the colors in the window may not be correct.

Animator Pro supports the concepts of frames, cels, and animated cels (Autodesk does not use the term "actor"), just like AWI, but the environment is much richer both in the tools available for creating or modifying objects and in the methods for merging animations and pieces of animations. It also supports 22 types of draw tools (listed below), color cycling, polymorphic tweening, and optical effects.

Animator Pro Draw Tools

Draw Tool	Description
Box	Draw a rectangle
Circle	Draw a circle
Draw	Freehand draw with various brush shapes
Drizzle	Freehand draw with varying brush width
Edge	Border a selected color with current ink
Fill	Fill all pixels of selected color with current ink
Fill To	Fill an area up to a border color
Gel	Draw current ink in increasingly transparent circles
Line	Draw straight lines in any direction with current ink and brush
Move	Move or copy images
Oval	Draw an ellipse
Petal	Draw a petal-shaped object with 3 to 32 petals
Poly	Draw a straight-line polygon
Rpoly	Draw an equal-sided straight-line polygon
Separate	Apply the current ink to all instances of a selected color
Shape	Draw a closed freehand shape with the current ink
Spiral	Draw a spiral with the current ink and brush
Spline	Apply ink in a spline curve
Spray	Apply current ink in a random spray pattern
Star	Draw a star with 3 to 32 points
Streak	Draw a broken trail
Text	Draw text in the current ink

Animator Pro also has the concept of *ink*, which describes the way that drawn objects are combined in the frame. There are 26 built-in types of ink, and externally developed ink functions can be added to the list. Seven such additional "ink files" are shipped with *Animator Pro*. The inks are listed below.

Animator Pro Inks

Ink Name	Description
Add	Add the index of the draw color to the pixel color
And	Perform logical AND between draw color and pixel color
Bright	Increase the value of colors within the draw object
Close	Close single-pixel holes in outlines of the draw color
Dark	Decrease the value of colors within the draw object
Emboss	Modify borders of draw object to make it appear raised
Glass	Apply the current color transparently
Glaze	Apply the current color with variable transparency
Glow	Perform color cycling in the drawn object
Gray	Increase the gray values of the screen colors
H Gradient	Apply gradient colors in a horizontal direction
Hollow	Create an outlined image

Jumble	Mix pixels on the screen randomly
L Gradient	Apply gradient colors horizontally contoured to the shape
Merge	Reveal another image over the main screen
Minus	Subtract the index value of the current color from pixel values
Opaque	Apply the current color directly
Or	Perform a logical OR between draw color and pixel color
Pull	Drag color in the direction the mouse moves
R Gradient	Create a radial pattern of gradient colors
Scrape	Reveal an image as you draw the object
Slice	Move vertical lines of pixels alternately up and down
Smear	Drag pixels in the drection the mouse moves
Smooth	Blur the image slightly
Soften	Blur the image
Spark	Produce a sparkling effect on screen
Split	Slide alternate H lines of pixels in opposite directions
Sweep	Replace isolated single pixels with surrounding color
Tile	Apply an image in a tiled pattern
Unbuzz	Process an image for interlaced display without flicker
Unzag	Perform antialiasing on an image
V Gradient	Apply gradient colors in a vertical direction
Xor	Perform a logical XOR between draw color and pixel color

You can see from these two lists that there is a tremendous range of possibilities when you combine draw tools with ink types.

Animator Pro is a single DOS application; you move between movie editing, cel editing, or background editing by making different menu selections. The main menu interface is shown in Figure 9.6. One frame from the sample animation magnet.fli is displayed along with the menu, which can be positioned anywhere on the screen. At the top of the screen is a menu bar that gives access to many more features of *Animator Pro*. At the top center of the menu box is a control panel for playing the animation or controlling the frame that is currently displayed. At the left is a selector for the current draw tool, and at the right is a selector for the current ink. You can customize the eight tools and eight inks shown in the main menu by selecting either Tools or Inks from the ANI selection on the menu bar. These selections give you dialogs that offer even more options for controlling the draw process. When the mouse is clicked and dragged on the screen, you are drawing directly into the current frame.

You begin a new animation in *Animator Pro* by choosing new from the ani menu. This creates a new animation containing just one frame. If you want a background color or image, you load that too. Then you set the number of frames for the new animation; any background image is automatically copied into all the frames. You then add the objects to be animated, which you can either draw directly into the frames, or you can load previously drawn objects from files. Using the time menu

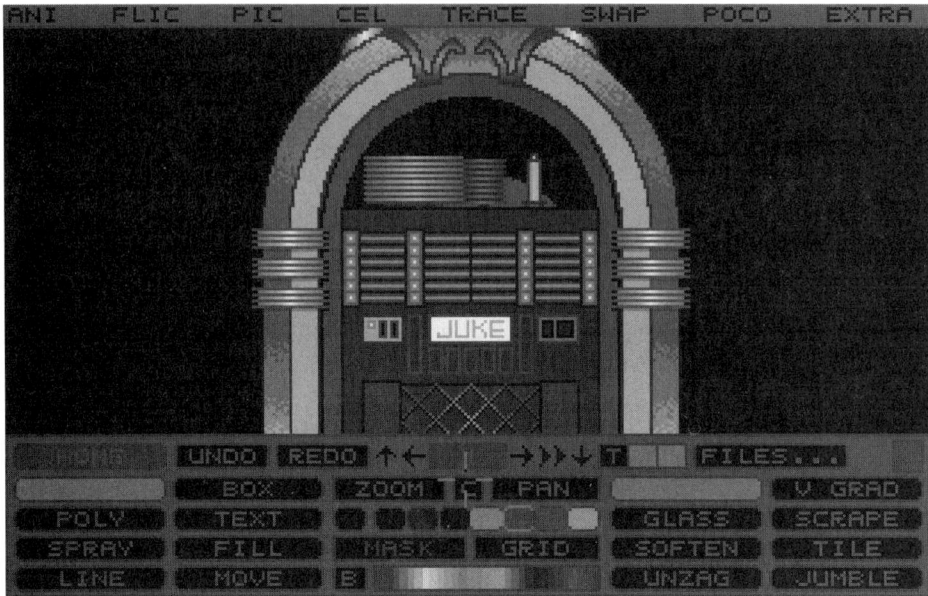

Figure 9.6 Main menu of *Animator Pro*

(which you access by right-clicking on the T box in the main menu), you can control which frame(s) will be affected by any actions you take.

Animator Pro provides a portfolio of ways to combine animations. For example, you can build pieces of your animation separately and then bring them together to play concurrently by *compositing* them into a single animation. You have a variety of ways to control how compositing takes place, including placement of animations in front of or behind others, adding transition effects when an animation starts or ends, etc. You can also combine animations by *joining* them—placing then end to end. You also have the transition options when joining. Although no single task in *Animator Pro* is difficult, the reason it takes a commitment to learn is that there are so many possibilities. You really need to learn a lot of them to appreciate that there is probably a way to accomplish any animation task you may need.

DISPLAYING ANIMATION

Once an animation has been created with the editing tool, you can display it in your application by using the appropriate player program. Some assembly tools have animation players built in, while others can play animation by using DDE

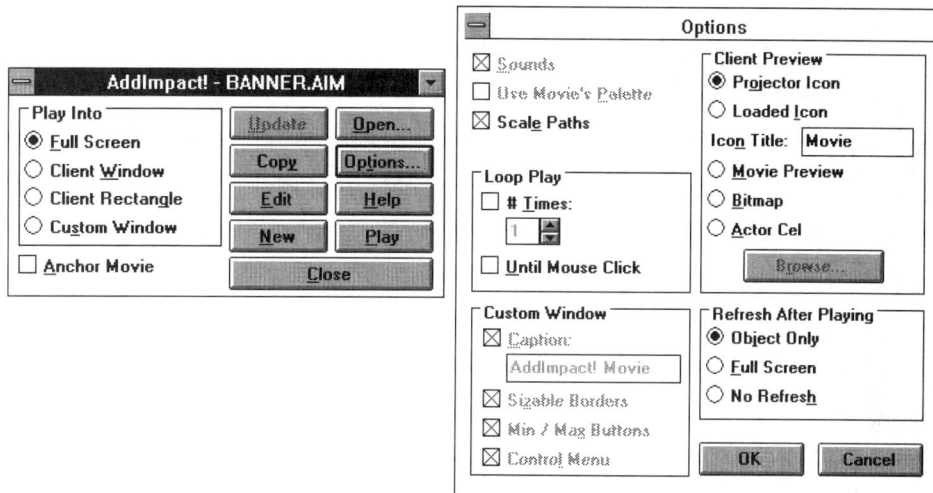

Figure 9.7 *AddImpact!* control panel and Options dialog

or OLE to access a separate player. One of the more interesting players is a companion to Gold Disk's *Animation Works Interactive* called *AddImpact!*.

Animation Player—*AddImpact!*

This program can run separately, or it can be installed as an OLE server that feeds animations (and sounds) to other applications. An important feature of *AddImpact!* is that you can control the destination of the animation, so you can have it play within the client application's window, on top of other material, if you wish. Or, you can set it up to play the animation with a transparent background on top of the full *Windows* screen. Finally, you can have *AddImpact!* create its own window if you want that.

In order to embed an *AddImpact!* animation into a document, you typically select the Insert object item from the client program's menus. This brings up the *AddImpact!* control panel shown in Figure 9.7. On the control panel you can select the animation file you wish to invoke and choose various options for how you want it played. The second window in Figure 9.7 shows the Options dialog.

As an example of an animation playing transparently over a word processing document, Figure 9.8 shows a baseball player hitting a home run, courtesy of *AddImpact!*

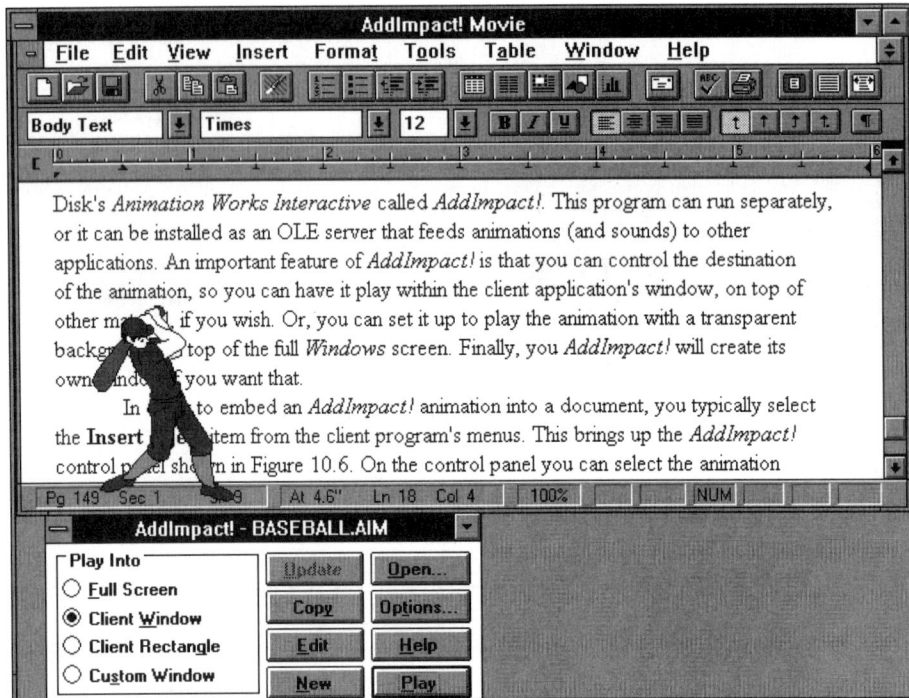

Figure 9.8 An *AddImpact!* animation (baseball player) running in a word processor document

Animation Player—Autodesk *Animation Player*

Autodesk animations can be played with the *Animation Player*, which is available for DOS or *Windows*. These players are not designed for concurrent running with other applications; they must be started separately, either by spawning them from another application or by calling them from the command line or *Windows* Program Manager. However, Autodesk has made the player code available in the form of a developer's library so that it can be integrated into other applications when they are being developed. Some authoring assembly tools have integrated this code; for example, you can play *Animator* files directly from *Authorware Professional*.

The control panel of *Animation Player* is shown in Figure 9.9; the dialog for Animation Settings is also shown in the figure. You can see that there are a lot of options for playing an animation. However, this version of the player always plays an animation in its own window—you cannot direct it to play in an existing window.

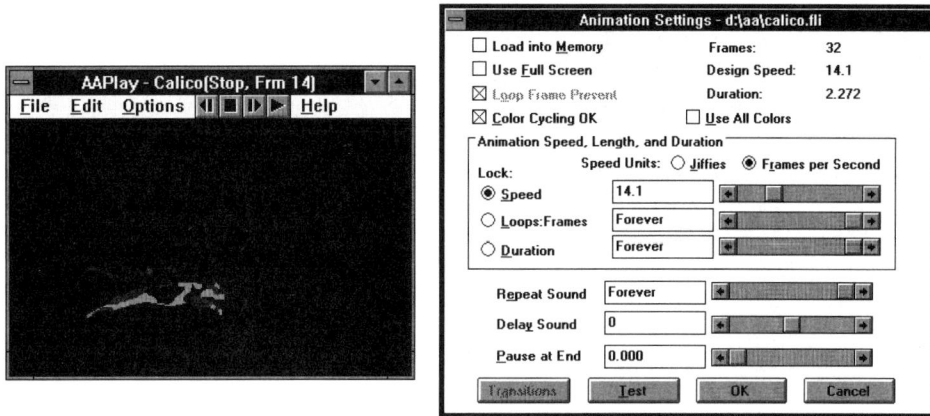

Figure 9.9   The control panel of Autodesk *Animation Player for Windows* at the left, and the Animation Settings dialog at the right

---

SUMMARY

Animations are an efficient way to add motion to your presentations; however, good animations are not easy to create. There are low-end tools that allow you to create simple animations without a lot of skill, but the professional-level tools require a substantial commitment to learning a complex task. If you have the time to devote to this, the results can be rewarding.

10

Integrating Objects from Other Applications

No single multimedia assembly tool is likely to have built-in features for everything you need. Even if a tool did have everything you want today, new capabilities will come out in the future that you will want to add. You would face the prospect of constantly updating or replacing your software—and at considerable expense. Fortunately, in multitasking environments there is a solution: interprocess communication (IPC). With IPC, you can use your favorite authoring assembly program to build applications and seamlessly integrate the features or capabilities of other tools right into your applications. Such "integration" is the subject of this chapter.

MULTITASKING ENVIRONMENTS

When a computer is able to run more than one program at a time, it is doing *multitasking*. What actually happens is that the computer rapidly switches between the several programs (called *processes* in the terminology of multitasking) so that, to the user, it appears they are running concurrently; and, to each program, it appears that the program has the entire computer. Multitasking is normally a responsibility of the operating system; for example, *OS/2*, *Windows NT*, and *DOS/Windows* do it, although to different degrees. It is also possible to have multitasking within a single program or process—this is called *multithreading*. *OS/2* and *Windows NT* support multithreaded applications; *DOS/Windows* does not. Some programs for DOS or *Windows* have developed their own internal multithreading, even though the operating system doesn't have it and with which in fact it will try its best to interfere. And, internal multithreading still does not allow more than one application to be running.

When you have multiple concurrent processes, it is natural to think about having them share data or commands. Since they are all running on the same CPU and in the same physical memory, it is possible to see several ways that processes could communicate, and this potential is a major advantage of multitasking over single-process architectures. Thus, if you are running a word processing program, and you need to play some audio (maybe as part of a help screen), your word processor doesn't have to know how to play audio; rather, via IPC, the word processor can call on an audio server to do it. Similarly, when you add a new capability to your system (maybe motion video), you just buy a motion video server that knows about IPC, and you can use it from inside any of your existing programs.

Before going more deeply into IPC, be aware that all multitasking systems are not equal. In the case of *Windows*, multitasking is not part of the underlying operating system (DOS); it is only part of the extension called *Windows*. The result is that any program (or DOS itself) can hog the entire system, and *Windows* cannot do anything about it. One example of this is disk accesses: If you ask DOS to load a large file from disk, it will do your bidding and stop everything else in the system (including even the mouse pointer) until your file is loaded. If you had something else running, such as playing audio, that will stop until the disk file is loaded. Therefore, multitasking in *Windows* is at the mercy of the programs that are running, and although several programs can be resident in memory at the same time, you may have to deliberately interrupt one program to effectively perform work in another.

In *OS/2* or *Windows NT*, the multitasking is built into the operating system itself, and it is *preemptive*, which means the operating system will regularly interrupt processes to ensure that every process always gets a fair slice of CPU cycles. In these systems, the multitasking is much more robust, and multiple running programs are truly concurrent. For example, if you begin playing audio (second process) while you are working with a spreadsheet (first process), you can still run an extended calculation in the spreadsheet and the audio will continue playing.

CLIENT/SERVER ARCHITECTURES

Multitasking operating environments typically have several ways to program IPC into applications. They also have defined protocol standards so that applications can communicate arbitrary types of data as long as they follow the protocol standards to set up the communications. One of these standards is *Dynamic Data Exchange* (DDE). DDE is a *handshaking* protocol where you have two processes communicating—one is the *client* and one is the *server*. The client is an application that wants a service, and the server is an application that can provide a service. DDE communication involves several steps that go something like this:

1. The client sends out a broadcast DDE message asking if there is a server that can provide a particular service. This message is communicated in a way that all running applications can see it.

2. An appropriate server responds and gives some details about its services in the form of a list of *topics*.

3. If the client acknowledges back to the server, a private communication path is set up for further exchange of commands or data.

4. Then the client requests the exact service it needs, and the server responds with the service, be it data, display, audio, or whatever.

5. When everything is completed, the private DDE link is terminated.

Many general productivity applications, such as word processors, spreadsheets, or databases have DDE built in—usually into a macro language so that users can set up the steps above for communication. This works, but it is a lot of detail for the user, and it usually takes some programming skill to get it right. Because of this, a more advanced protocol is now available, called *Object Linking and Embedding* (OLE, which, as mentioned in an earlier chapter, is pronounced "oh-lay").

OLE

The concept of an *object* is widely used in the latest programs. An object is an encapsulated data entity that has its own properties and behavior and can be manipulated as one thing by the computer user. Programs that use objects are called *object-oriented*. Typical objects are individual data files (text, spreadsheet, etc.), an image (also a data file, but with properties that describe how it is displayed), or an audio, video, or animation clip. An application can build a complex document that incorporates a number of objects of different types and origins. This metaphor is exactly what is needed to build an authoring assembly tool, and, in fact, most assembly tools are object-oriented.

One of the properties of an object is its origin—where did it come from? In an OLE environment, an object can come from anywhere on the system (or on the network), in any storage location, and it can be created by any OLE server application. This generalization opens up your system so any client application can have access to any object, and the object details do not have to be understood by the client. However, the client and server applications do have to understand OLE—the OLE protocols must be designed into those applications. I'll explain what that means from the user's point of view.

Applications that want to be OLE servers contain code that registers them with the operating system when they are installed on the system. This *registration database* is readable by potential client applications so they can find out what services are available on this system. To implement OLE in its user interface, a client application will typically have an Insert Object item in its Edit or Insert menus. That menu selection will bring up a list of the types of objects one can select for use in the current application. The application builds this list from the information in the registration database. When the user makes a selection from this list, a communication path is established with the server application, and a dialog (from the server) opens for the user to select the exact object. If the user makes a selection now, the chosen object will be copied (via the communication path) into the client's document. (I'm using the word *document* as a generality here—a document could just as well be a multimedia script or some other authoring assembly format.) This is the *embed* part of OLE. Notice that the user did not have to work with DDE at all. The code for that is designed into the two applications and is invoked automatically when the user makes the dialog selections.

But there's more. Now that the selected object is embedded in the client's document, the user can modify it by double-clicking on it to enter an edit mode. This action will again start up the server application, but this time it will be editing the embedded object, not the original one. When the user is finished editing, she closes the editing application, returning her to the client application, and the object copy in her document is updated. This all happens because the client application remembers the origin of the object and uses DDE to set up the editing session; these features must also be programmed into both applications.

Because OLE is relatively new and it takes some special programming inside the applications that will use it, not all applications on the market have it yet. When buying authoring software, you should check and confirm that the products you buy are going to support OLE.

DDE is older, and more products support it. With DDE you can do the same things that you can with OLE, but it takes more work during authoring, because DDE is a much lower-level protocol. However, this is also an advantage because it's more flexible, and with DDE you can do other things with IPC that you cannot do with OLE.

I have not yet explained the *linking* part of OLE. Linking is an alternate way of including an object in a client document *without* making a copy of it. This can be important in several situations: You may want the same object to appear in several documents and have them all update automatically if you make changes to the original. That will not happen if you embed them, but it does happen if they are linked. When a client application opens a document containing linked items, it also opens and displays the linked items. Any changes previously made in the linked items will appear. You may also want to link objects when you are short on hard disk space. Each time you embed an object, a copy is made in the client document—if the object uses a lot of storage (a high-resolution image, for example), you will be duplicating that storage on your hard disk.

Of course there are also reasons *not* to use linking. A linked object is identified by its path name on your hard disk. If you move a document to another system with a different directory structure, the client application may not find the linked objects. Also, when you distribute the document, you will have to distribute the originals of any linked items (assuming that they will not exist on a foreign system). When you distribute a document with embedded objects, everything is in the single document file. Another case where you should embed rather than link is when you want to make different modifications in each embedded copy of an object.

Linking is activated differently than embedding. To set up a link, you must manually open the server application, select the desired object, and copy it to the *Windows* clipboard. Then you can close the server, go to the client application, and choose Paste Special or Paste Link from the Edit menu. The object is now linked. Most client applications do not directly support editing of a linked object—you have to start the server manually, make your edit, and then repeat the copy-link operation.

Using OLE with Multimedia Objects

A good example of an OLE server for multimedia is Gold Disk's *AddImpact!*, which was designed specifically for that purpose. *AddImpact!* is a *Windows* program that can deliver animations with audio to any application that has OLE client capability. *AddImpact!* shows up in an Insert Object list as AddImpact! Movie. If you select that item, the *AddImpact!* control panel shown in Figure 10.1 appears.

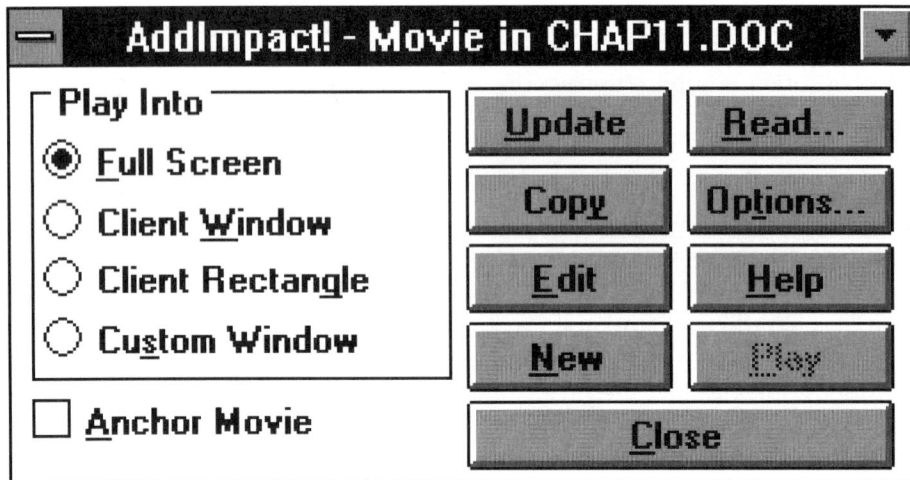

Figure 10.1 The *AddImpact!* control panel

To proceed with embedding, you click the Read... button to access a "Select an AddImpact! Movie" dialog where you can choose the animation file to be embedded. When you make a selection in this dialog, a preview window shows the first frame of the animation. Once you are satisfied with the selection, clicking OK returns you to the control panel. If you now click on Update, the embedding is completed, and a small icon appears in your document. The icon is actually a pushbutton—if you double-click on it, the animation will play.

There are many options available to modify the way the animation plays. From the control panel you can choose whether the animation plays to the full screen, to the client document's window, to a rectangle in the client document, or to its own custom window. You can also specify that the starting point of the animation be anchored to its icon button, regardless of where that button appears on the screen. A dialog with more options appears if you click the Options... button in the *AddImpact!* control panel. The Options dialog is shown in Figure 10.2.

From the Options dialog you can specify whether to play sound with the movie (it has to be authored into it) and whether to play the animation repeatedly (loop it). If you have specified a custom window, you can define some of the window's properties. You can also specify a custom icon and icon title to appear in the client document. The default icon is a movie projector, but you can also specify a special bitmap, the first frame of the movie, or a cel of a specified actor in the movie. All of this makes it very easy to add animations and audio to your documents.

You might have noticed that an embedded animation in a word processor or spreadsheet document appears as an icon that must be double-clicked for the animation to play. That is OK if you want it that way, but many times you would

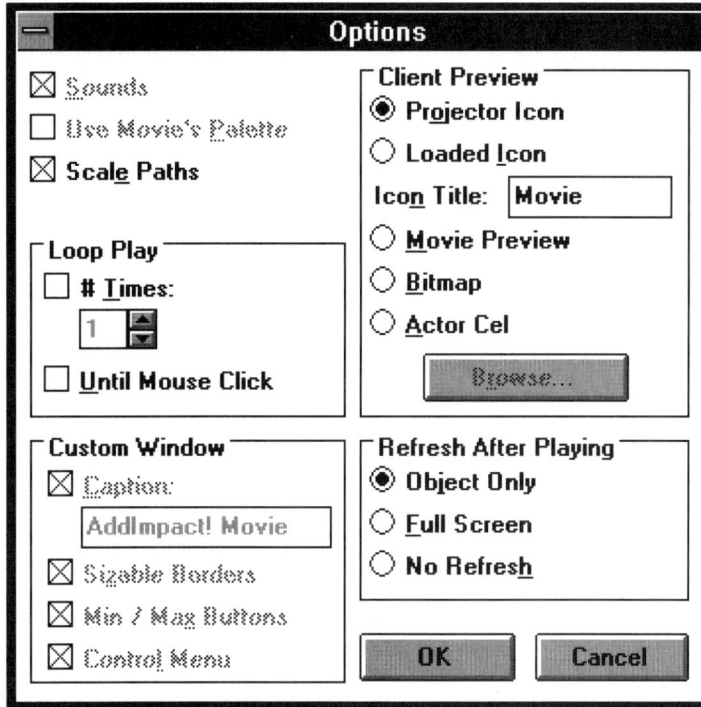

Figure 10.2 The *AddImpact!* Options dialog

like the animation to play automatically so that the user does not have to do anything. Some of the presentation packages that support OLE have solved this problem. In *PowerPoint*, for example, if you embed an animation into a particular slide, the animation will play automatically when that slide is shown. You cannot control the playback in any other way. For example, if you wanted the animation to play some time *after* the slide was shown, you would have to use a subterfuge such as starting the slide first with no animation in it, and then presenting an identical slide with the animation. You transition to the second slide when you want the animation to play.

Static objects that don't play, such as images, drawings, or text, are double-clicked to enable editing. But a playable object uses the double-click to activate playing. You edit a playable object by selecting it and then looking in the Edit menu of the client application. There should be a specific item added to the Edit menu to start editing of that object. This is another feature of the OLE protocol.

There are some additional factors to consider when you need to distribute a client document containing embedded *AddImpact!* animations to different systems. You need to be sure that all the resources (cels, actors, backgrounds) required by the animation are included in the embedded object and that the *AddImpact!* server is available on the other machine. *AddImpact!* has features to handle both of these problems. First, when you are creating or editing an animation with the *AddImpact!* editor, you can specify to save the animation with all its resources embedded in one file. If you plan to use this object with OLE, you should do that. Second, the *AddImpact!* server can be freely distributed, but that requires specifically installing it on every target machine. *AddImpact!* provides an easier way: You can embed the server directly into the target document; that way, it is always available.

ENABLING WITH DDE

Many applications that don't support OLE can still have the embedding feature by using DDE. The result is the same; it's just a little more tedious to do. Because the process is different, I will call it *enabling* rather than embedding. To explain how enabling works, I'll describe an example with the MEDIAscript OS/2 Server module and Microsoft *Visual Basic* under OS/2. These same procedures will work with *Windows* applications under *Windows*. With OS/2, this example shows that you can even communicate via DDE from an OS/2 application to a *Windows* application running in an OS/2 *Windows* compatibility box. (*Visual Basic* is a *Windows* application.)

The *MEDIAscript* Server is an OS/2 application that can present any kind of multimedia object or combinations and sequences of objects. You can even tell it to run a complete multiwindowed application, authored with the *MEDIAscript OS/2* Authoring Interface (AUI) module. You control the Server by sending it text commands, or lists of commands, which are called *scripts*. Ordinarily, you create scripts ahead of time using the AUI, save them in files, and then, when you want to run a script, just tell the Server the script's file name and it will run it. The script name can be given to the Server from the OS/2 command line at the time you invoke the server (for example: mms filename), or you can send a script name via DDE. The procedure for doing the latter is described below.

First, a little more about the protocols for DDE. There isn't really any standard, but because all applications use the same API to the operating system, there are some generic steps that everyone has to take. Applications support DDE either by being a *server* (service provider) or a *client* (service receiver), or sometimes both. *MEDIAscript OS/2*'s Server module can function as either client or server. (You might wonder how a server can be a client—this occurs when the server is running a script that calls for client communication with another server application.)

There can be multiple DDE connections (called *sessions*) active at the same time in the system; in fact, one application can participate in several at once.

Because DDE communication involves two applications exchanging a number of different message types (to set up the communication, exercise it, and finally terminate it), DDE requires a little programming in the applications. Authoring assembly tools like *MEDIAscript OS/2* or *ToolBook* can use their authoring interface and their authoring language for this purpose. General productivity applications, like *Excel*, typically provide a *macro language* that can be used to program the steps of an activity like a DDE session. The result is the same—the language statements are created once by an author and encapsulated somehow (in a file or in a button definition) for repeated use by the end user.

A DDE session is started by the potential client application sending out an INITIATE message via DDE. This message is "broadcast" by the operating system, so that all running applications will receive it. The INITIATE message includes the name of a *topic* for which the client is interested in acquiring a server. Potential server applications examine each INITIATE message that comes their way, and if a server sees a request for a topic that it can handle, it responds with an INITIATE_ACK acknowledgment message. The ACK message contains information so the client can communicate directly with the server (it is no longer broadcast)—the connection is now established.

Now the client has several choices: For example, it can ask for additional information about the server—the *System* topic requests the server to send a complete list of topics that it supports. If the client already knows enough about the server, it can immediately request whatever it needs from the server. In this example, with *MEDIAscript OS/2* as the server, we can go right ahead and send *MEDIAscript* a script file name along with the run command. *MEDIAscript* will then run that script and give us whatever multimedia services are described in the script. When it is finished with the DDE link, the client must send a TERMINATE message to end the session. This tells the operating system to remove the link and free up any system resources it was using.

The previously described sequence assumed that the server application was already running and watching for INITIATE messages. Sometime a server will not be running; in this case, the client application must start it. This is not a DDE function, but most applications are facilitated to request the operating system to start another concurrent application. This is usually an execute command in the client application's macro language. The following example demonstrates how a *Visual Basic* application can play motion video using the *MEDIAscript OS/2* Server and DDE. (This requires *OS/2* 2.0 or higher.)

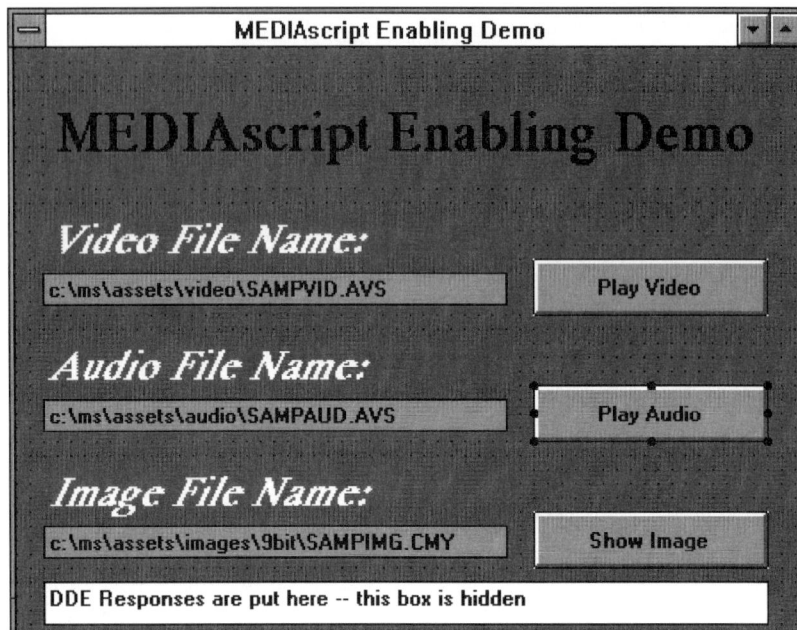

Figure 10.3 A *Visual Basic* video player using DDE

Enabling Example

A simple dialog was created in *Visual Basic* to receive the user's selections for type of material to present, along with the relevant file name. This dialog is shown in Figure 10.3. When the user clicks on a button, Play Video for example, a *Visual Basic* subroutine performs the DDE calls to tell the *MEDIAscript* server about the name of a script that will perform the selected operation. The *VB* subroutine is shown in Listing 10.1.

Understanding Listing 10.1 is simple once you know how the *Visual Basic* statements work. As you can see from the dialog in Figure 10.3, there is a hidden text control at the bottom of the dialog that receives (and initiates) the DDE link. That control has the name "Response." The property Response.LinkMode sets the mode of DDE communication *and initiates it.* LinkMode = 0 cancels any existing DDE communication, so the first statement in the subroutine simply ensures that no previous link remains open. Then the Response.LinkTopic property specifies ApplicationName | TopicName that will apply to the next link to be initialized. The statement Response.LinkMode = 2 specifies that *VB* should initiate communication with the application: MEDIAscript on the topic: Script. The value 2 for LinkMode says that this will be a one-time communication without

```
Sub PlayVideo_Click ()
 Dim runfile As String
 On Error GoTo AfterVideo
 Response.LinkMode = 0
 Response.LinkTopic = "MEDIAscript|Script"
 Response.LinkMode = 2
 runfile = "set str(0)=" & " & VideoFileName.Text & "
 Response.LinkExecute runfile
 runfile = ".video"
 Response.LinkExecute runfile
AfterVideo:
 Response.LinkMode = 0
 Exit Sub
End Sub
```

Listing 10.1 A *Visual Basic* subroutine for enabling

any automatic updating. (Notice that the statement On Error Goto AfterVideo takes care of trapping errors. If an error occurs in any statement after that, control will jump to the AfterVideo: label where the subroutine is gracefully exited.) So, if the Response.LinkMode = 2 statement executed without error, we can then build the commands to send to the *MEDIAscript* Server. The desired command for playing video is the word "video" preceded by a period. This invokes a script named video.ms that contains the code for playing video. However, this script assumes that the name of the file to play is in the *MEDIAscript* string variable str(0), so we first have to set str(0). This script is shown in Figure 10.4. (The video player can be anything you want, including a control panel having buttons for pausing, resuming, rewinding, etc., but in Figure 10.4 it only plays the video to the end or until the user clicks an "Exit" button to destroy the video window.)

The *VB* property LinkExecute sends a string to the DDE server. This statement is used twice to send the *MEDIAscript* set command to initialize str(0) and then to run the script video.ms. You can see from this example that there is considerable programming required to use DDE, compared to what is necessary when both applications have OLE built in. However, if you don't have OLE, then this is the way you can still enable multimedia in your applications.

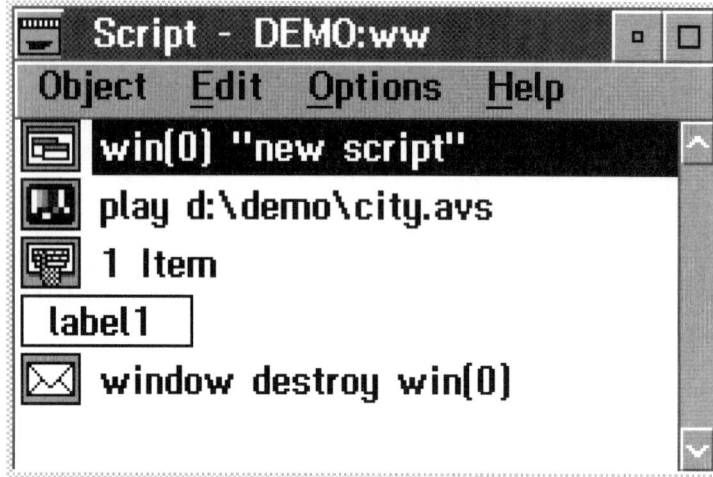

Figure 10.4 A *MEDIAscript OS/2* script video.ms for a simple video player

SUMMARY

You can see that embedding and enabling are very powerful techniques for causing applications to cooperate in a multitasking environment, but it takes some work on the part of the author to set things up. If you can find authoring products that do the things you need without using DDE or OLE to other applications, you will have a simpler and easier-to-use environment. But, for the greatest flexibility and future expandability, you should still choose authoring products that support DDE and OLE so that they can be used to add future capabilities that are not currently in your authoring products.

11

Choosing Authoring Tools

You must begin the process of selecting tools for an authoring environment by examining the author himself and what he wants to do in multimedia creation. This chapter identifies those questions and places them into a format that you can use to assess your own personal requirements as an author. When the questions have all been answered, you can build a "profile" that you later can use to evaluate different software for your environment. This chapter also examines the ingredients of the profile, which relates your needs to the characteristics of authoring software, and describes a *Windows* program (ats.exe on the accompanying CD) for performing this analysis and selecting authoring tools. The design of the ats.exe program is described in detail in Appendix B.

The first thing that will become clear is that you have to think through your objectives for multimedia authoring. It is not possible to begin selecting the components of an authoring environment until you know what you will be using them for. If you don't know this already, reading through this chapter will help you define your objectives. If you run the authoring tool selection program, it will allow you to experiment with the questions and pursue a number of "what if" possibilities.

Although you can build a powerful authoring environment by assembling a collection of many specialty tools, it will prove to be more complex to manage and use than an environment with only a few broad-based tools. It also may be more expensive. Tools such as *IconAuthor, Authorware,* and *MEDIAscript OS/2* are designed to be self-contained environments that provide basic capabilities for all the tasks of authoring. If your needs are for sophisticated applications, these programs provide the best starting point for your environment.

THE PROCESS OF SELECTION

There are undoubtedly many ways to go about tool selection; however, we will use a single approach here, beginning by defining the author's capabilities, what he wants to do with multimedia, what platform(s) he will use, and where he will be getting his media content materials. Using that input, we will then create a list of multimedia features that are required in the applications he will author. Then we will create a list of authoring features required in this author's environment to support his skills and what he wants to do. We call this list the author's profile.

The authoring profile is a list of authoring features. It can be matched up with similar lists created for candidate authoring tools; in that case, they are lists of the features provided by each tool. The process of matching tool features with required features is the heart of the selection process. Since it is unlikely that a single tool will provide everything an author needs, the matching process must deal with not just one tool at a time, but combinations of tools. The tool selector program assists you by presenting the initial list of questions, proposing the features list and the authoring profile for you to review and edit, and finally giving you an environment in which you can interactively match up tools with your profile and keep track of how good the matches are. Now let's look at each of the four steps in more detail.

WHAT KINDS OF APPLICATIONS?

The most important question is: "What do you want to use multimedia for?" This question can be broken down into more specific questions by first identifying the purpose of your applications, who your end users are, and then by considering the multimedia features you will need in your applications. For example:

Application purpose

- Will you be doing business presentations?
- Will you be doing information delivery?
- Will you be doing sales or merchandising?
- Will you be doing training or education?
- Will you be doing entertainment?

End users (audience)

- Will your application users be only passive viewers?
- Will your applications be used interactively by the general public?
- Will your applications be used interactively by grade school students?
- Will your applications be used interactively by high school students?
- Will your applications be used interactively by professionals?

Application features

- Do you need linear presentations?
- Do you need menu selection?
- Do you need random-access interactivity?
- Do you need a database capability?
- Do you need hypertext capability?
- Do you need audio?
- Do you need stereo audio?
- Do you need realistic still images?
- Do you need motion video?
- Do you need graphic drawing?
- Do you need animation?
- Do you need variables and calculations?
- Do you need hard copy output?
- Do you need data communications?
- Do you need student management?
- Do you need mouse control?
- Do you need touch screen control?
- Do you need keyboard entry?
- Do you need computer network capability?

Looking at the above items as individual questions, you should answer "yes" to as many as apply to your work. Of course, the more "yes" answers you give, the more you are asking for in the authoring environment. An easier way to handle this is to answer only the purpose and end-user questions and let the other questions be answered automatically by the computer. This is possible because there are fairly common templates for how multimedia is used for different purposes and for different users. The authoring tool selector program sets it up so that you answer the purpose and end-user questions and the computer then fills in the standard answers for the others; however, you still can change the other

Table 11.1 Templates for authoring characteristics versus purpose and end user

Characteristic	Business Presentations	Interactive Applications for		
		Public	Schools	Professionals
linear presentation	yes	yes	yes	yes
menu selection		yes	yes	yes
interactivity		yes	yes	yes
database		yes		
hypertext		yes		
audio	yes	yes	yes	yes
stereo audio		yes	yes	yes
still images	yes	yes	yes	yes
motion video		yes	yes	
graphic drawing	yes	yes	yes	yes
animation		yes	yes	
variables			yes	yes
hard copy output	yes			yes
communications		yes		yes
student mgmt.			yes	
mouse control	yes	yes	yes	yes
touch screen		yes	yes	
keyboard entry			yes	yes
computer network	yes			

answers if you don't like something the computer chooses. Table 11.1 shows the default templates for different end uses and users. Of course, you can alter these if they don't match your style of applications.

WHO IS THE AUTHOR?

The next category of questions deals with you, as the author. We need to know your background and skills and any particular preferences you may have. The following questions apply to that

Author characteristics—check any computer programming skills that you have:

- None?
- BASIC?
- Pascal or C?
- Other?

Check other computer skills that you have:

- DOS?
- Windows?
- OS/2?
- Do you use a word processor?
- Do you use a spreadsheet program?
- Do you use a database program?
- Do you have experience with any multimedia programs?

Check other related noncomputer skills:

- Graphic art
- Writing
- Photography
- Videography
- Sound recording
- Animation design

MEDIA SOURCES

After checking the above characteristics that apply to you, the remaining thing to do is to identify your needs for different media, and what sources are available to you. This will affect your need for special tools to perform media processing and formatting. For each medium, you need to establish whether you will be using clip art from a media library, other outside sources, and/or creating your own. Check clip, outside, and/or create as they apply:

(media sources)	clip	outside	create
Audio	☐	☐	☐
Still Images	☐	☐	☐
Motion Video	☐	☐	☐
Animation	☐	☐	☐

GENERATING THE PROFILE

At this point, we can calculate your authoring profile. The profile itself is a list of items (shown in Table 11.2), each of which is given a value of 0 or 1 based on the

Table 11.2 Items that define an author's profile

Category	Item
operating system	DOS
	Windows
	OS/2
authoring metaphors	slide show
	hierarchical
	book-page
	window
	timeline
	network
	icon
	language
interactivity features	buttons
	menus
	hypertext
	touch screen
text objects	font and style selection
	advanced text effects
	text boxes
	multiformat in one object
	text from a file
chart objects	create
graphic objects	display of graphics
	vector drawing
	bitmapped drawing
	grouping of objects
	clip art library
	shapes
	professional level
animation objects	display of animation
	animation editor
	clip animation library
image objects	display of images
	image editing tools
	image compression tool
	image capture tool
	clip image library
audio objects	WAVE audio
	MIDI audio
	audio compression
	stereo audio
	audio editor
	audio capture tool
	clip audio library

continued

Category	Item
motion video objects	video compression tool
	video capture tool
	video editing tools
	clip video library
variables and math	strings
	string parsing
	integers
	arrays
	structures
student management	student database
authoring language	accessible to author
	scripts
	procedures/functions
	high-level functions
	low-level functions
media management	media database
	media library
window authoring	create
	properties
	multiple windows
	parent-child windows
	window controls
database features	compatible with others
	custom format
interprocess communication	OLE client
	OLE server
	DDE client
	DDE server
	MCI
hard copy output	during authoring
	in an application
distribution features	runtime module
	single executable
	data encryption
	media packaging

author's answers to the questions. In the selection process, your profile will be matched item by item to a similar profile (using the same list of items) created for each authoring software package under consideration. Each item in the list is a possible feature of an authoring tool. The actual items are in the right-hand column; the left column items are headings. If an item in your profile has zero value, it means that you don't need that feature.

To help you understand the profile items, each one is discussed below.

Operating System

Each tool is designed for a particular operating system: DOS, Windows, Windows NT, or OS/2. Some systems can run applications designed for another system; for example, Windows can run DOS applications.

Authoring Metaphors

This is the conceptual model used during authoring of an application. Assembly tools usually have a particular metaphor that they focus on. Some tools support several metaphors. The following discussion of individual metaphors will explain how an assembly tool supports each metaphor.

slide show metaphor—This is the metaphor of a linear presentation. Tools using this metaphor assume that the presentation can be broken down into a series of "slides," which are separate screens that are presented sequentially. Depending on the capability of the assembly tool, a slide can be anything from a single image or text screen up to a complex multimedia display including images, text, audio, video, and animation. The limitation of this metaphor is that slides always have an order of presentation that will be followed by default. Some slide show tools provide a degree of interactivity by allowing buttons that can jump from one point in the presentation to another. Features of slide show authoring include a slide sorter, outline views, and individual authoring for each slide.

hierarchical metaphor—This metaphor assumes that the target application can be organized into a tree structure. It is best suited to menu-driven applications, where a main menu branches to a series of secondary menus, etc. Assembly tools designed for hierarchical applications will have special features that facilitate building of menus and controlling their use.

book-page metaphor—In this metaphor, an application is organized into one or more "books," and books are organized into separate screens called "pages." Pages have a sequential order just as in a physical book, and in this regard the metaphor is much like the slide show. However, there is usually more support for interactivity between pages, as when flipping through a real book.

window metaphor—In the window metaphor, the target application is organized into a series of "windows" that are separate screen objects. Within each window, the authoring is more like a slide show. The important feature of this metaphor is that multiple windows can appear onscreen at the same time, even containing concurrent activities. Tools for this metaphor will have extensive features for authoring windows, window controls, and their contents.

timeline metaphor—Applications or presentations that consist principally of animation, audio, and/or video can be authored in terms of a timeline. Events in the target application are authored and placed in a time sequence. Of course, when you give the end user interactive control, the timeline no longer applies; however, it can still determine the default behavior when the user does nothing. Timeline authoring tools will have a time display on which you place "events" that are authored separately.

network metaphor—The word *network* refers here to the structure of an application, not a communication network. This metaphor allows the target application to be organized in a "go anywhere from anywhere" free-form structure. There is no built-in order of presentation or structure. Since the assembly tool places no limitations on structure, the author has to build his own, which probably means he has to do more work. However, this is the most flexible of all the metaphors for building a rich application containing many levels of interactivity.

icon metaphor—Assembly authoring consists of creating multimedia "objects" and placing them into a structure. In the icon metaphor, the objects are identified by graphical icons that usually give a clue to their contents and, during authoring, they are shown in a flow chart display that identifies the paths from one object to the next. This works well for applications whose structure can be displayed in two dimensions. The key features of the icon metaphor are the icons themselves and the flowchart display.

language metaphor—Some assembly tools use a language for creating the application structure and contents, and this itself is a metaphor. Depending on the level and power of the language, this can be a flexible and capable approach; its principal disadvantage is that the author must learn the language, as the key feature of this metaphor is the language.

Interactivity Features

There are different devices to provide end-user interactivity. Nearly all tools today support the use of keyboard and mouse, and some support touch screens. The following items are some of the authoring features that need to be considered for interactivity authoring.

buttons—Buttons are on-screen objects that will produce some response when the end user clicks the mouse on them or touches them. For example, the pushbutton control in Windows dialog boxes is an example of a button. Authoring of buttons involves defining what the button looks like onscreen, where it will be located, and what it will do when clicked. Assembly tools that support buttons will provide features to do all three things.

menus—I have already discussed menus as the key feature of hierarchical metaphor authoring. This profile item will be checked if a tool has features that assist the authoring of menus.

hypertext—Hypertext is a way of navigating in an application that contains a lot of text display. It provides for certain words in a text display to have button behavior. When the end user clicks or touches the word, some action will take place, such as going to a more detailed presentation on the subject identified by the word touched. Hypertext authoring tools will have extensive features for displaying text, marking (called *tagging*) text buttons in the text files themselves, and defining actions for each one. Although many assembly tools can simulate hypertext behavior by the use of conventional buttons embedded in a text display, we do not check this profile item unless the tool provides for tagging of text files.

touch screen—Almost any tool can use a touch screen display if the touch screen driver operates as a mouse emulator. A touch screen is different from a mouse in that it has no buttons. Further, some touch screens can respond to how hard the user presses on the screen. Thus, a touch screen can do both more and less than a mouse. This profile item will be checked only if a tool supports native touch screen operation in addition to mouse emulation.

Text Objects

Nearly all applications require the use of text. Features for handling and display of text are important parts of authoring assembly and image tools and are discussed in the items below.

font and style selection—In operating systems such as Windows and OS/2, font and style capabilities are built into the system and their use is expected of every application that works with text. This profile item will be checked if the authoring tool supports these system features.

advanced text effects—Advanced effects include scaling, distorting, rotation, text on curves, special styles, etc. This profile item will be checked if the tool offers any of these features.

text boxes—In some cases you need to display a block of text that stays in a defined area of the screen. If the text does not fit in one line, it should wrap to new lines to remain within the defined area. If there is more text than will fit in the defined area, there should be provision for scrolling. These are the features of text boxes.

multiformat in one object—Sometimes you need to highlight one or more words in a line of text by changing text size, color, or style. With many tools, you would have to break the text up into several objects to achieve this. This profile item is checked if the tool supports change of size, color, or style within a single text object.

text from a file—The ability to display the contents of a text file is important to many kinds of applications. It makes it possible for the same application or application segment to display many different pieces of text based on previous selection by the end user.

Chart Objects

The display of numerical data in graph or chart form is important to many applications. This item is checked if the tool supports automatic creation of charts from numerical data supplied at runtime.

Graphic Objects

A fundamental requirement of any multimedia assembly tool is to display graphics. Some assembly tools and many special graphics tools can create as well as display graphic objects. The following profile items list the more important graphics features.

vector drawing—This means that the graphic drawing is rendered at runtime from a file of drawing commands. It has the advantage that the drawing file is small, and the actual drawing can be modified at runtime to suit various requirements, such as the size of the drawing space, etc. During authoring, vector drawing also has the advantage that any part of the drawing can be selected and modified without affecting the rest of the drawing.

bitmapped drawing—Bitmaps are either already-rendered vector drawings or digitized photographs or video images. They can be displayed quickly, but they are less flexible in terms of modification at runtime. During authoring, bitmaps can be drawn on by bitmapped drawing tools. Note that images (see below) are also bitmaps, and there are many tools other than drawing for working with images.

grouping of objects—This is a vector drawing feature that allows a number of draw objects to be selected at the same time and made into a group that can then be edited as one object—for example, to change position or color.

clip art library—Because drawing takes a degree of skill that every author may not have, there are libraries of already-drawn items that can be combined, modified, and manipulated for use in applications. Generally these are in vector form because that provides the greatest flexibility in use.

shapes—Some vector draw tools provide a library of shapes, such as arrows, stars, etc., that can be sized and positioned with the mouse the same as you do with a rectangle primitive.

professional-level graphics—This profile item is checked if the tool provides features that are suitable for professional graphics artists. Examples are two-monitor display, color shading tools, etc.

Animation Objects

Animation is important because it is an efficient way to add dynamics to your applications, without the massive data requirements of digital video. Many assembly tools that have vector drawing capability and can be programmed to do looping can produce simple animations. However, the items that follow apply only to more complex animations created with formal animation tools.

display of animation—This profile item will be checked if a tool has built-in capability to display any of the formal animation file formats, such as Autodesk *Animator* .FLI files.

animation editor—Creation of an animation takes special tools to assemble the parts of the animation, control the placement and timing, and output standard animation files. This item will be checked if the tool includes such an editor.

clip animation library—Because animation creation takes a degree of skill that every author may not have, there are libraries of animations that can be combined, modified, and manipulated for use in applications.

Image Objects

An image is a bitmap, created either by drawing with a paint tool, capturing from live video, or digitizing from a photograph or other hard copy. The items below are features for working with images.

display of images—Most assembly tools can display images that were created elsewhere. Normally this includes the capability to position the image on the screen, crop it, and possibly scale it to size.

image editing tools—An image editor is the same as a bitmapped editor. It includes file management and file conversion for image files, the ability to crop and scale images, image processing tools to adjust image parameters on an area or a pixel basis, and various drawing tools to modify or add to an image.

image compression tool—Because image files are large, the ability to compress for storage is important. Some image tools include the JPEG image compression algorithm to compress image files up to 20:1.

image capture tool—Capturing images requires a video camera and digitizing board or an image scanner. Special software is required to use these devices; it is sometimes built into other authoring tools such as image editors or assembly tools.

clip image library—Because good images are often difficult to acquire, there are libraries of images that can be combined, modified, and manipulated for use in applications.

Audio Objects

The items below are the features that can be built into authoring tools to support audio.

WAVE audio—WAVE audio is captured from analog audio signals by simple digitizing without compression. This item is checked if the tool is capable of playing or processing WAVE audio.

MIDI audio—MIDI audio is a series of commands for controlling a music synthesizer to produce orchestral music. This is a form of compression; a MIDI file for music is much smaller than the same music when digitized. This item is checked if the tool is capable of playing or processing MIDI audio.

audio compression—WAVE audio can be compressed up to 4:1 by applying a compression algorithm to it. This item is checked if the tool has capability for compressing audio.

stereo audio—This item is checked if the tool is capable of using stereo (two-channel) audio.

audio editor—The ability to cut, copy, and paste audio streams is valuable in preparing audio clips for use in an appliaction. Other techniques such as resampling, adjusting volume or stereo balance, or mixing two or more channels are sometimes available. This item is checked for tools that have any of these capabilities.

audio capture tool—Audio capture requires a digitizing audio board. Special software is required for its use. This item is checked if the tool can control an audio digitizing board.

clip audio library — There are libraries of special sounds that can be combined, modified, and manipulated for use in applications. This item is checked if the tool contains such a library.

Motion Video Objects

The items below are the features that support motion video.

video compression tool—Successful motion video on a PC requires compression. This item is checked if the tool has the capability to compress a motion video stream.

video capture tool—Capture of motion video requires video digitizing hardware and either a very fast CPU and hard disk or special hardware for on-the-fly compression. This item is checked if the tool has capability to control video capture hardware.

video editing tools—Video editing includes cut-copy-paste, combining videos, adding transition effects, combining audio with video, etc. This item is checked if the tool has any of these capabilities.

clip video library—There are libraries of video that can be combined, modified, and manipulated for use in applications. This item is checked if the tool contains such a library.

Variables and Math

Many applications have to keep track of information entered by or created by the end user at runtime. Variables are required to do that. When numerical variables are used, there is usually also a requirement to do math. The items below are some of the assembly tool features needed with variables.

string variables—Strings are text variables. The tool should have the ability to set up string variables that can be modified at runtime and the ability to display them as formatted text. This item is checked if the tool has any of these features.

string parsing—In order to respond to command information in the form of strings—either input by the user or from a text file—a tool should have functions for reading through a string and interpreting its contents. The reverse capability to build a string from its parts is also necessary. This item also can include conversion of strings into other data types.

integer variables—Integers are the simplest form of numerical variables. This item is checked if the tool has author-definable integer variables and at least four-function math.

array variables—Many applications have to present or work with tables of data, either strings or numeric. These are usually stored internally in the form of arrays that can be indexed item by item for processing. This item is checked if the tool supports author-defined arrays.

structures—More sophisticated data storage requires the ability to group variables of different types into structures that can be handled as single objects. This is normally associated with language-based authoring. This item is checked if the tool supports structures.

Student Management

A requirement in education applications is to keep track of a number of students who are using the application. This usually takes the form of a student database, which the application maintains, including student names or IDs and data about student progress and performance.

Authoring Language

Language-based authoring is at once the most powerful and the most difficult authoring assembly approach. Therefore, many tools that have a language provide some kind of shell above the language, which performs simple authoring tasks without exposing the language. The language is there for the sophisticated author who needs to do something that the shell cannot. The items below are some of the features of language authoring.

language accessible to author—This item is checked if the tool's language is available for use directly by an author. This is necessary for an author to benefit from the power of the language.

scripts—Scripts are editable files written in the language. This item is checked if the tool provides language scripts that can be edited by an author.

procedures/functions—Tasks that are used repeatedly should be able to be packaged as separate procedures or functions that can be called from anywhere in the application. This item is checked if the tool supports procedures or functions.

high-level functions—Many authoring languages have addressed the programming difficulty issue by providing some high-level commands that perform complex tasks with one (or a few) statements. For example, an audio command can do everything needed to play a single audio file without any further authoring beyond specifying the file name. This item is checked if the language has such high-level commands.

low-level functions—One advantage of a language should be that it gives access to anything in the system running the language. This means access to memory, storage, devices, DLLs, etc. These things call for "low-level" (detail)–type commands that can reach anything in the system. This item is checked if the language contains such low-level features.

Media Management

Multimedia applications typically require a lot of data, packaged in many separate files. Most of this is the media content—text, images, audio, video, animation. Some tools provide features to assist an author in managing his collections of media data.

media database—This feature is a database that keeps track of media files for an application. Normally, additional data fields are included to provide text descriptions of objects and keywords for searching for specific subjects. For visual objects like images, graphics, or video, a visual index of "thumbnail" images may also be maintained.

media library—This feature is a media database specifically created to contain media objects for use by all the applications in an environment.

Window Authoring

The following items are features needed for authoring one or more windows in a windowed application.

create windows—The tool contains features for specific creation of a window, specifying size, position, colors, etc. This is needed if the author wishes to retain control over windows in his application.

window properties—There are many properties associated with windows beyond the size, position, and colors mentioned above. For example, you can specify border style, background image or pattern, title bar style, system menu, etc. This item is checked if the tool supports control of all the major window properties.

multiple windows—This item is checked if the tool supports having more than one window on screen at the same time.

parent-child windows—Child windows are constrained to remain within the parent window, regardless of the size or position of the parent. This item is checked if the tool supports creation of child windows.

window controls—Windowing systems like Microsoft Windows or OS/2 provide for a large number of different control types, such as pushbuttons, check boxes, radio buttons, list boxes, scroll bars, etc. This item is checked if the tool supports most of the standard window controls offered by the operating system.

Database Features

Certain applications require built-in database capabilities. For example, a videotape indexing program should be able to store information about each tape and search it for specific kinds of content. This requires features to create database arrays, input into them, search them, and display results. Although any language-based system that has low-level commands could be used to program this, our interest here is only in high-level features that allow building of databases without extensive programming.

compatible with other databases—This item is checked if the tool can import or export data files from database programs such as *dBASE*.

custom formats—This item is checked if the tool can create its own custom-format database without extensive programming.

Interprocess Communication

IPC allows communication with other concurrently running applications in the environment. With these features an author can command other applications to provide data or services to support his application.

OLE client—The authored application can be a client to another application via OLE.

OLE server—The authored application can provide services to other applications via OLE.

DDE client—The authored application can be a client to another application via DDE.

DDE server—The authored application can provide services to other applications via DDE

MCI—While MCI is not technically an IPC protocol, it achieves similar results in that it gives an authored application access to devices that the assembly package does not directly support. This item is checked if the tool supports the sending of MCI commands.

Hard Copy Output

This refers to support of a printer, either in the authoring system or in the target system.

hard copy during authoring—The tool supports printout of important data or screens during the authoring process. This is usually used for documentation purposes.

hard copy in an application—The tool supports the use of the printer by an authored application. This may be used, for example, to provide printed maps or directions from a kiosk that advertises restaurants in an area.

Figure 11.1   Opening logo screen of the Authoring Tools Selector program

Distribution Features

These features assist in preparing an application to be distributed to other systems.

runtime module—A special module is provided for running applications on systems that do not contain the complete assembly tool.

single executable—The tool can package an application into a single file for distribution.

data encryption—The distribution files are not readable by others and cannot be modified except by the author.

media packaging—The tool will build an environment containing all the files needed to distribute the application.

THE AUTHORING TOOL SELECTOR APPLICATION

The authoring profile described above can be implemented in a spreadsheet-like computer application, which can also include a comparison of your authoring profile to the characteristics of one or more authoring tools. This concept has led to the Authoring Tools Selector application, which is a *Windows* program developed using Microsoft *Visual Basic.* An executable version of the program and its control files (described in Appendix B) are on the accompanying CD-ROM disc. There are two steps to using the program: In the first step you click check boxes to enter your objectives, your skills, and your preferences; in the

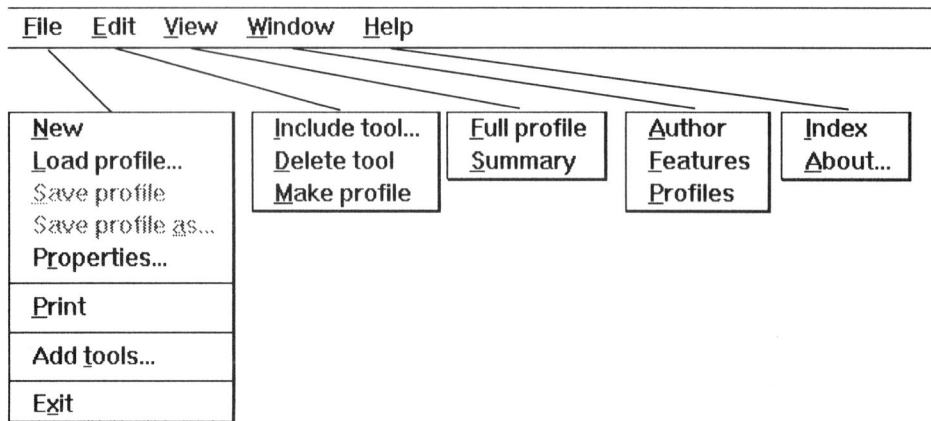

Figure 11.2 The main menu of the Authoring Tools Selector

second step, an authoring profile for you is calculated and displayed, and you can compare it to similar profiles for various available authoring tools. The application also contains an editor for you to use if you want to create profiles for new authoring tools that you may be considering in the future.

The selector program starts up with the logo screen shown in Figure 11.1. When you click the button on the logo screen, you move to the main screen, which has the menu bar shown in Figure 11.2. If you are using the program for the first time, you create a profile by going to the Window menu and selecting the Author window, which is the only item active.

The Author's Input window is shown in Figure 11.3; it has check boxes for each of the questions about the application types you want to develop, who your application users will be, what skills you have as an author, what operating system(s) you plan to use, and what sources of multimedia you will be using. Click any boxes that apply.

Clicking Next takes you to the Multimedia Features Needed screen (Figure 11.4), which lists the authoring features you might need. The first time you go to this window, you can click the Use Defaults button to tell the computer to fill in this screen automatically from the Author's Input information. You should carefully examine the result and make sure that you agree with it. If there are any problems, you can make changes, but do not click the Use Defaults button after that because it will restore the computer's choices. When you are satisfied with this window, click Next to proceed to the Profiles window (Figure 11.5).

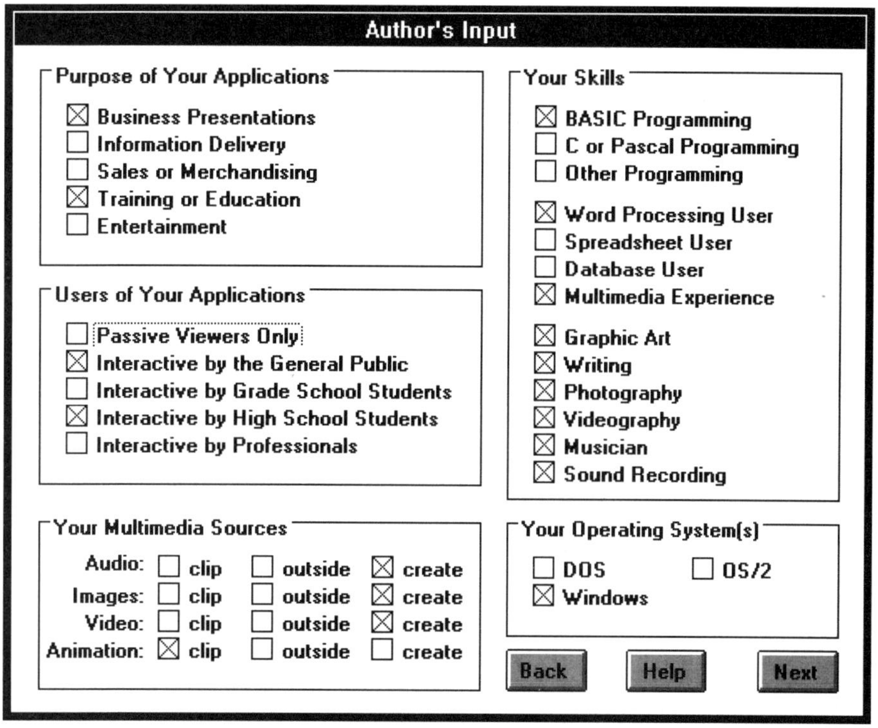

Author's Input

Purpose of Your Applications
- ☒ Business Presentations
- ☐ Information Delivery
- ☐ Sales or Merchandising
- ☒ Training or Education
- ☐ Entertainment

Users of Your Applications
- ☐ Passive Viewers Only
- ☒ Interactive by the General Public
- ☐ Interactive by Grade School Students
- ☒ Interactive by High School Students
- ☐ Interactive by Professionals

Your Multimedia Sources
- Audio: ☐ clip ☐ outside ☒ create
- Images: ☐ clip ☐ outside ☒ create
- Video: ☐ clip ☐ outside ☒ create
- Animation: ☒ clip ☐ outside ☐ create

Your Skills
- ☒ BASIC Programming
- ☐ C or Pascal Programming
- ☐ Other Programming
- ☒ Word Processing User
- ☐ Spreadsheet User
- ☐ Database User
- ☒ Multimedia Experience
- ☒ Graphic Art
- ☒ Writing
- ☒ Photography
- ☒ Videography
- ☒ Musician
- ☒ Sound Recording

Your Operating System(s)
- ☐ DOS ☐ OS/2
- ☒ Windows

[Back] [Help] [Next]

Figure 11.3 The author's input window of the Authoring Tools Selector

Multimedia Features Needed

- ☒ Linear Presentations
- ☒ Menu Selection
- ☒ User Interactivity
- ☐ Database
- ☐ Hypertext
- ☒ Audio
- ☒ Stereo Audio
- ☒ Still Images
- ☒ Motion Video
- ☒ Graphic Drawing
- ☒ Animation
- ☒ Variables and Calculations
- ☐ Hard Copy Output

- ☐ Interprocess Communication
- ☒ Student Management
- ☒ Authoring Language
- ☒ Touch Control
- ☒ Multiple Windows
- ☐ Network Capability
- ☐ Audio/Video Capture

Click Use Defaults to automatically fill in this form. You may modify anything that is not to your liking. Then click Make profile.

[Back] [Use Defaults] [Make Profile]

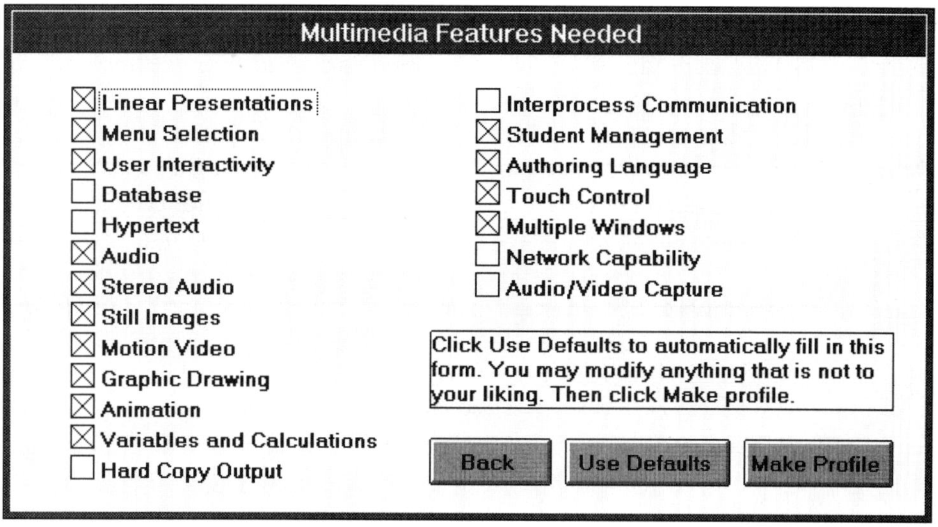

Figure 11.4 The Multimedia Features Needed window of the Authoring Tools Selector program

Items -- ACL1.PRF	Author Profile	FreeLance	Photo Styler	Authorware	MM ToolBook	T
Description of tool		Slide show	bitmap	Flow chart	Book/page	
Operating system	** 1 **	** 1 **	** 1 **	** 1 **	** 1 **	
. DOS	--	--	--	--	--	
. Windows	1 <	1	1	1	1	
. OS/2	--	--	--	--	--	
Authoring metaphors	** 3 **	** 1 **	*******	** 1 **	** 2 **	
. slide show/storyboard	1 <	1	--	--	--	
. hierarchical	1	--	--	--	--	
. book-page	--	--	--	--	1	
. window						
. timeline/animator						
. network						
. icon flow chart						
. language						
Interactivity						
. buttons						
. menus						
. hypertext						
. touch screen						

Authoring Tools Selector — 70%

File   Edit   View   Window   Help

Authoring metaphors

The authoring metaphor determines the style of authoring. Your choice of metaphor depends on the kind of work you will do as well as your personal preference. Note that some tools provide more than one metaphor.

Change this profile item   Cancel

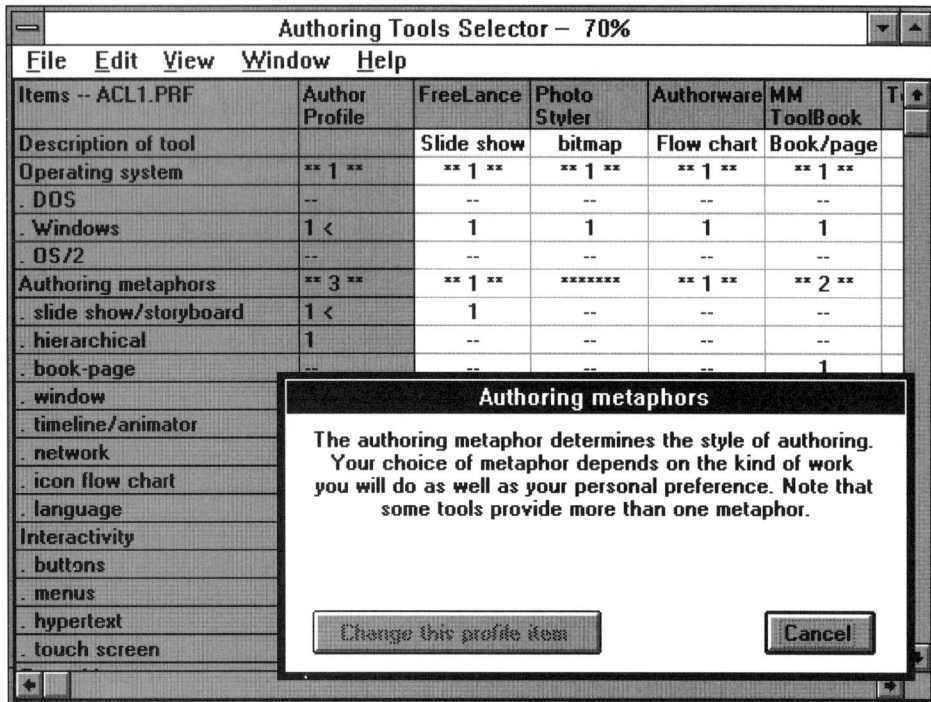

Figure 11.5   The Profiles window of the Authoring Tools Selector program

In the Profiles window, you see a spreadsheet grid giving the same list of authoring profile items that was shown earlier in this chapter. The second column has a value for each item—1 or 0; these have been calculated by the computer. If an item is 0 (indicated by a dash), it means that the selector program has determined that you do not need that item; items that you do need get a 1. Examine this list, and, if anything seems incorrect, you can either go back to the previous screens and make an appropriate change, or you can change the item directly on the profile screen. To do the latter, click on the profile item; this brings up a dialog that contains a definition of the item and also a button that will toggle the item between the values 0 and 1. If you change anything about the earlier questions, the profile screen will be recalculated when you return to it.

As you proceed through the following steps, selecting software that fills some of the needs will cause those items' profile numbers to get checked off. Thus, the objective of software selection is to find one or more packages that put check marks on all the items that have numbers.

Evaluating Actual Software

Once you have developed your authoring profile, you are ready to evaluate existing authoring packages compared to your profile. A simple approach yields helpful results. Make up a profile for each authoring package you are considering, in the same format as your Authoring profile. Each item can be answered simply yes (1) or no (0), depending on whether the software has the feature or not. A quick evaluation is then simply made by multiplying the value in your profile with the value in the software profile for each item. This is exactly what the Tools Selector program does.

If you total all these items, you have a score for the evaluation. However, you need to know what to compare that score to. One approach is to add up all the values in your profile to make a target score. You compare a package's score to that number—100 percent would indicate that a package did everything you needed; less than 100 percent means that the package is lacking some of the things you need.

It is unlikely that one package is going to do everything, and you need a way to consider a group of packages to fill your needs. Multiple packages are a reasonable approach in a multitasking authoring environment; you just need to be sure that the packages work together. One way to ensure this is to select software from a series such as the IBM Ultimedia Tools Series, which have all been certified to work together. If you begin your evaluation by considering the major authoring packages first, you can then focus on the holes that are left by looking at the items that had values in your profile but were 0 in the software's profile. These are the holes, which the selector program shows as profile numbers, without check marks.

For example, most authoring assembly tools do not support advanced graphic drawing. If you have drawing skills and need such capabilities, you will need to select a stand-alone drawing package. The profiles for such packages will have a lot of 0s in them, but they will have 1s where you need them. The selector program allows you to do a second (or third, etc.) evaluation, but using only the unchecked items from the previous evaluation. This way, you can progressively select software to cover everything you need.

The selector program already contains profiles for a number of authoring tools packages. A dialog (shown in Figure 11.6) containing a list of these can be seen by choosing the Include Tool item from the Edit menu. As you select from this dialog and double-click (or click the Include button), the software profiles are placed in the extra columns on the profile grid, and the package name appears at the top. The check marks on the profile items are also updated to account for the features provided by each package. If you want to remove a software package already shown in a profile column, click at the top of the column and then choose Delete Tool from the Edit menu.

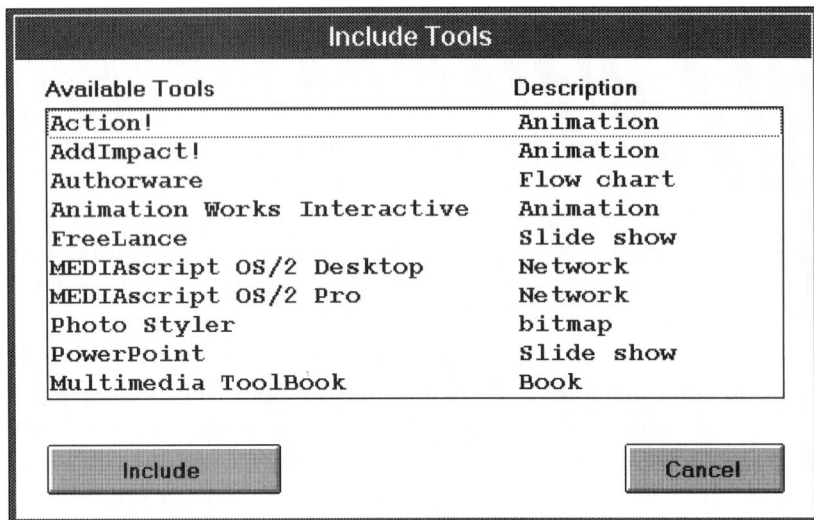

Figure 11.6 The Include Tools dialog of the ATS program

All the software package profiles are kept as text files, with the file name extension .TLL, which you can edit or create by using the Add Tools item in the File menu. Thus, you can update the profiles as new packages come out or existing packages are changed or updated. The list box in the Profiles window displays all the .TLL files it finds in the default directory. The selector program allows you to experiment with different combinations of tools to see which ones will best fit all your needs. Using the CD-ROM, you can also see descriptions and demonstrations of the tools and test-drive many of them with actual working models.

Appendix B more fully describes the ATS program, in case you are interested in more detail of what it does, or if you want to make more changes than you can do with the Add Tools window.

SUMMARY

The selection of software for an authoring environment depends on the kind of work you are going to do, your skills, and the sources of material available to you. Using some simple logic, these few items will expand to a list of authoring features that you need. A second list can then be developed in the format of a specification for authoring software. That list is your Authoring Profile, and it is easy to compare your profile to a similar list prepared for any software package that you are considering. A selector program has been built to help you develop your profile and to compare it with profiles for existing authoring packages.

12

Using Your Authoring Tools

Most authoring environments will include a number of different tools to accomplish all the multimedia tasks needed by your work. There are three important issues in getting a multitool environment to work effectively, which are:

- Operating system compatibility
- Data compatibility
- Author interface uniformity

Each of these is discussed below.

OPERATING SYSTEM COMPATIBILITY

Some of the operating system considerations were covered in Chapter 3; this chapter takes those issues a little further and introduces some other thoughts. An application program is inherently designed to operate with a particular operating system—it uses the API of that operating system to control all its use of system resources. For example, a DOS program knows only about the DOS API and cannot make use of any of the features of *Windows*, even if *Windows* is present. The newer operating systems (*Windows*, *OS/2*, or *Windows NT*) have provided a way to run DOS applications without leaving the new OS; they set up a special environment for them that contains the DOS API. This works well for simple DOS programs, but it sometimes breaks down when the DOS application has sophisticated requirements for memory, drivers, or other special features. This latter situation applies to many authoring tools, particularly those that support special hardware such as sound or video boards.

It would be simple to choose *OS/2* or *Windows NT* as your native OS, since both these systems make the claim that they will run DOS, *Windows*, or their own applications at the same time with multitasking. However, you will find that those statements are not always true—some applications have such special needs that they will not run under anything except their native OS. There's no way to prove this except by actually trying the tool under the proposed non-native OS. Even that is not always simple, because the new OSs provide ways to create special configurations for non-native applications; but you have to experiment with the configuration options to see whether your proposed situation will work. You can spend an amazing amount of time with this task, it can take a lot of technical skill, and success is still not always assured.

In general, I would not recommend DOS as your native operating system for authoring. Even though some of the DOS tools have their own graphical user interfaces that are just as good as *Windows* or *OS/2*, you will be limited to running only one tool at a time, you may have to reboot a lot to change configurations for different tools, and there is no clipboard for interchange of data between tools. DOS is good only if you can find a single tool that does everything you need.

My recommended operating system is *OS/2* 2.1 because of the following things:

- It has preemptive multitasking
- It will run DOS and *Windows* applications most of the time
- More good native *OS/2* authoring tools are becoming available
- It is a stable and robust system

With the appropriate tools, you can still create multimedia applications under *OS/2* that will run with *Windows* or DOS—you are not restricted to building only *OS/2* applications. Of course, when you build applications under *OS/2* to run in different environments, those applications cannot benefit from any of the features of *OS/2* when they are running in their target environment.

DATA COMPATIBILITY

For a group of tools to work together, they must be able to share the same data for text, graphics, images, audio, video, or animation. There are four ways that data can pass between applications: in all OSs by means of a disk file, in *Windows* or *OS/2* by means of *Object Linking and Embedding* (OLE), *direct manipulation* (also called *drag/drop*), or the *clipboard*.

The *Windows* or *OS/2* clipboard is a feature of the system whereby you can select data in one tool, *cut* or *copy* it to the clipboard, and then go to another tool that can recognize the clipboard data and *paste* the data into the second tool. After working on the data in the second tool, it can be returned to the first one by reversing the process. The clipboard must be programmed into each of the tools when they are designed, but, fortunately, nearly all tools have done this because the clipboard is such an important feature.

OLE was discussed in detail in Chapter 10; it provides a way for data assembled in one tool to be immediately editable by its originating tool without leaving the assembly tool. However, all of the functionality to make this possible must be programmed into each of the tools when they are designed. Because OLE is still new, not all tools have it. It also inherently links a data object to a parent tool, so with OLE you cannot edit the same data in any tool other than its parent. (You can do it by working on the disk file directly, but this does not work on an object that has been embedded into a document file.) This could be a problem if, for example, you have a special image processing tool that you would like to be able to use on any image, regardless of that image's "parent" tool. OLE is not the way to do that.

Direct manipulation refers to the process of selecting an object with the mouse by clicking on its icon and then "dragging" the icon by holding the mouse button while moving the mouse. When the icon is over a suitable target icon, such as the icon for a tool that can edit the object, you release the mouse button, which "drops" the object onto the target icon. This action causes the target tool to start up with the data object loaded for editing. Direct manipulation is a very intuitive way to move data between tools, and it is getting more support in the newer tools for *Windows* and *OS/2*. (It also has to be programmed into the tools at the time they are designed.)

Many tools use proprietary data and file formats that offer them certain advantages, but make it impossible for another tool to utilize the data. For example, *CorelDRAW!* has its native file format .cdr; this format contains all the information to make a drawing completely editable in *CorelDRAW!*, but few other programs can read .cdr files. Many tools also offer export and import features in their File menus—this provides for interchange of certain foreign formats. In the *CorelDRAW!* example just cited, you probably need to export your drawings in a more generic format to use them in other tools. At the same time, you probably will also want to keep a copy of each drawing in the .cdr format to make sure you can edit it in the future. Export/import gives a wider range of compatibility but, because it is accomplished by doing a file conversion at the time of exporting or importing, it is more awkward (you usually have to choose the format from a list) and slower to use. It is also possible to build some data conversion into the clipboard feature so that it will occur automatically at the time of cutting, copying, or pasting. This is convenient, but it may still be slow.

There are also file conversion utilities, such as Hijaak PRO for images. These programs can process a large number of formats (over 70 in the case of *Hijaak PRO*), but because they are separate applications, the task of file management becomes even more awkward and slow. When you are dealing with a large number of files, any conversion or special handling quickly becomes tedious and time consuming. But right now, there is often no other answer. You may not be able to find tools that do everything you need without some amount of export/import or conversion activity.

When you are using several tools to process the same data, you have to think through the steps you will take to get the data into and out of each tool. You should consider that at the time you are selecting tools, because there are some tool combinations that just will not work, or they will require a separate file conversion tool. Unfortunately, checking out data compatibility issues may not be easy to do because the information is often buried deep in the documentation or help files for the tools.

Ultimedia Tools Series Compatibility

Because one of the objectives of the IBM Ultimedia Tools Series is that the tools will work together as seamlessly as possible, it is useful to see what they have done about data compatibility. The Tools Series architects have created specifications that require a limited number of data formats of each type to be supported by all tools in each data category. The tools may accomplish this either as native formats or by means of export/import. The important point is that they have determined ahead of time that the tools will exchange data if you stick to the specified formats. The Ultimedia Tools Series specification also specifies that all tools must support certain DDE and OLE (optional) features, drag/drop, and MCI.

Table 12.1 shows a summary of the Ultimedia Tools Series requirements for different operating systems. Common User Access (CUA) is the IBM specification for the design of graphical user interfaces. It provides for uniformity in the techniques for performing common operations with a GUI. National Language Support requires that a tool be designed for easy conversion to foreign languages for sale outside the United States. This usually means that all the text content of a tool (dialog headings, warning messages, button names, etc.) should be centralized so that a single text library can be translated to different languages (done by the manufacturer). It also requires that the design of dialogs take into account that text in some languages may require more or less space than English does.

Direct invocation refers to the act of double-clicking on an application's icon to cause the application to start up. *Indirect invocation* is the act of double-clicking

Table 12.1 Summary of Ultimedia Tools Series requirements

	Platform		
Element	OS/2 2.1	Win 3.1	DOS
Common User Access (CUA)	yes	yes	yes
National Language Support (NLS)	yes	yes	yes
DDE	yes	yes	no
OLE	no	optional	no
Drag/Drop	yes	yes	no
Clipboard	yes	yes	no
RIFF file format	yes	yes	yes
Media Control Interface (MCI)	yes	yes	no
Multimedia I/O (MMIO)	yes	yes	no
Direct Invocation	yes	yes	no
Indirect Invocation	yes	yes	no

on a data icon to cause the parent application to start up with the data object that was clicked available in the application's workspace.

Data File Compatibility in the Ultimedia Tools Series

Ideally there should be a single data file format for all multimedia objects. This is theoretically possible if the file header is designed to specify enough so that different tools and applications can recognize their own files and can find enough information in the header to understand all the characteristics of the data that follow. This ideal has not been accomplished to date, but there are several attempts underway. One initiative is the *Resource Interchange File Format* (RIFF), which is available on many platforms and is extensible to any data type. However, not all data types have yet been standardized under RIFF.

The Ultimedia Tools Sseries architects specify a single format for most types of multimedia objects that should be usable by each tool of that type; they use RIFF formats where they are available. For certain tools, standardizing on a generic format causes limitations because those tools have special features that may not be possible except when using the tool's proprietary data format. In the interest of compatibility, these limitations are accepted. Below is the current status of the UTS recommendations for each data type:

Animation—The .fli/.flc and .awm/.awa formats are chosen as interim standards.

Application Scripts—These are the files created by an assembly tool to hold the details of the authored application's structure. No standard is set at this time.

Charts or Graphs—No standard is set at this time.

Digital Video—The standards for hardware motion video are AVS PLV 2.0 and AVS RTV 2.0. The standard for software motion video is AVI Indeo (RTV 2.1).

Images—The standard format is the RIFF Device Independent Bitmap (RDIB). The standard image characteristic is 640 × 480 × 256 colors, uncompressed. Of course, other resolutions, color combinations, and compression algorithms can also be supported by RDIB. It is intended that MMIO and MCI will support all RDIB parameter values that apply to the installed hardware. In practice, other commonly used formats are allowed because they are supported transparently under OS/2 MMPM/2.

MIDI Audio—The standard file format is RIFF MIDI (RMID). MIDI editors should be capable of supporting both base-level and extended-level MIDI.

Vector Graphics—Tools should be capable of exporting RDIB files but are not required to import them. Tools should also support DXF for 3-D graphics and DRW for 2-D graphics.

Waveform audio—The standard file format is RIFF WAVE (WAVE), supporting mono or stereo, PCM, 8- and 16-bit samples, and 11-, 22-, or 44-kHz sampling rates.

AUTHOR INTERFACE UNIFORMITY

Although GUI systems like *Windows* and *OS/2* have a lot of built-in functionality for handling windows, dialogs, and controls, creative programmers would be able to use these features to build a wide range of different user interfaces that weren't at all uniform. To stem that possibility, both IBM and Microsoft publish design guides for application designers that specify the preferred ways to use the user interface tools. The IBM manual is *Object-Oriented Interface Design: IBM Common User Access Guidelines* (often referred to as the CUA Guide), and the Microsoft manual is *The Windows Interface: An Application Design Guide.* Fortunately, the approach is similar in both of these manuals, and, even more fortunately, most application designers for *Windows* or *OS/2* have followed the recommendations. The design guides specify such familiar things as:

- How to name and arrange a menu bar
- Standards for the design of file management dialogs (Open, Save, etc.)
- How to use the different dialog box controls
- Providing feedback to the user
- Providing on-line help to the user
- Use of the keyboard in a GUI
- The standard way to implement the user interface for OLE and many other window features

The Ultimedia Tools Series specifications require that all tools follow the CUA Guide. This is required even for DOS applications (if they have their own GUI). In general, it has worked, and most of the common features of GUIs work the same in different applications and between *OS/2* and *Windows*.

TYPICAL SCENARIOS FOR USE

Figure 12.1 shows most of the possibilities for authoring all the classes of multimedia. Your collection of tools will have to complete all the steps shown for the classes of data you will be using. Note that each of the lines between boxes in this diagram represents an interface where you must assure that the source and destination data ports have compatible formats.

Many tools combine several of these steps—for example, an audio editor may also handle mixing. Also, assembly tools will often do some of the data preparation steps, although in some cases they may not do as much as you need. When one tool does several steps, you don't have to worry about the data interfaces within the tool—the tool designer takes care of that. Thus, multiple-task tools will reduce the number of interfaces that have to be considered. Even though a major tool, such as one for assembly, may do some tasks other than assembly, you may still need separate tools to do certain tasks at a more sophisticated level. The scenario options for each data class are covered in the next sections.

Audio

Regardless of whether you capture your own audio or acquire it from a clip library or some other external source, you will probably need an audio editor tool to modify your audio clips or to mix two or more clips into a single file for use by your application. Some assembly tools can control the start and end points of an audio clip at runtime, but this may mean that your audio file(s) are larger than

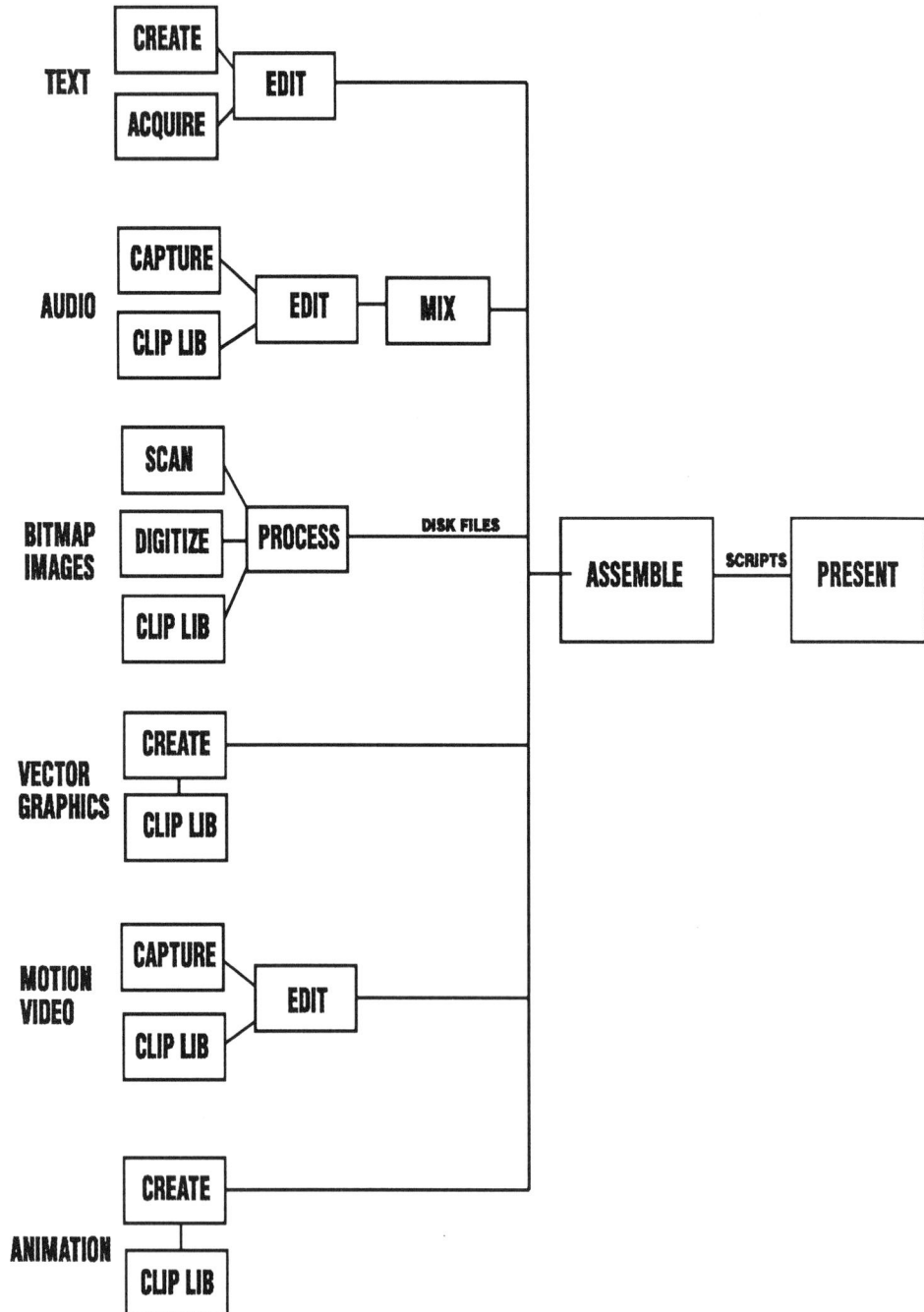

Figure 12.1 Typical steps for authoring multimedia data objects

they have to be. If storage space is at a premium, you will want to cut your audio clips to size with an editor.

When you buy a sound card for your system, you will usually get software for capture and editing. Similarly, *Windows 3.1* contains a capture tool (*Sound Recorder*) and an editing tool (*Wave Editor*). There also are third-party tools that will do more sophisticated editing if you need it.

Text

Applications that use large amounts of text need special assembly tools that can handle large text objects and special editing tools for processing the text input. Sometimes you can do the text processing with a word processor, but that can become tedious if elaborate tagging has to be done. For smaller text objects, such as bullet charts or simple captions or message boxes, you can usually just type the text directly into the assembly tool, and no special text tools are needed. In this case, you just need to be sure that your assembly tool will do what you want with text — text capabilities of assembly tools vary widely.

Bitmapped Images

If you are going to scan or digitize bitmapped images, you will need special hardware and software for controlling it. Sometimes the hardware will come with an image tools that can directly access the hardware driver. This is the case with image scanners, for example, which often support a software standard called *Twain.* If you install a Twain driver for your scanner, it will then be accessible from any image tool that also supports Twain.

Vector Graphics

Most assembly tools have built-in vector graphic capabilities. In many cases this will be all you need and, if it is, you don't have to worry about vector file formats at all because the interface is hidden inside your assembly tool. However, if you want really sophisticated drawing capabilities, you will need to add a more powerful drawing tool to your environment. Another situation for which you may need a fancier draw program is when you want to use a large clip art library. When selecting draw programs or clip art libraries, be sure that the file formats supported are compatible with your assembly program.

Motion Video

Digital motion video can be reproduced with software only or with special hardware. (The hardware approaches give better performance.) If you are going to capture motion video from live or taped sources, you must have some hardware. Most assembly tools do not support motion video capture or editing (*MEDIAscript OS/2* is an exception), so you will usually need video software if you plan to create or edit digital video. Playback of motion video is normally handled by making MCI calls to the driver that came with your video hardware or software; therefore, you must be sure your assembly tool supports MCI.

Animation

Assembly tools do not usually have animation creation capabilities, except for the very simplest of moving objects. If you want to create animations, you will need a tool for this purpose. Depending on your assembly tool, animations may be displayed by a built-in driver, MCI, or DDE/OLE. You should research that question and determine that there is file format compatibility between the tools or drivers you select.

A TYPICAL ENVIRONMENT

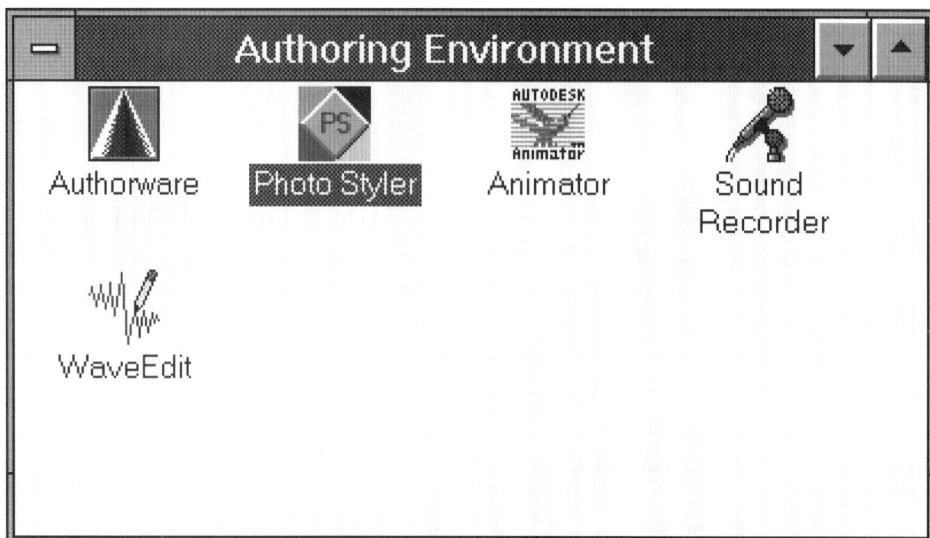

Figure 12.2 A Windows group box for a typical authoring environment

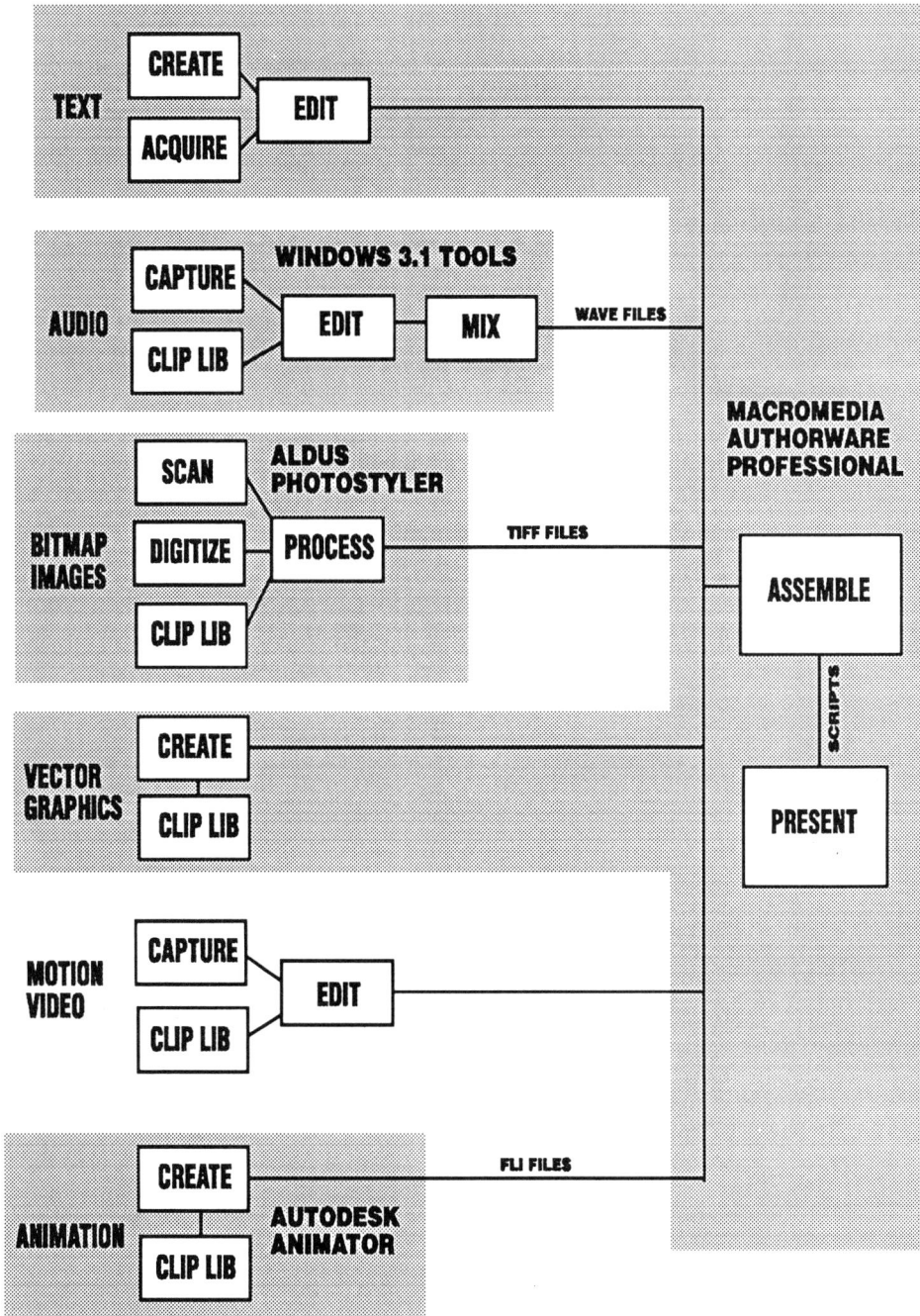

Figure 12.3 Figure 12.1 with shading added to show tools for a typical environment

A typical Windows group for an authoring environment is shown in Figure 12.2. Figure 12.3 is the same diagram as Figure 12.1, except that shading has been added to show how the tools in this environment cover the various tasks. The assembly tool for this environment is Macromedia *Authorware Professional*, which will also be used for all text preparation and vector drawing. However, Aldus *PhotoStyler* is included for bitmapped image capture and editing. Autodesk *Animator* is available for creating animations, and the *Windows 3.1* tools, *Sound Recorder* and *WaveEdit*, are used for sound processing. For each of the interfaces between tools, which are accomplished with disk files, the format is shown. Since the environment will not be supporting motion video, that area is not shaded. You may find it useful to make a diagram like this for your environment, and identify how your tools cover the tasks and the types of interfaces you will use.

Notice that Figure 12.3 is doing the same thing that the Authoring Tools Selector program in Chapter 11 does. The difference is that while Figure 12.3 is more visual, it summarizes the tasks of authoring into only 20 items, whereas the Tools Selector displays nearly 100 characteristics of authoring tools.

SUMMARY

This chapter discussed the issues of selecting and running a multitool environment, which may be summarized as:

- Operating system compatibility
- Data compatibility
- Author interface uniformity

A diagram showing the tasks of authoring was also introduced; this diagram is useful to show how the tools you select cover the authoring tasks and where the data interfaces will be.

13

Authoring Linear Presentations

Although linear presentations seem simple, they require all the steps of the authoring process described in Chapters 1 and 2. You begin by choosing the concept of the presentation by answering questions such as:

1. Who is the audience? The style and the level of your presentations will depend on the audience and their degree of interest in what you are presenting. For example, a typical business audience will already be interested in the subject and you probably don't have to use any devices to attract them. However, a presentation for a public kiosk may well require some bells and whistles to attract an audience to the kiosk.

2. How will the presentation be given? The first part of this is the output format for the presentation: Is it hard copy, computer screen, or NTSC or PAL video? The only one that can be interactive is the computer screen, and this also may be the easiest format to manage. If you will be presenting the computer screen to large audiences, a computer monitor will be too small. The answer is to use a video projector, preferably one that can project the computer VGA screen directly. (Some projectors only work with NTSC or PAL video, which requires a conversion box and does not have as high quality as a computer screen.) The second factor is whether the presentation will stand alone, or be given by a live speaker. A stand-alone presentation probably needs synchronized audio, whereas a live speaker provides most, if not all, of the audio.

3. Will the presentation primarily use text bullet charts? Bullet chart presentations are easy to author from an outline. If this is your style, you can find extremely easy and fast tools to do it.

4. Will any screens have images in them? A bullet chart presentation can be greatly enhanced by adding images to the display. Most tools support doing this, but it adds the problem of having to decide what the images will be and where you will get them.

5. Will you use audio? If you want to run recorded audio with your presentation (or part of it), you need audio hardware and software. You also have to decide what the audio is and where you will get it.

6. Will you use video? If you want to run motion video with your presentation (or part of it), you need video hardware and software. You also have to decide what the video is and where you will get it.

7. Will you use animation? If you want animation with your presentation, you have to decide what the animation is and where you will get it. If you will build your own animations, you need animation tools for that.

8. Is any interactivity required? The only interactivity needed by a simple presentation with a live speaker is a way to change slides. All presentation tools support that. However, you may want the ability to reverse as well as go forward, or maybe you even would like to be able to go to any specific slide at any time. Many of the tools support that too, but it makes the authoring process a little more complicated. If you need even more interactivity, it's probably not fair to call it a linear presentation.

The next stage is the design of your presentation. Usually this can be accomplished by creating an outline. In the case of text bullet charts, the outline can show the entire content of the presentation, and many tools can give you a finished presentation directly from the outline. This chapter uses an example that is a simple presentation on fire safety in the home. This presentation is intended for a general public audience, in schools, or as part of the material on kiosks in shopping malls. The outline for this is shown in Listing 13.1.

```
Fire Safety in Your Home
Why worry about fire safety?
  Because YOU can prevent fires in your home
  Because YOU will be most affected if a fire
   occurs in your home
Common Hazards
 poor housekeeping
```

```
heating
lighting
power
cleaning materials
fumigants/insecticides
Poor Housekeeping
 combustible items near heat sources
 exits blocked, locked or nailed shut
 outside gutters filled with debris
Heating
 improper use of portable heaters
 poor ventilation
 chimney blocked or dirty
 unsafe chimney construction
Lighting
 faulty wiring
 improper use of high-intensity lights
 decorative lights too close to combustibles
Power
 illegal or faulty wiring
 overloaded circuits
 extension cords under rugs
 worn plugs on electrical cords
Cleaning Materials
 poor ventilation or storage
 piles of dirty rags
 improper use of combustible/flammable
  cleaners
Fumigants/Insecticides
 inadequate ventilation
 materials used on or near open flame
 improper use of foggers
```

Listing 13.1 Outline for the Fire Safety presentation

Each heading in the outline represents a slide, so there are a total of nine screens.

The next step of general authoring is to obtain content material. If you are just doing bullet charts, the outline is it. However, if you have images, audio, video, or animations, you must collect them.

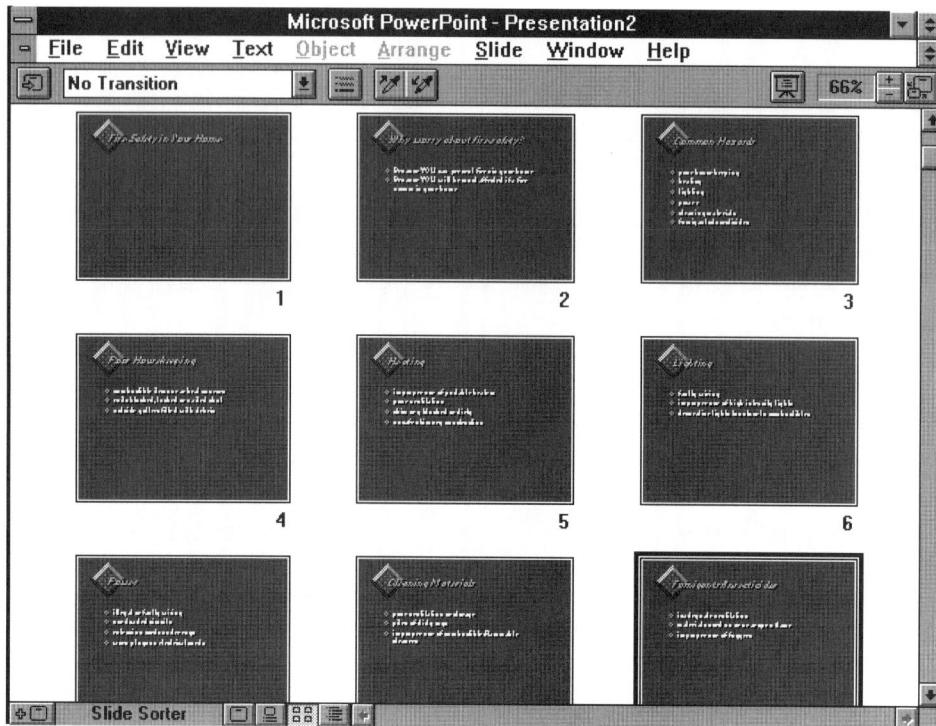

Figure 13.1 A *PowerPoint* presentation generated automatically from an out-line

Then you do the assembly step. Presentation authoring tools such as Microsoft's *PowerPoint,* Lotus *FreeLance,* or Software Publishing's *Harvard Graphics* will automatically build your presentation from the outline. All you do is import your outline from a word processor, select a style from the built-in library of screen designs, and presto! you have a presentation. It only takes 45 seconds. Figure 13.1 shows the slide sorter view for the presentation generated automatically from the outline of Listing 13.1.

ENHANCING YOUR PRESENTATION

You don't have to stop there, though—you can modify almost anything about the presentation or any individual slide, and if you want graphics, images, audio, video, etc., you can continue to add these features to your presentation. It is still very easy. Figure 13.2 shows the same presentation as Figure 13.1, but a different slide template has been selected and a picture has been added to each slide. The

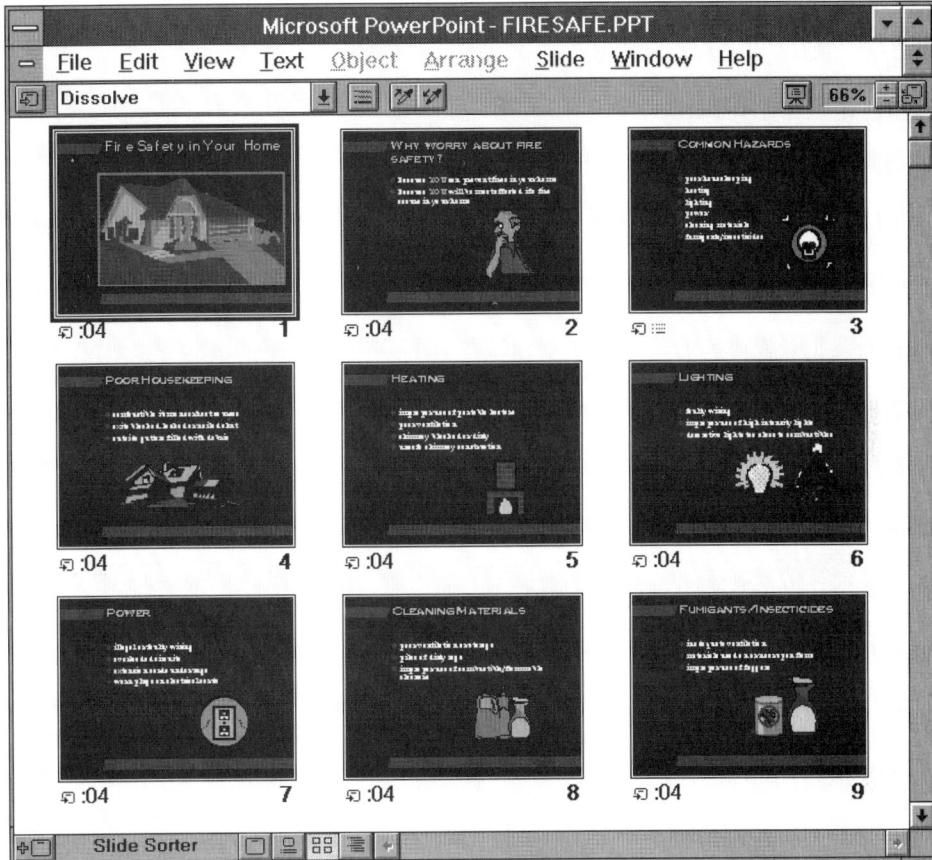

Figure 13.2 The Fire Safety presentation with pictures added to each slide

pictures are vector graphics from clip art libraries; they were sized and positioned in *PowerPoint.*

Once you have created the presentation, you will want to test it to make sure that it does what you want. You can do this by previewing it in *PowerPoint,* or by running it with the *PowerPoint Viewer,* which is a run-only program that you can distribute freely with your presentations. If you need to make any changes, you can revisit any part of it in *PowerPoint* for editing.

Adding Transitions

One easy way to enhance your presentation is to add transitions between slides. Without transitions, each new slide is presented with a rapid vertical wipe over the previous one. Instead, you can choose from dozens of dynamic effects to

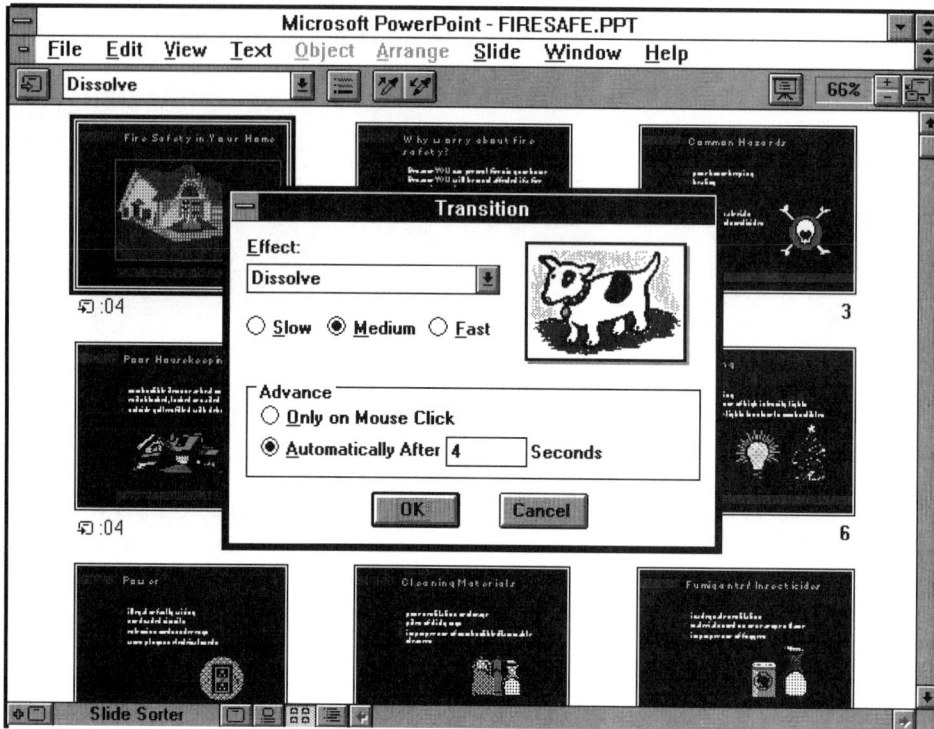

Figure 13.3 *PowerPoint* screen showing the transition dialog

control the way each slide appears. You first select the slide you want to control and then (see Figure 13.3) you either select the the drop-down list that contains the word "Dissolve" in Figure 13.3, or you click the toolbar button just to the right of the drop-down list. Choosing the button brings up the dialog shown in Figure 13.3, where you can choose not only the transition type, but control its speed and specify whether the slide changes after a specified time, or waits for a mouse click.

With dozens of transitions available, you may be tempted to use a different one on every slide in your presentation. This is usually not a good idea, though, because it becomes distracting. It is better to use the same transition throughout, or maybe use the same type of effect but alternate its direction from one slide to the next—for example, a horizontal wipe to the right is followed by a horizontal wipe to the left, and then another wipe right, etc. You can also specify a separate transition for the showing of the first slide. It is usually OK to use a different effect for this one, since it only occurs once. The example uses a dissolve for the first slide and a diagonal wipe effect for all the rest of the slides. In Figure 13.3, the small icon at the lower left of each slide image indicates that a transition has been

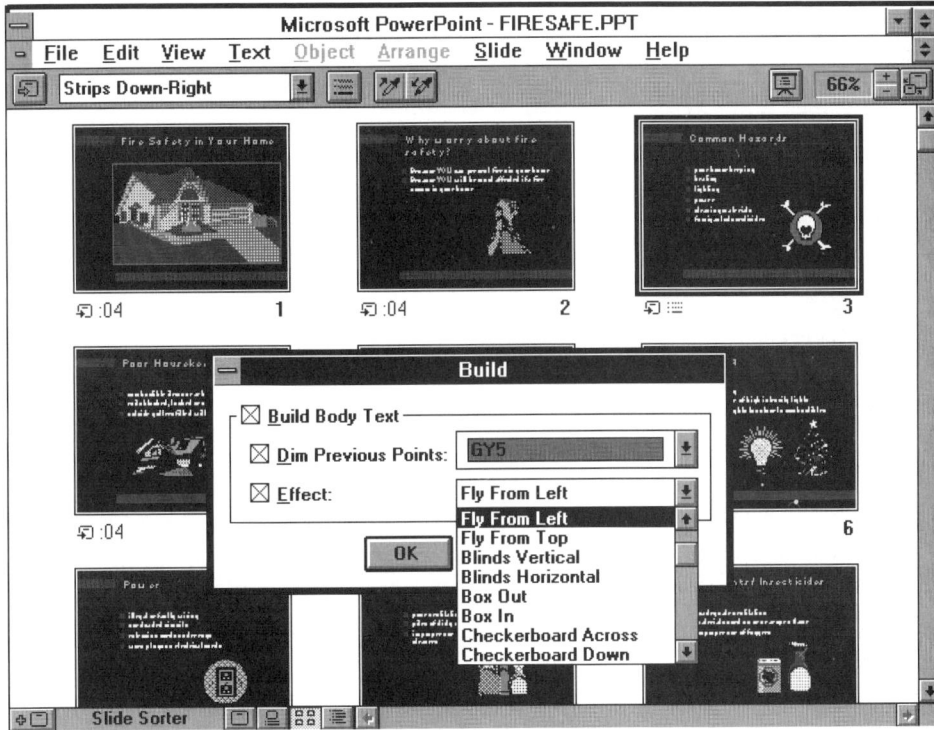

Figure 13.4 *PowerPoint* screen showing the text build dialog

assigned to that slide. Also, the number next to the icon specifies a timeout value for the slide, if any.

Text Builds

When you have a multiline bullet chart, you may not want to present it all at once, but rather reveal each bullet line as you get to it in the speech. This is called *building* the slide, and it can be done with *PowerPoint* by choosing the icon just to the right of the transition drop-down in the toolbar. That button brings up the dialog shown in Figure 13.4, which is used for setting the parameters of a text build. You enable a build for the selected slide by clicking the check box Build Body Text. You can then also opt to dim the previous points by clicking that box and then choosing a color to use for dimming. You also can specify an effect for the showing of each line of text by checking the Effect box and choosing the effect from the list. The effect "Fly From Left" causes each line of text to be

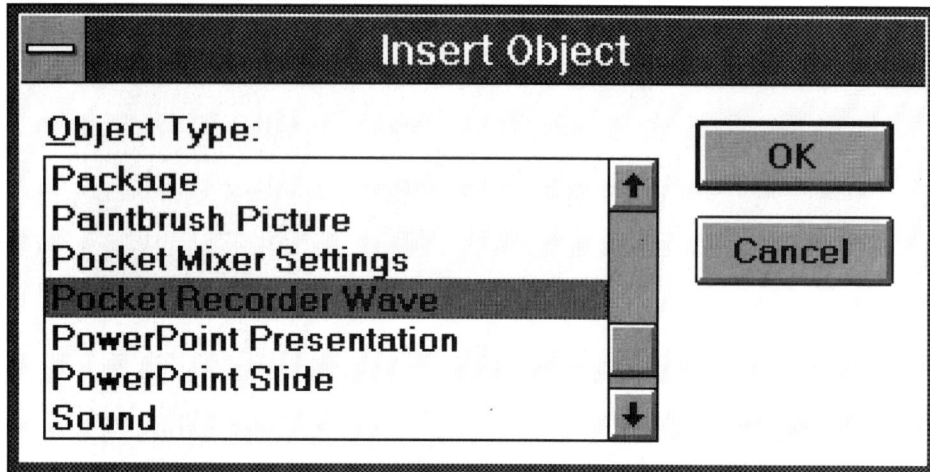

Figure 13.5 The Insert Object dialog to select an object for embedding in *PowerPoint*

animated, moving horizontally in from the left of the screen. There are many other effects choices.

Notice that if you have chosen a timeout value for a slide that has a build, the build will proceed rapidly, and then the total slide will time out. If the slide has no timeout value (waits for mouse click), then it takes a mouse click to activate each step of the build. The build feature has been added to slide 3, which also has no timeout value. Notice that the build icon appears below slide 3 and there is no number, indicating there is no timeout for that slide.

Adding Sound to a Presentation

You can also add sound to any slide of the presentation. The sound will begin playing when the slide is first shown. *PowerPoint* does not contain a sound driver; rather it depends on OLE to do this. Let's add a sound introduction to the first slide of the presentation. In the Edit menu, choose Insert, and select Object from the subordinate menu. That opens the dialog shown in Figure 13.5, listing all the classes of objects that can be embedded in the presentation via OLE. Choose the Pocket Recorder Wave item. The Pocket Recorder is a tool that comes with the Media Vision Pro Audio Spectrum 16 sound card. The *Pocket Recorder* dialogs will appear over your slide, as shown in Figure 13.6. Using the *Pocket Recorder*, you can either embed an existing audio file, or you can create a new audio file. Embedding occurs when you choose Update from the Edit menu in *Pocket Recorder*.

Figure 13.6 The dialogs for *Pocket Recorder* appearing over a *PowerPoint* slide

Adding Animation or Video

The procedure for adding video or animation to a presentation is the same as described above for audio. If you have OLE-aware animation or video tools in your environment, they will automatically appear in the Insert Object dialog of *PowerPoint.* You select the type of object you want, the tool's dialog will appear, and you choose or create the object and click Update—that's all there is to it.

SUMMARY

Using a presentation authoring tool such as *PowerPoint, FreeLance Graphics,* or *Harvard Graphics,* linear presentations can be quickly authored directly from a written outline. All the tools provide many features for enhancing the presentation by adding professional styles, images, graphics, audio, video, animation, charts, or almost any other kind of object that can reside in your computer. The tools are easy to learn and will quickly enable you to develop your own multimedia presentations.

14

Authoring for Training or Education

Computer-based training (CBT) is a field that had its beginnings before the personal computer came on the scene, when the only computers were large systems shared by many users. Application architectures and authoring metaphors for CBT are well established and they are supported by dedicated software on many personal computer platforms. This chapter explores the needs of computer-based training and education and focuses on the special authoring requirements posed by those applications. In order to simplify the terminology, I will use the acronym CBT to refer to either training or education.

WHAT'S DIFFERENT ABOUT TRAINING?

The user of a CBT application expects to *learn* from the computer—she is a *student,* and I will refer to her that way to highlight that CBT is different from general multimedia. The computer's display and sound capabilities present the subject matter to the student and its interactive capabilities collect the student's responses and provide appropriate feedback to help the learning process. An effective CBT application will try to make learning seem easy, even fun, for the student.

Learning is facilitated by breaking a subject down into a series of single thoughts that can be approached sequentially. Each thought should be presented and the student's understanding of it tested before proceeding to the next thought. Testing is usually accomplished with multiple-choice questions that the student can answer with a mouse click or by typing a single character. If the student is not getting it (as indicated by wrong answers to test questions), additional help should be given and testing repeated until the student answers correctly. The structure: present-test, present-test, . . . etc., is one of the unique characteristics of CBT, and assembly tools for CBT applications often have this built-in. These are called *teaching units* in this chapter.

A CBT workstation is often used by a number of students, for example, all the members of one class. Each student may not have exclusive use of the workstation for a long enough time to complete a whole subject; she will have to give up the system to other students and resume her learning at a later time. Thus, a CBT application must keep permanent records for all the students who are using the system. It should be easy for a student to stop at any time and save her status so she can return to the system later and pick up at the teaching unit where she left off. Another reason for record keeping is so a teacher or training manager can track student progress and performance. These tasks are called *student management* and, although they can be programmed in any assembly tool that has variables and file I/O, assembly tools designed specifically for CBT will have a student management module already programmed and available as part of the authoring interface.

TRAINING APPLICATION ARCHITECTURE

Based on the preceding discussion but adding features to support a full application, a typical CBT application may be described by the block diagram shown in Figure 14.1. Use of the application always begins with the Student Login module, which is part of the student management process. A student must identify herself to the application before entering the actual training modules; her previous status (if any) will be acknowledged, and she will be able to resume where she left off. The application also has a Navigation module that is accessible by the student at any time; this allows her to go to any subject that she has already completed, for example, to review a subject. However, the student management functions can prevent her from jumping ahead to subjects that are beyond the one on which she is currently working.

The Navigation module also can provide student access to general features of the application, such as a glossary, the student's status report, or an overview of the entire application. Notice that a student quits the application by going to the Navigation module and choosing Quit. This saves the current student's status and returns to the Student Login module for another student to take over the system.

Each subject is further subdivided into individual teaching units, which are the present-test structures described above.

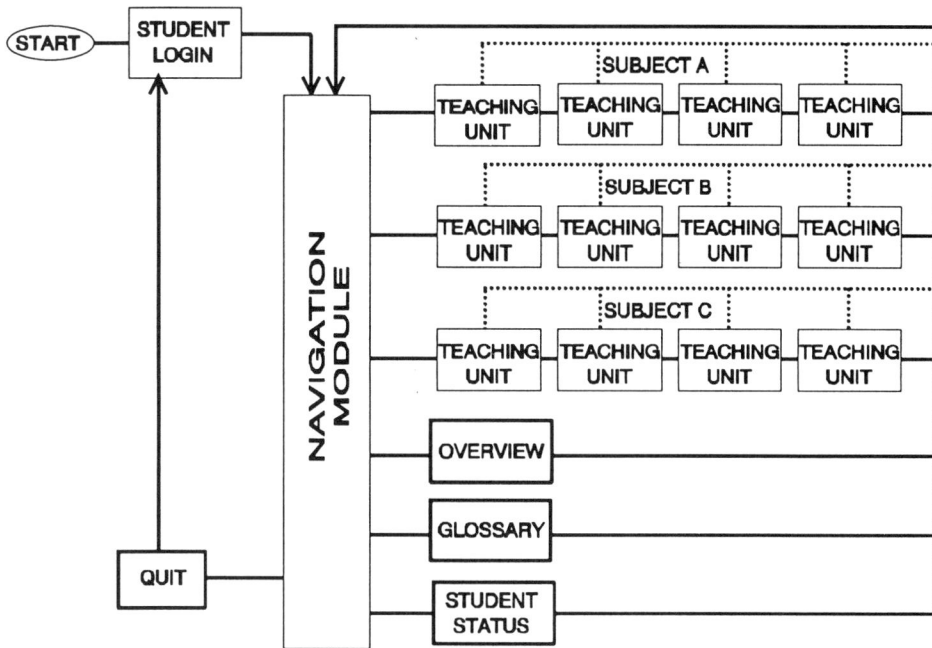

Figure 14.1 Block diagram of a typical CBT application

A Teaching Unit

Figure 14.2 expands on the internal architecture of a single teaching unit. When the student first begins the unit, she sees a multimedia presentation of the subject of the unit. The presentation for a single unit should be short—one or two minutes—and, when it is finished, the test part of the unit is presented. The student must respond correctly to the test question in order to complete the unit, in which case the unit is marked correct in the student's record. If her response is incorrect, a help presentation is made and the test is restarted. Incorrect answers are counted to keep track of how well the student is doing.

It is best if each incorrect response has its own specific help message (different from the unit's main presentation). Help messages should be simple and short; usually a brief audio clip or one text message box or screen will be enough. At all times in the testing mode, the student should have the option to repeat the main presentation of the unit. An Exit button is also available to quit the unit, although the student will get no credit for the unit if she uses this way out. She also will not be able to proceed to the next unit.

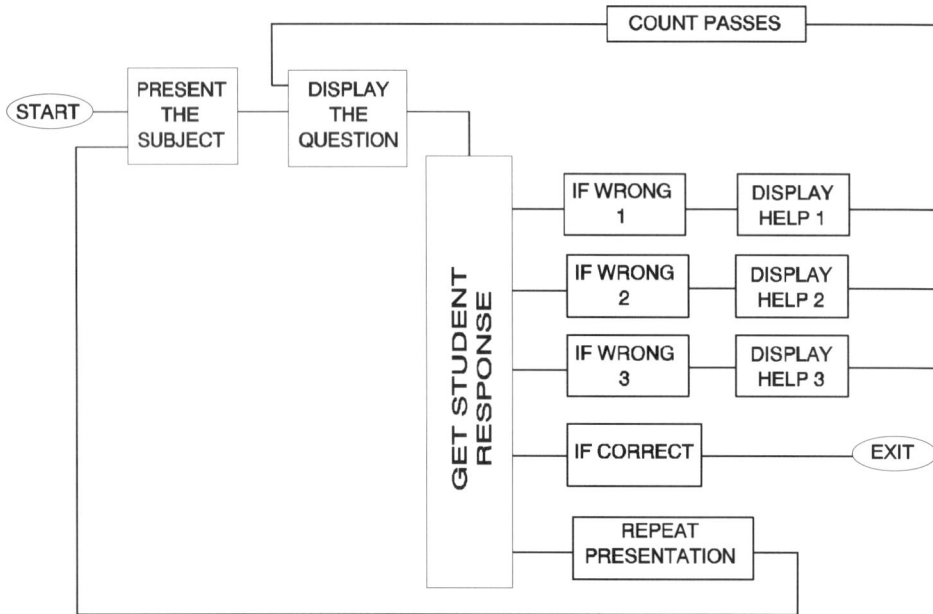

Figure 14.2 Block diagram of a teaching unit

To keep the student from becoming annoyed by too much testing, the tests for a single unit should be simple—only one or two questions. More comprehensive tests can be given periodically in a string of units, or at the end of a complete subject. These tests follow the same architecture as the ones in a single unit, except that there may be more questions and the options for handling of incorrect responses may get more complex.

AUTHORING TOOLS FOR TRAINING

CBT applications can be authored with any full-featured assembly tool that supports interactivity, variables, and file I/O. The teaching unit structure described above is best authored by designing an engine script that runs from a control file. Then a separate control file is written for each teaching unit, containing the parameters of the unit's main presentation, the test screen(s), and a table of responses to incorrect answers for the unit. The remainder of the authoring involves building the navigation module and a student management module. If these parts of the application are done properly, they can be reusable for other applications by changing control files and navigation structures.

Assembly tools intended for CBT include features such as test building as an integral part of their authoring interface. *IconAuthor* by AimTech and *Authorware Professional* by Macromedia are two examples, which run under *Windows*. These are both expensive tools, but they include comprehensive capabilities for creating almost any kind of test structure. Another example of a CBT assembly tool is *Quest* by Allen Communication, which runs under DOS. *Quest* has a built-in student database that provides for student registration, scheduling, status tracking, and course management.

TEACHING UNIT EXAMPLES

A simple example was created with *Authorware Professional*. An excerpt from the "Star-Spangled Banner" is played, and then the question "Who wrote it" is asked. The screen is shown in Figure 14.3. A three-button multiple choice selection is presented. If the student answers correctly, a graphic is presented, and, after a three-second delay, the screen is erased. If the choice is incorrect, a message says that, and the student is asked to try again. The *Authorware Professional* flowchart for the example is shown in Figure 14.4. The following explains the flowchart.

The flowchart begins at the upper left; the first icon is an Audio icon that plays the "Star-Spangled Banner" excerpt. It is authored for "wait for end" so nothing will happen until the audio finishes. This is the "present subject" part of the teaching unit. The next icon is a display icon that puts the question, "Who wrote the 'Star-Spangled Banner'?" on the screen. The icon after that (the one with the question mark in it), is an interactivity icon.

This interactivity icon has three parts, shown to its right; the parts are pushbuttons, whose names are shown in the list at the right of the icons. Each pushbutton also activates a display icon when it is clicked by the student—they display the relevant messages. Since the second choice (Francis Scott Key) is the correct one, it is identified as such and told to quit the interactivity icon. The other choices, which are incorrect ones, return to the question after displaying their messages. When the student makes the correct choice, a graphic is displayed and control moves to the wait icon, which waits three seconds, and then the screen is erased, using a mosaic effect.

All the parameters above are selected in the *Authorware* dialogs that are accessed by double-clicking on the various icons. The screen is drawn in a Screen Editor window and the entire process is very easy. Since all the parameters for this example are stored in each icon's data, it is a "hard-coded" script; you would

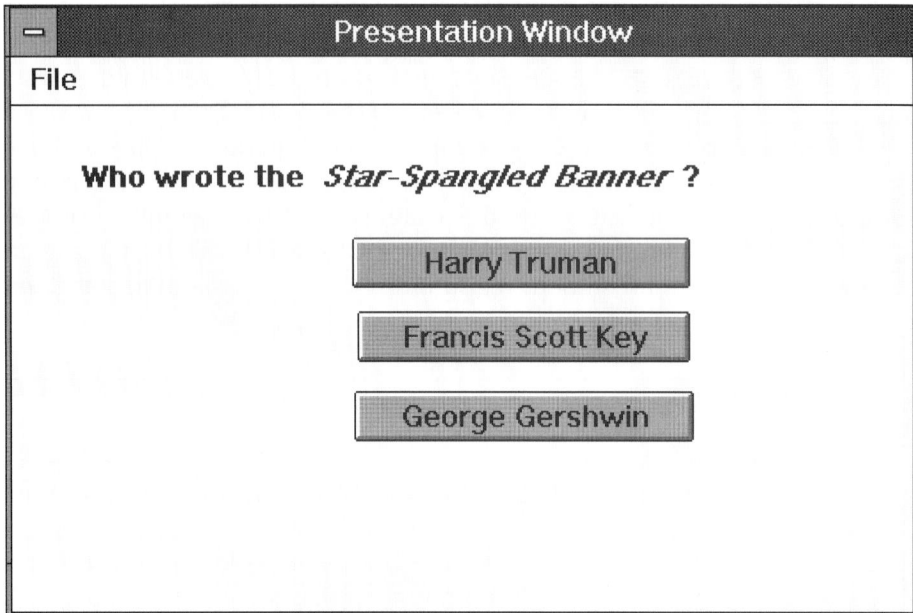

Figure 14.3 Screen of the sample teaching unit

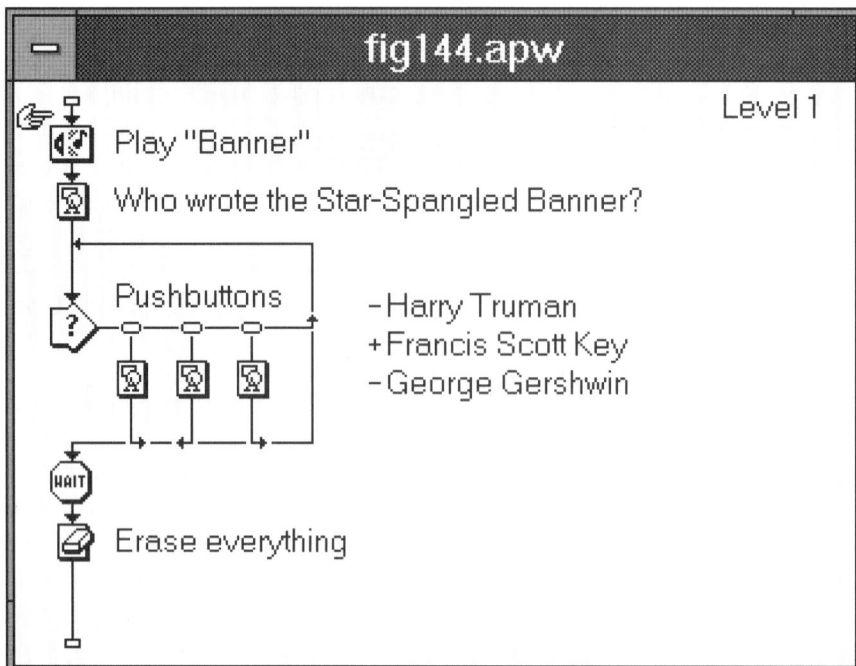

Figure 14.4 *Authorware Professional* flowchart for the sample teaching unit

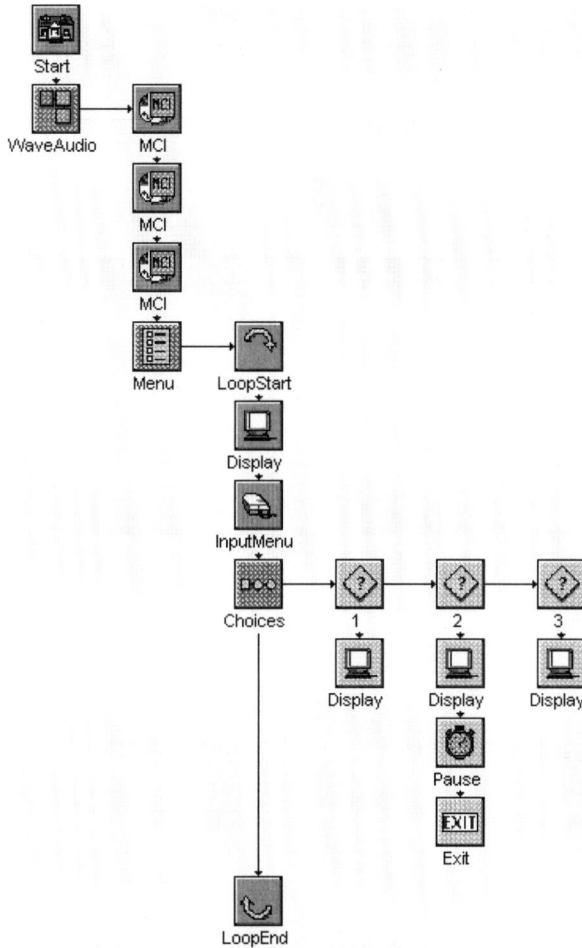

Figure 14.5 *IconAuthor* flowchart for the sample teaching unit

have to repeat the complete authoring process for every teaching unit in your application. With *Authorware Professional,* it is easy to turn this into an engine script driven by a control file by defining all the parameters in the icons as variables. Before running each teaching unit, the variables are initialized from a control file to specify the content of that unit. Authoring of multiple units then only consists of creating the control files, which can be done with a word processor.

The same example authored with *IconAuthor* is shown in flowchart form in Figure 14.5. The flowchart begins at the upper left with four icons that play the audio file using MCI. The four icons are created in one action by *IconAuthor* when you select the WaveAudio icon; you only have to enter the file name. Then a

Menu icon sets up a Loop and Choices structure—this group of icons is also automatically created when you choose the Menu icon. The Display icon shows a bitmapped image for the test screen; it is an image that was created with the *IconAuthor* graphic editor and saved in a separate file.

The InputMenu icon defines the coordinates of the buttons in the image; you enter these using the Input Template editor, which displays the menu image and lets you use the mouse to choose the button areas. The order in which you choose the button areas relates to the numbered selections in the flowchart. Finally, you attach additional icons to the structure to define the action for each of the choices.

SUMMARY

Training or education applications pose special requirements for creating interactive questions and for maintaining a student database. An architecture for training applications was presented and programming examples using *Authorware Professional* and *IconAuthor* were described.

15

Authoring for Information Delivery

Although information is all around us, it's not always as accessible as we would like it to be. For example, you are in a library to look for information about chocolate-point Siamese cats. There are thousands of books, but which ones have the information you need? You can go to the library catalog files (often on a computer now) and look for books that have "Siamese Cat" or just "Cat" in their titles—that is a start. However, there are probably many other books that contain more information on your subject, but the keywords are not in the titles. How much better if you could search through the *content* of all those books, looking for your exact subject and getting not just references to book titles and page numbers, but an interactive display of the actual paragraphs or chapters referenced. Of course, we know that can be done if all the books in the library are stored in a digital format searchable by a computer. That time is coming, and in that respect today's information delivery applications are a peek at the future. This chapter discusses the characteristics of information delivery, identifies the special authoring features needed, and gives some authoring examples from information delivery applications.

WHAT'S DIFFERENT ABOUT INFORMATION DELIVERY?

Information delivery is the process of using a computer to provide a user with access to specific information. Doing this is appropriate when:

- Computer searching is required
- You need fast retrieval of specific information

- You want easy and friendly access
- The target database is too large to be effectively distributed by other means
- You need a large database to be as physically small as possible

Notice that three of these reasons are important even when the database involved is small. The bottom line is that computer access is fast and easy for any size of database. In many cases, that alone is the reason for using a computer. For example, placing interactive computer kiosks in a shopping mall instead of the common directories or maps gives the consumer many more options for finding a store or stores selling the goods he needs. A modest database of all the stores coupled with lists of the items they sell is searched by the computer when the consumer tells the kiosk what he is looking for. The resulting display cannot only list the stores, but it might indicate which stores have sales on and offer directions for getting from the kiosk to each store. The consumer can get some of his questions answered without actually walking to each store and asking someone. This saves time for salespeople, too.

Many information kiosk applications exist because updating of the information data can be easily accomplished. In the shopping mall example just cited, updating is done by periodically going around to all the kiosks in the mall with a floppy disk containing the update. The information is kept on a hard disk in each kiosk. There is a separate system in the offices of the mall that processes updates; it has its own version of the kiosk application, modified to assist a nontechnical operator in managing the update process. Upon command, this system will automatically create the floppy disk for updating. The program for the updating system was designed at the same time as the kiosk application, using the same authoring tools.

In a situation where the delivery systems are not physically nearby (worldwide, for example), updating can be done by telephone communications or by shipping floppy disks or CD-ROMs out to each system. The authoring of the delivery application must include an update mode that operates automatically when the update disk is inserted, so that no authoring skills are required in the field.

An example that exploits the small physical size of large digital databases is the use of a computer to access the maintenance and service documentation for a vehicle or a system. The paper documentation for an airliner fills many shelves in the maintenance shop, but in digital form it is stored on a few CD-ROM discs. A computer accessing those discs is so small and light that it can even be placed on board the aircraft, so that full documentation is available wherever the aircraft goes. Further, periodic updating of the data is accomplished inexpensively by distributing updated CD-ROM discs to all aircraft.

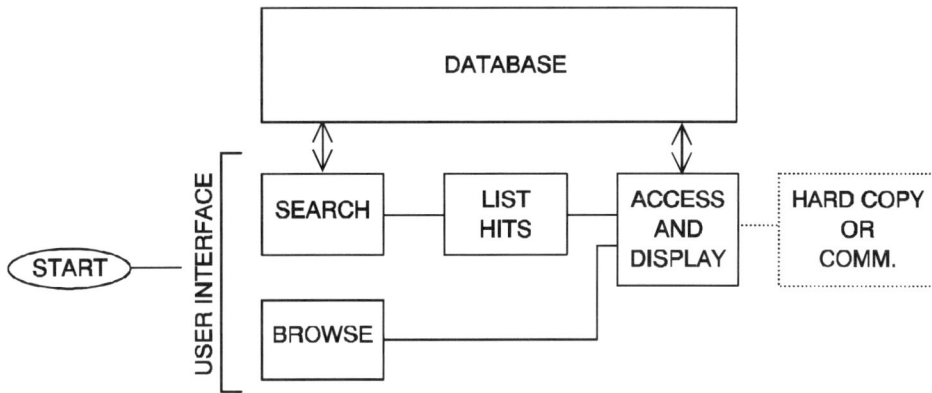

Figure 15.1 Block diagram of an information delivery application

INFORMATION DELIVERY ARCHITECTURES

Because an important objective of information delivery is to simplify and speed access for the end user, most applications have custom user interfaces that exactly match the characteristics of the database and the user. This makes it difficult to present a general architecture for an application. However, by avoiding the details of the user interface, the block diagram of Figure 15.1 can be created.

The figure represents an application having only one database. Many times, an application will have several databases, each with its own unique user interface mechanism. In the shopping mall example, the main database is the list of stores. This database needs to have a user interface that supports an elaborate search mechanism so the customer can find who sells the product he is looking for. But, there also are databases of restaurants and entertainment sites; these have different access needs and their user interfaces are different. The shopping mall kiosk might further present information about the history and the statistics of the mall; these subjects probably don't need a search mechanism at all. When a customer selects one of these subjects from the kiosk's menu, he would just get a linear presentation of the material.

Referring again to Figure 15.1, the user of this application is given just two choices—he may choose to manually browse the database or he can utilize the search features of the application. As he browses through the data by following the database structure, usually a tree, the current material is immediately displayed for him. If he uses the search mechanism, he defines his criteria and the search system displays a list of the items found, if any. This usually is done while he still has access to the search mechanism, so that he can modify his criteria until the list of hits is reasonable to him. Once he is satisfied with the list, he can switch to a browse mode for just the items in the hit list. Essentially he has created his own subset of the database, containing only items he is interested in.

Some databases may be too large to access by the single-step method described above. These databases will have an *index*, and the browse and search tools will first access the index rather than the full database. If the index is well-prepared, it can substantially speed up access to a large database. Preparation of a large database is a formidable task and there are special tools available to assist in such processes as indexing.

Hypertext

An enhancement to the browse mechanism is *hypertext*. When the user is in the browse mode, he may see, in the text or images of the database, subjects that he would like to explore further. With hypertext, potential items of this sort are specially marked in the display, indicating to the user that he can click on them to immediately get further information. A good example of this is the on-line help systems that are in most applications under Windows or OS/2. Tagged items are displayed in a different color and the cursor shape changes when the cursor is over a tagged item.

Hypertext requires special modifications to the database and to the display mechanism. Tags must be added in the data to mark hypertext items; the tags must include some kind of code that points to the database location the display mechanism should go to if the user clicks on the tagged item. The display mechanism must include features to highlight the tagged items and to respond to the user's clicking on them.

Not all assembly tools support hypertext; one that does is *ToolBook*. Figure 15.2 shows a screen from one of the sample books in *ToolBook*, with a hypertext word (*ToolBook* calls it a *hotword*) highlighted and the associated authoring dialogs open. The dialog at the lower left lets you set the properties of the hotword, and the window at the bottom right shows the script that activates when the user clicks the hotword. In this case, the script simply jumps to another page in the same book.

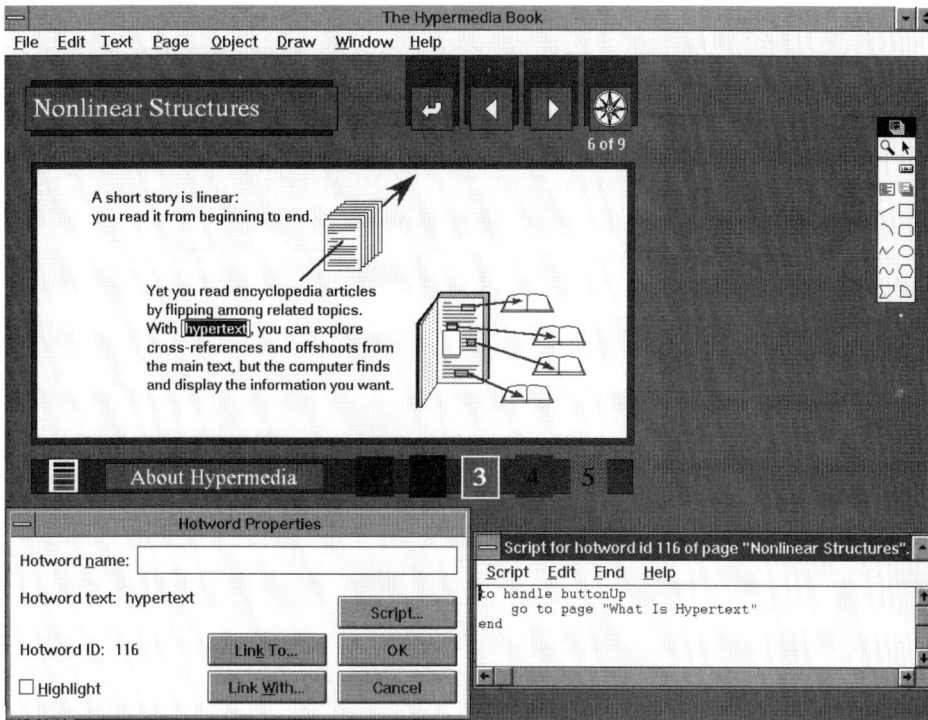

Figure 15.2 The *ToolBook* authoring screen showing a hotword highlighted and its associated authoring dialogs

AUTHORING TOOLS FOR INFORMATION DELIVERY

Authoring features needed by information delivery are:

- Flexibility—In order to make the data access as easy as possible for the end user, the author should create a custom user interface that is tailored to the type of data and the user. In many cases, the presence of a computer should be hidden from the end user; this means that the screen should look like a TV screen and the user control should be via touch screen.
- Data I/O—The information delivery application needs to access its database in many formats of mass storage. For updating, the delivery application should be able to read the updating information and respond to it and the update-creation application should be able to create the distribution data stream or disk.

- Special functions—Many applications require support for features such as text searching, hypertext, printer output, or data communications. Authoring assembly products must be able to author these features.

Because of the large number of sophisticated features listed above, information delivery authoring usually calls for the high-end assembly tools, or even single-purpose tools, for tasks such as searching or hypertext. Some tools suitable for information delivery development are: *Authorware Professional*, Multimedia *Tool-Book*, *MEDIAscript* (all versions), and *IconAuthor*.

AUTHORING OF MENUS

An important part of the user interface for most information delivery applications is a menu structure, so many assembly tools have special features for building menus. Since a menu consists of a screen or window that has a series of interactive controls (buttons, check boxes, etc.), the highest-level authoring approach for menus would be to combine in one object the creation of the screen with the assignment of controls. However, most assembly tools do not do that; instead, they make the drawing or loading of the screen a separate object from the assignment of controls. This is a more flexible approach because it allows the author to use any tool to create the screen.

Making the screen separate does have a problem, though—the author must perform a separate task to tell the menu object about the locations of the controls on the screen. This is usually accomplished with the mouse by displaying the screen during authoring and tracing the outline of each control into the menu object. Alternatively, it can be done by typing in coordinate values for the controls (if they are known).

With that background, let's look at some examples of menu objects in different assembly tools. The first one is *Authorware Professional*. Figure 15.3 shows part of a flowchart for a menu in *Authorware*. The approach here is actually a compromise with complete separation of assignment and screen drawing. The screen is separately loaded by a display icon (the icon at the top of the chart), but the controls are drawn by the menu object (the icon with the question mark in it and the icons to its right, called an *interaction* object in *Authorware*). This way, the control coordinates are already known in the menu object without the author having to do anything other than drawing them. You add a control by dragging a display or map icon over to the right of the interaction icon and dropping it. This causes a new control labelled "untitled" to appear in the presentation window. You can adjust the size or position of that control with the mouse. While

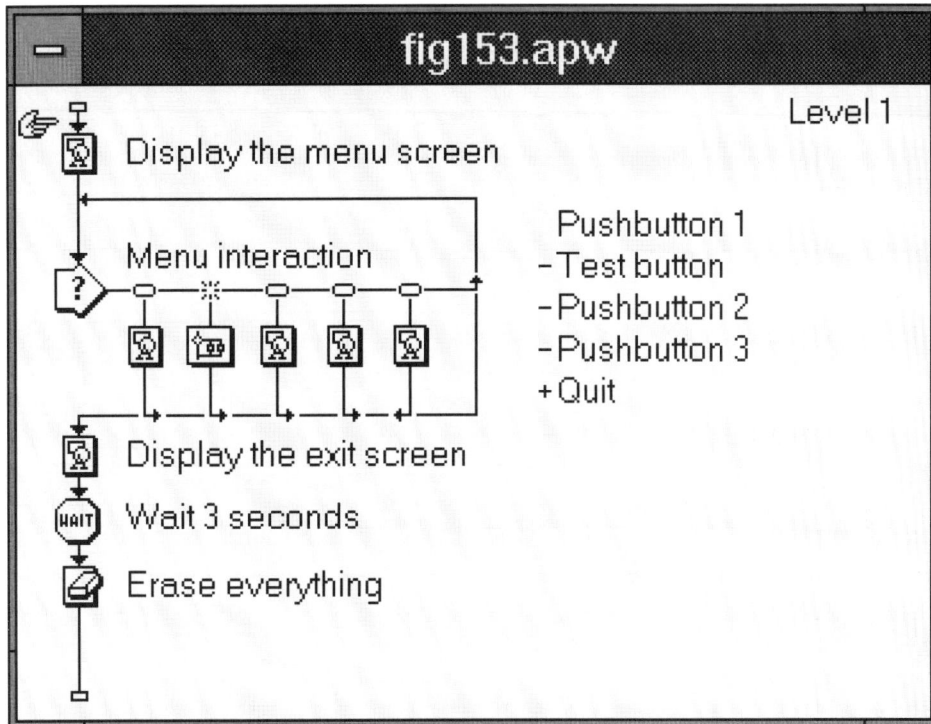

Figure 15.3 An *Authorware* flowchart for a menu

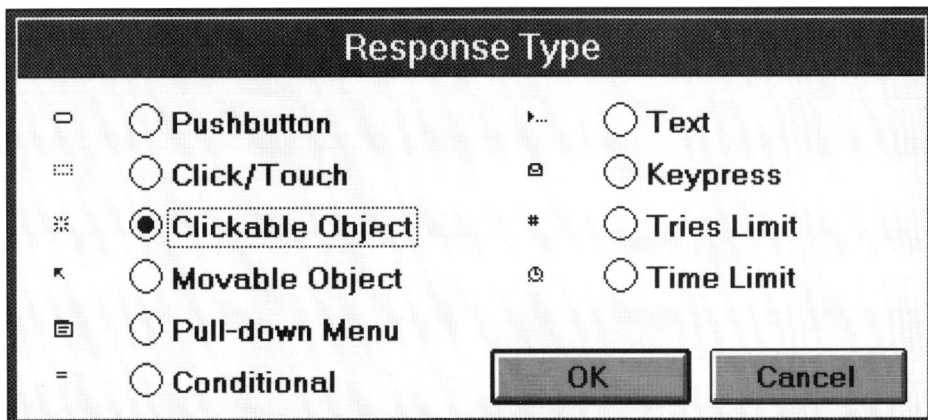

Figure 15.4 The *Authorware* dialog for selecting the type of an interaction

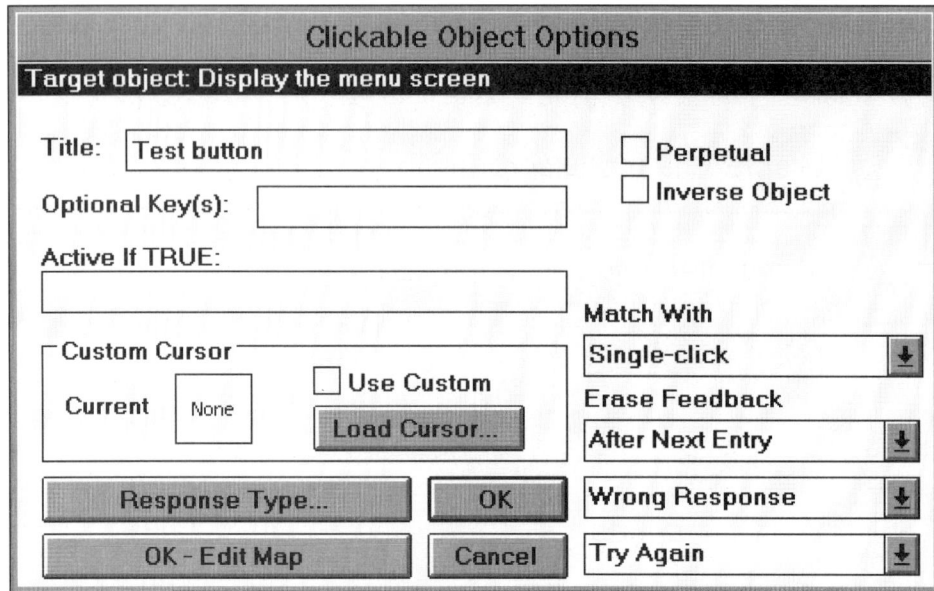

Figure 15.5 The *Authorware* dialog for specifying the properties of a Clickable Object

you are creating or editing controls, *Authorware* gives you access to several dialogs so you can set the control type and its properties. The first of these is for choosing the type of user response, and it is shown in Figure 15.4.

In the Response Type dialog, you can specify that the object is one of the following:

- Pushbutton—a standard Windows pushbutton
- Click/Touch—any rectangular area of the screen can be a hotspot that the user clicks on for a response
- Clickable Object—any *Authorware* screen object of any shape can become a hotspot
- Movable Object—any screen object can be set up for the user to drag it to a specified location to produce a match response
- Pull-Down Menu—a pull-down menu is attached to the interaction icon by this response type
- Conditional—an expression of variables is evaluated for a possible match response
- Text—the user is expected to type some text into a text entry area
- Keypress—this will respond when the user presses a designated key or keys

- Tries Limit—this is used to set a limit on the number of times the user may try a response
- Time Limit—this is used to set a time limit on the user's response

You can see that there are many types of interactions. One interaction icon can have as many of each type as you need and each interaction can have its own parameters.

SUMMARY

Information delivery is an important application class, which exercises all the potential of a multimedia system. Since the audience of an information application is often the general public, creation of an easy-to-use GUI is critical to the success of the application. This calls for the most capable assembly tools having a full set of features for authoring windows, menus, and interactions.

16

Trends in Multimedia Authoring

If by now you have not become fired up with the excitement of digital multimedia authoring, this book has failed its purpose. But keep in mind that multimedia authoring is still young and the tools have a long way to go before they are as easy to use and pervasive as other computer tools such as word processors or spreadsheets. In this chapter I will discuss some of the trends that may help you visualize where multimedia may be headed in the near future. I'll begin by discussing some of the supporting technologies for multimedia.

TELEVISION

You may be surprised that I list television as a supporting technology for multimedia. In fact, many of the elements of multimedia were in use in the television industry for years before we began putting them on computers. This particularly applies to audio and video production—these technologies are very mature in the TV industry. However, we must acknowledge that there is a major difference, also—TV is basically an analog technology that doesn't mate gracefully with digital computers. But the biggest trend of all is changing that—television technology is going digital!

Digital techniques are already widely used in video production for TV (and other end uses), particularly for generation of special effects. All broadcast studios and postproduction facilities have digital effects equipment that create the effects and transitions that we see all the time on TV. Until recently, this equipment, although digital, was not computer equipment—it was special-purpose (hardwired) digital hardware. Now, however, we have PC technology that can perform many of the effects under software control, and PC-based effects units are appearing in broadcast facilities.

But TV broadcasting itself, and cable TV, is still analog. That will soon begin to change with the adoption of a digital standard for high-definition TV (HDTV), which is a new high-performance TV system that is currently being standardized in the United States, Japan, and other countries. This will bring computers and TV even closer together. Worldwide television is an even larger market than worldwide computing, so to the extent that they become more technologically similar, we can expect that the rate of improvement in both markets will get even higher. End users will benefit from lower-cost, higher-performance products.

MULTIMEDIA PLATFORMS

The growth pattern of many new markets has been characterized by a phase of product proliferation followed by a period of consolidation. In the growth phase of a market, there are often more different products introduced than the market can support in the long term; the weaker ones are weeded out over time because they just don't sell very well. PC hardware platforms have been relatively stable for a few years (IBM PC/AT compatibles, IBM PS/2, Macintosh, Amiga, etc.), but proliferation is once again occurring because of new operating system introductions for the PC platforms (I consider the operating system to be part of a platform) — *OS/2* and *Windows NT*. In addition, a host of new multimedia platforms have been introduced for a possible consumer market for digital multimedia. These latter products are not intended for use as personal computers at all—they deliver multimedia titles to the consumer. Table 16.1 shows some of the variations.

Based on currently known development activities, there will be more platform introductions before a shakeout begins. This is primarily because of the possibility that a mass consumer market will develop for digital multimedia players.

The proliferation of platforms is a serious problem for software developers, since each platform has its own unique software interface. A developer must either face the considerable expense of producing separate products for each platform, or she must choose which one(s) to target. Several strategies have been developed to help this problem—all are based on writing applications in a special language that can be compiled separately for specific platforms. This doesn't eliminate the need to produce different products for each platform, it simply makes the development process easier since you write the application code only once and the rest of the process (compiling) is just mechanical.

Table 16.1 Multimedia Platforms

Personal Computer (PC) Platforms	Consumer Platforms
IBM-compatible—DOS/Windows	Sony MMCD
IBM-compatible—Windows NT	Kodak Photo CD
IBM-compatible—OS/2	Philips CD-I
Apple Macintosh	3 DO
Various workstations	

Rather than compiling for each platform during the development process, another approach is to write code on each platform that can interpret a common language at runtime. This is the objective of the *ScriptX* project of Kaleida Labs. Application developers write their programs in the *ScriptX* language, which can immediately run on any platform that has a *ScriptX* driver installed. *ScriptX* is nearing introduction as of this writing, but it is too early to tell how well it will be accepted. In any case, it seems that something like it will solve the problem of incompatible platforms in the near future. This will allow platform manufacturers to offer products that compete at the hardware level but become compatible at the application level through software.

THE CONSUMER MARKET FOR MULTIMEDIA

Digital multimedia is often viewed as the way that the capabilities now enjoyed by the consumer in the form of television can become interactive. A truly interactive consumer multimedia product can offer much more than television for entertainment, information delivery, and education. Using CD-ROM distribution, multimedia titles can be published on a wide range of subjects so that consumers will no longer be limited to the titles that are broadcast—they can view any subject at any time, based on their own choice and no one else's.

For many years, the consumer market has been a holy grail sought after without success by PC manufacturers—many people now hope that digital multimedia will be the way for PC products to find a place in every home along with television. Subject to the issues discussed below, I think this will happen in the next five years. One of the problems is that the PC market and the consumer (home) markets are so different that it is naive to think the same product can serve both. Table 16.2 shows some of the differences.

These differences are the reason that unique non-PC hardware products are being introduced to the consumer market, as shown in Table 16.1. However, it

Table 16.2 PC and consumer markets

PC Market	Consumer Player Market
Must have long product life with regular updating (for a price) and growth potential—it is a capital investment.	A player is a one-time purchase. It must have low cost with long service life without updating.
Requires expandability and flexibility.	Plug-and-play supercedes expandability and flexibility.
Although a single standard is desirable, the infrastructure can support several standards for the same market.	A single standard is essential to support the mass market required to achieve consumer volumes and price levels. This applies to both platforms and applications.
Distribution channels can provide technical support. Customers often have technical capability.	Distribution channels cannot provide technical support, nor would the customers know how to use it anyway.

is still attractive right now for application developers to try to serve both markets with the same products, and various approaches to run the same software on different platforms are being tried out. Trying to combine the markets for software is desirable because the consumer market is just starting out with few platforms in service while the PC market has millions of platforms in use. Thus, an application that serves both markets can achieve immediate volume in the PC market while the emerging consumer market is an opportunity for future growth. This may work in the initial stages, but in the long run, as the consumer market grows as large or larger than the PC market, application products will become different for the two markets. PC applications will be more complex with more features and more technicality, while consumer applications will be simplified for ease of use. This will also support price differences between the markets—PC users will pay more for the additional features in their products compared to consumer products of the same genre.

AUDIO

Large numbers of audio boards for WAVE audio are now being sold in the PC market. For users, installing audio is an easy and low-cost first step into multimedia. However, WAVE audio is wasteful of storage space, and users quickly wish they could compress it. The technologies for audio compression are well developed for other audio markets such as the telephone and can be easily implemented in software on a PC. But the software approach proves awkward on platforms that do not have good multitasking capabilities and, in any case, it uses up a lot of CPU and system resources for something that is routine. A better approach is to put hardware on the audio board to do compression and decompression. Many of the newer audio board introductions now have digital signal processing (DSP) chips on-board to perform compression and decompression. This turns out not to be very expensive, and I expect it will sweep the market in a few years.

Audio is becoming such an important part of the PC that systems will soon integrate it into the motherboard, and it will no longer use up an expansion slot. This trend will occur for all the hardware capabilities required by multimedia—we'll see CD-ROM drives become standard in every PC; even video compression and decompression hardware will be built-in.

VIDEO

Motion video today is at once the most exciting multimedia capability, the most expensive one, the most demanding one for the rest of the PC, and the hardest one to author. All of these problems are being addressed in current development projects, and the future will show major improvements. However, there are limits which cannot be overcome, and motion video will continue to be probably the most demanding use of a PC.

The use of video compression technology is required to produce practical motion video on a PC. As with audio, video compression can be done in software—this is amply demonstrated by the *Video for Windows* product currently available. Contrary to audio, though, software video compression or decompression will use up *all* the resources of the fastest PC and still not do as much as you would like. This will continue to be the case even as PC processing power improves by 10:1 or more over the next five years. Therefore, I feel that hardware assists for video compression and decompression are essential. Current product introductions are addressing this: Video boards capable of real-time capture and compression are already available in the $500 price range, and I think this is just the beginning.

The technologies of video compression are well known, but the possibilities of combination are so complex that none of the systems currently available could be said to be fully optimized. Development is continuing in many quarters, and better algorithms are appearing regularly. For this reason, compression hardware designs should retain a degree of flexibility so that future improvements are possible without completely scrapping everything. This is best achieved by using the DSP approach where the hardware provides general video processing capability and the algorithm is described to it by software. Boards that have the Intel i750 video processor use this approach. That way, future algorithm improvements can be introduced to existing hardware through software updating.

In spite of the preceding paragraph, hardware for video compression is being built to the JPEG and MPEG standards with the algorithms cast in silicon chips. There's nothing wrong with this, but users just have to realize that a lot of potential for future improvement still remains in video compression, and they may have to replace their hardware in the future to benefit from it.

As video compression technologies improve, the gains will probably be turned to producing better-quality, higher-resolution full-screen pictures at the same data rates used today (150 – 500 KB/second). Tradeoffs in frame rate, pixel size, and number of colors will always be available to lower data rates where necessary.

MASS STORAGE

Mass storage technologies continue to improve steadily but slowly—larger capacity, better reliability, lower prices. Optical technologies are also increasing their penetration into the market as their costs are reduced. The CD-ROM optical read-only drives are rapidly becoming part of every PC, and new drives have much faster performance. They still are not in the same league as magnetic hard drives, but both access times and data transfer rates have improved by two to three times. The latest CD-ROMs are quite practical for their intended use of high-volume information delivery.

Optical drives, both read-only and read/write types, will continue their improvement and cost reduction, but there is little chance that their speed performance will equal magnetic hard drives in the next five years. Instead, they offer the advantage of massive storage capacity with a low-cost removable medium. This will cause increased penetration into the market, but almost always along with a hard drive in the same system. The prospect of an optical-only high-performing mass storage system is still far off. Recognizing that the real advantage of optical drives is their high storage capacity, we will see new drives that have increased storage beyond the 680-MB limit of today's CD-ROMs.

INTEGRATED CIRCUITS

The integrated circuit (IC) industry is still tracing the curve of Moore's law, which it has followed for more than 25 years. This "law," was first articulated by Gordon Moore of Intel Corporation; it predicts a two-fold improvement in devices on a chip every two years or so. That growth is moving RAM memory technology from the 4 MB per device, which is common today, to 16-MB chips, which are already available to 64-MB and even 256-MB devices that exist in the laboratories. There is no indication that the pace is slowing down. It means that the RAM require-ments of multimedia systems will be met at lower and lower costs, and systems that have 8 megabytes today may well have 16, 32, or 64 megabytes in five years. That translates to better multitasking capability and greater speed in manipulat-ing large multimedia objects in real time.

The same IC density growth is supporting the continued increase in CPU speed. The latest CPU introductions now have parallel architectures to eliminate processing bottlenecks and even include their own cache RAM on-chip. As CPU chips grow from the several million devices per chip to 10 million and beyond, CPU speed will go higher and higher. Some manufacturers are predicting that the CPU of the year 2000 will have a speed of 1000 MIPS! This will provide a fantastic opportunity for system and software developers to offer features that haven't even been dreamed of today. The PC of the future will perform the multimedia tasks we struggle with today in the background while doing even more fantastic processes at the same time. It just means that everything we can do on a PC today will become easier and lower in cost in the future.

DISPLAYS

We are presently in a transition period in which the preferred display configura-tion is moving from VGA (640×480 pixels, 16 colors) to Super VGA (offering resolutions up to 1024×768 pixels and color formats up to 24 bpp, but not at the same time). Low-cost super VGA video adaptors are available with video accelera-tor chips that pretty much overcome the speed penalty in using higher resolution and/or higher colors. As I discussed in earlier chapters, the amount of resolution you actually need depends on how close you sit to the display screen. Thus, for the typical desktop situation, 640×480 resolution on a 14" screen will be around for a long time. However, everyone can benefit from having more colors, and I expect the next several years will show a transition from 16 colors (4 bpp) to 256 colors (8 bpp), to even 32,000 colors (16 bpp) or 16 million colors (24 bpp). That will happen as users include more photorealistic images in their presentations. For realistic imaging, 16 colors doesn't cut it at all, 256 colors work if you take some care, and 32,000 colors or more make it easy.

More displays larger than 14" are being introduced all the time, especially in the 17" range. This is because of a trend to use higher than 640×480 resolution in applications that require a lot of concurrent activity. The resulting competition in large monitors is bringing prices down, and of course that will cause more of them to be sold, which will cause even lower prices, etc. Thus, I expect a slow trend to larger monitors on the desktop, particularly for applications like multimedia authoring where the display screen is often filled with many windows.

DIGITAL NETWORKS

Networks have suddenly come of age even for small organizations with only a few PCs. Easy-to-use networking software such as *Windows for Workgroups* from Microsoft have contributed to this trend. However, we should consider the subject of computer networks to be much broader than that—a network is any means of real-time mass distribution or communication of digital data. Because there will soon be a worldwide system of digital video distribution for HDTV and other new digital services, facilities for high-speed digital transmission will be low in cost and available almost anywhere. Of course, the high data rates of multimedia, especially motion video, will still tax these networks, but there will be many uses for which it will make sense to centralize huge depositories of multimedia information that can be accessed by users over a network. This will be true in any organization that builds multimedia applications or presentations. One such case is the educational institution—the depositories of information for education (*libraries* is a good word)—which will benefit from being converted to digital formats accessible remotely via networks. Although a lot of this is probably beyond the next five years, the trend will be clearly evident in five years.

As fiber optic distribution channels are put in place for telephone and cable TV uses, we will see high-speed digital connections directly into every home. This will broaden even further the potential users of multimedia, to include all consumers. It is not too early to think about how the consumer multimedia devices now being developed will be able to exist on a digital network. Again, wide use of such technologies are more than five years off, but we will soon see trial systems and a lot of development activity.

TELECONFERENCING

Building on the growth of high-speed digital networks, the technologies of multimedia will support the holding of business meetings and conferences via the network. This is called *teleconferencing*, and it is practiced today using expensive single-purpose facilities, usually analog. Digital teleconferencing with personal computers will take over because of their vastly lower cost. As hardware add-ins and software are developed for this use, teleconferencing will become the mode of operation for more and more businesses. The low cost will make it something any business can afford.

MULTIMEDIA AUTHORING TOOLS

As in platforms, we are in a proliferation stage for authoring tools. New products are introduced almost every day, there are few standards in place, and the market seems to be going in all directions at once. I am sure there are not enough users to support all this activity over the long term, and I expect there will be some shaking out. However, all this development is exploring all the ways to perform authoring tasks, and the result should be authoring tools that are both more powerful and easier to use.

As I have said earlier in this book, it takes a complete *environment* to perform authoring, typically involving several tools. It becomes most important that all the tools work together, easily passing data and command information where necessary. This is a standards issue. We need initiatives like the IBM Ultimedia Tools Series that offer a collection of tools from many vendors, which are guaranteed to work together in an environment. Another approach, of course, would be for one vendor to make a tool or an integrated set of tools that does *everything*. That appears unlikely, and, anyway, many authors would not want to be locked into one vendor that way.

STANDARDS

As you can see from the foregoing discussion, multimedia technologies are developing at a rapid pace, which causes the field to be quite turbulent and makes it difficult to set standards. Although every company that introduces a new technology hopes that their approach will become the industry standard overnight, it seldom happens. Many industries have strong trade associations or technical societies that provide the leadership necessary to develop standards among the many competing companies, and they do it before mass product introductions are made. Unfortunately, the personal computing field does not have such entities, and standards are reached only with great difficulty. Some of the larger companies (IBM, Apple, HP, AT&T, Microsoft, etc.) try to provide the leadership, but it is difficult for them to buck the tide of innovation coming from the smaller companies. As users, we wouldn't want that to happen anyway. Thus, standards in personal computers are decided by the marketplace, which inherently causes a turbulent market until the clear leaders emerge. That's where multimedia is today.

But there are some bright spots on the horizon. For example, the MCI software interface, spearheaded by Microsoft, is becoming standard by virtue of IBM adopting the same protocol in OS/2. However, hardware manufacturers still have to face the writing of two MCI drivers, one for Windows and one for OS/2. But once that is done, authors can use the same commands to activate the hardware from either operating system. Similarly, the IBM Ultimedia Tools Series is addressing the matter of standardizing in the authoring environment. The *ScriptX* language from Kaleida Labs is another software-based approach to standardization so that the same applications can run on many platforms. *This problem will be solved!*

SUMMARY

It is now clear that multimedia is going to be one of the most important attributes of personal computing in the 1990s and beyond. It is a tremendous opportunity for those of you who are becoming familiar with it now. Although you will face significant challenges in applying multimedia to your needs, you will be positioned to grow as the market expands, and the rewards will be great. Happy multimedia computing!

Appendix A

The CD-ROM

This appendix describes the CD-ROM included with this book and tells how to use it.

WHAT IS THE CD?

The CD is a special version of the IBM Ultimedia Tools Series Sampler CD, produced by IBM specifically for distribution with this book. It includes:

- A tutorial on multimedia application development
- A product selection tool that can search and navigate a database of information about the products in the Ultimedia Tools Series. The database contains product overviews, product demonstrations and guided tours, and often a working sample of the product for evaluation.
- The Authoring Tools Selector (ATS) that assists you to build and evaluate an environment of tools and compare it to your specific authoring needs. This is described fully in Chapter 11 and Appendix B.
- A multimedia glossary
- Capability to print out a fact sheet on a selected product

It is a powerful on-line encyclopedia of multimedia software tools, terms, and information.

SYSTEM REQUIREMENTS

To utilize this CD and exercise all of its features, your system must include the following:

- An IBM PS/1, PS/ValuePoint, PS/2, IBM Ultimedia System, or 100% compatible computer with a 386 or higher processor
- At least 2MB of RAM and 540KB executable low memory under DOS

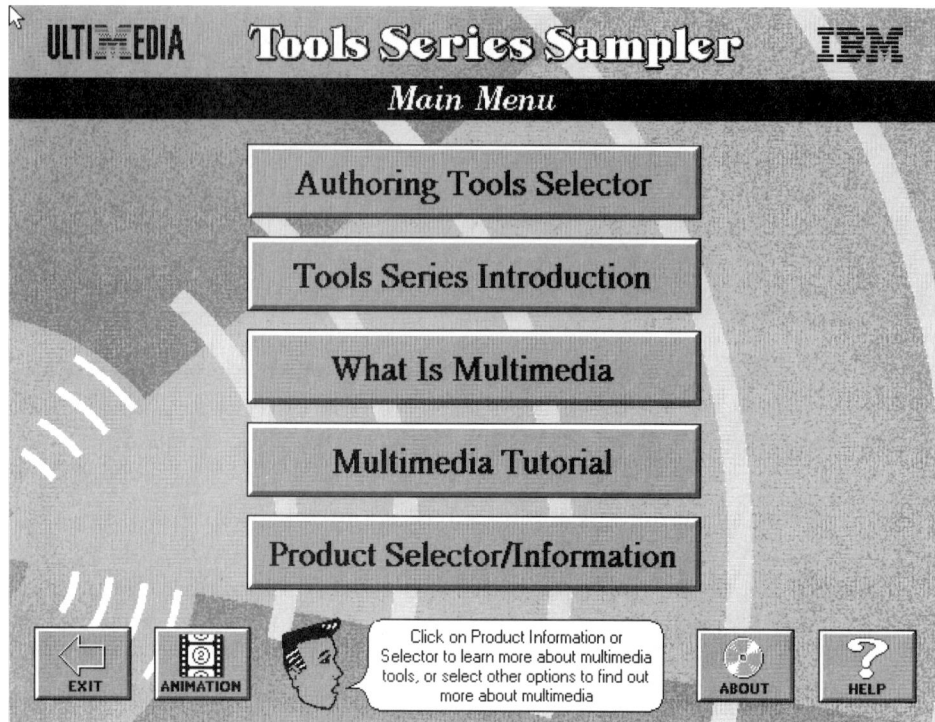

Figure A.1 The main menu of the CD

- Hard disk drive with at least 10 MB of available temporary space
- Sound card with speakers
- CD-ROM drive
- Mouse
- Printer (optional)
- DOS 5.0 and Windows 3.1 or OS/2 2.1 with MMPM/2 1.1
- Appropriate driver software for your CD-ROM and sound card

STARTING UP

To start the CD from either DOS or Windows, you must be in a native DOS session (not DOS under Windows). Then you move the current drive to the CD, type the word: "UTSDOS", and hit Enter. To start the CD from OS/2, you open a DOS full-screen session, change the current drive to the CD type "UTSDOS" at the command prompt, and hit Enter.

The startup process takes a few seconds to check your PC configuration and do some housekeeping. Then, the first time you use the CD on your system, you will be asked to designate the hard drive where you want the temporary working files. A directory called "TOOLSHOP" will be placed on the designated hard drive—when you are running the CD, certain files will be copied to this directory. When you exit the CD, this directory will be cleared, but the directory itself will remain.

The menus of the Sampler CD are mostly self-explanatory. Figure A.1 shows the main menu, which provides access to each of the capabilities. Notice that the message balloon at the bottom center of the screen gives you an explanation of whatever object is currently under the pointer. This is all that you will need to figure out the operation of the CD.

The
Authoring Tools Selector

There are two programs on the CD to assist you in selecting authoring tools for your environment. Appendix A described the IBM Ultimedia Tools Selector, and this appendix describes the ATS Authoring Tools Selector. The former program provides selection based on the characteristics of the tool, and the latter program provides selection based on the characteristics of the author. You probably will want to use both of them.

WHAT ATS DOES

ATS asks you a series of questions that determine your needs as an author. These questions are about your skills in the various tasks of authoring, what type(s) of applications you will be authoring, who your end users are, where you will be getting your content material, and your operating system preference. The questions are described fully in Chapter 11. After you have answered the questions, ATS develops a profile for you in terms of 90 authoring tool characteristics. These also are described in detail in Chapter 11.

Your profile then can be used to measure authoring tools for the degree that they match your needs. You select a group of tools and ATS tells you how well they suit your needs by calculating the percentage of your profile that is filled by the tools. You can experiment with different choices in a "what if" mode to choose the best environment for you. Profiles and tool selections can be saved for later use and they can be printed out for hard copy presentation.

USING ATS

ATS is invoked from the CD main menu (see Appendix A) by clicking the ATS button. This starts a Windows session running ATS. Alternatively (see below), you can set ATS up on your hard disk to run in your own Windows session independently from the CD. However, this latter approach does not allow you to switch easily between ATS and the IBM Selector, which you will find is a valuable thing to do.

ATS begins with the Logo screen (Figure 11.2); when you click OK or hit Enter, the Profiles screen (Figure 11.6) is shown. This is the main screen of ATS; it contains a menu bar that gives access to all functions.

If you are starting the progran for the first time, you should click the Window menu and choose the Author's Input window (Figure 11.4). This window asks all the questions described above and it is the main input screen for the program. You should think about each of the questions and check or uncheck it as it applies to you and your work. When you have finished with the questions, you click the Next button to proceed.

That takes you to the Multimedia Features window (Figure 11.5), which contains more questions. You can choose to answer them directly, or you can click the Use Defaults button and ATS will answer them for you based on your entries in the Author's Input screen. In any case, you should still examine the results in the Multimedia Features window and edit them until you are satisfied with the answers. Notice that, once you have edited this screen, you should not click the Use Defaults button again because it will remove your edits and return the screen to the default condition.

When you are satisfied with Multimedia Features, you click the Make Profile button and ATS calculates your profile and fills in the Author Profile column of the Profiles screen. This is based on algorithms built into ATS, which may or may not create a profile that suits you. Therefore, you should examine the profile items and make sure that the ones checked (indicated by a "1" in the Author Profile column) are correct for you. An Author Profile item can be changed either by clicking on the description of the item, which displays a dialog defining the item and gives you a choice of changing it by toggling the item on or off. (You can also do that by clicking on the profile item itself.)

At this point you have built your profile and it is a good time to save it for future use. You do that by clicking Save or Save As on the File menu and giving a file name. The dialog will also ask you to fill in your name (optional) and any remarks you wish to save with the profile. The contents of the Author's Input, Multimedia Features, and Profiles windows are then saved.

Now you are ready to try out some tools on your profile. From the Edit menu, select Include Tool. A dialog (Figure 11.7) opens containing a list of all the tools available. When you select a tool from the list and click the Include button, that tool's profile is placed in the first available column of the profile. The number of matches of that tool's profile to your author's profile is counted and a percentage is calculated for the match count versus the total of checked items in your profile.

Each item that is matched in your profile is marked with a left carat character, so you can look down the profile and see the status of each item. If you select an additional tool, additional items may be matched. The percentage is updated using the total of matches for all the tools selected. Usually you will begin the tool selection by choosing an assembly tool that you think you would like to use. You can reach this decision by using the IBM Selector program and examining all the assembly tools available. Most assembly tools have a wide range of capabilities, so you should get a fairly high percentage from the one tool (usually more than 50 percent).

Now you should examine your profile for unmatched items and select a second tool that matches one or more of the unmatched items. For example, you may need an animation editor and the assembly tool you chose does not have this. Therefore, select an animation specialty tool as your second tool. The percentage will go up. You can continue by trying to fill other unmatched items. The IBM Selector program will help you find tools of each class you require. You can continue this process until you have matched every item to give you 100 percent.

Sometimes this is not the best approach. You could end up with a lot of different tools, which will be expensive and may not be very convenient to use. You may do better by starting with a different assembly program that delivers a higher percentage to start with. Obviously, a lot of experimenting is needed, but it may pay off with a less expensive and more convenient environment.

As you select tools to include in your environment, ATS checks that each tool selected is compatible with your operating system. If it is not, a warning message is displayed, and the tool will not be included in your environment. If you get this warning too often, you should consider changing the operating system you plan to use.

RUNNING ATS FROM YOUR HARD DISK

When running from the CD access program, a directory is created on your hard disk to hold the ATS working files. This is a subdirectory to the CD's working directory: \TOOLSHOP—\TOOLSHOP\ATS. Ordinarily, the CD access program deletes all the demonstration files in \TOOLSHOP when it terminates, leaving only a few files that will speed access the next time you use the CD. However, the subdirectory ATS is left intact; this is necessary so that profile files you create with ATS will not be lost when the CD access program finishes.

ATS.EXE is contained in that directory and you can run ATS from there without running the CD access program. All you have to do is create a program object in one of your Windows groups to access ats.exe from that directory. You should also define the working directory to be the same one.

CUSTOMIZING ATS

Some of the features of ATS are table driven from text files that you can edit to make changes in the program itself. In particular, the list of items for the profiles is contained in the file items1.txt. This file also contains the algorithm that ATS uses for creating the author's profile and the text that appears when you open the description dialog for a profile item. With a text editor that can handle long lines (up to 512 characters), you can modify this file and customize the profile list. However, before you jump into that, you should be aware that it also will probably require editing the files that contain the profiles for all the tools. There is one of these files for each tool—more than 90 of them!

Each line of items1.txt represents one item of the profile list. The format of each line has four parts as shown below:

```
[code]Item name|algorithm|Descriptive text
```

The first item (code) indicates whether the item is a class heading that will appear in the summary or whether it is an item. For a class heading, the code is nothing; for an item it is a period followed by a space. For example, the operating system items from items1.txt are:

```
Operating system||You must decide on the operating systems
you will use. Tools are designed to run on a particular sys-
tem, so the OS choice will restrict the tools you may con-
sider.
. DOS|a13|DOS is the original PC operating system, although
it has gone through many updates. DOS does not have a native
graphical interface, but some tools provide their own. DOS
also does not have multitasking.
. Windows|a14|Microsoft Windows is a graphical interface sys-
tem that runs on top of DOS. It has limited multitasking, and
it also can run most DOS programs.
. OS/2|a15|IBM OS/2 is a true multitasking operating system.
It is capable of concurrently running DOS, Windows, or OS/2
programs.
```

In the listing above, each item is only one line; the word wrapping is introduced by the need to fit the text on this page.

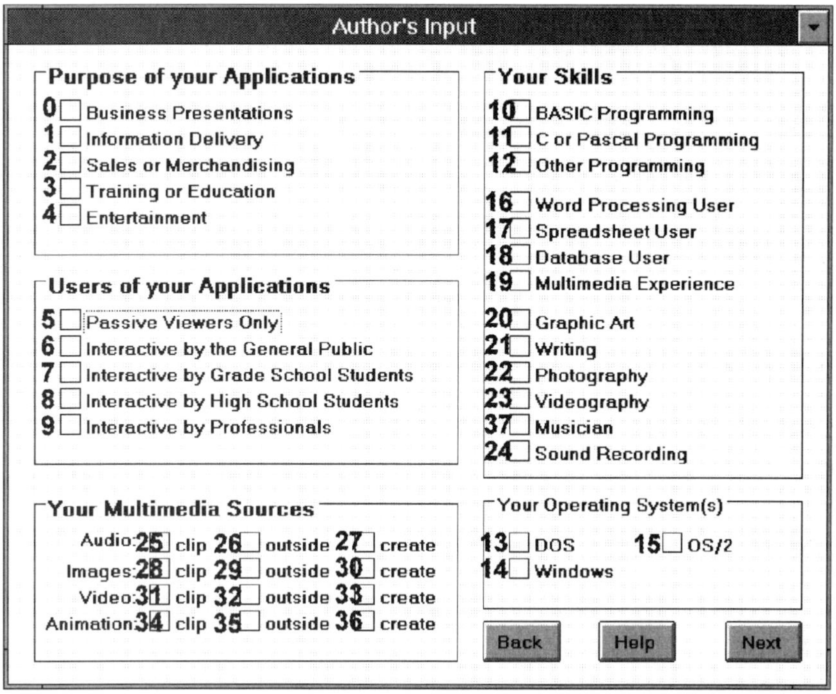

Figure B.1 The Author's Input window showing the numbering of items

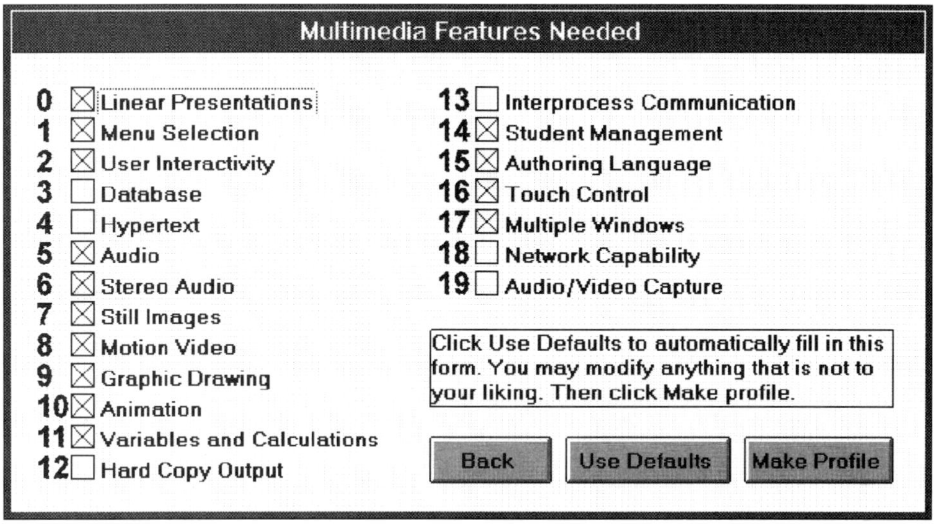

Figure B.2 The Multimedia Features window showing the numbering of items

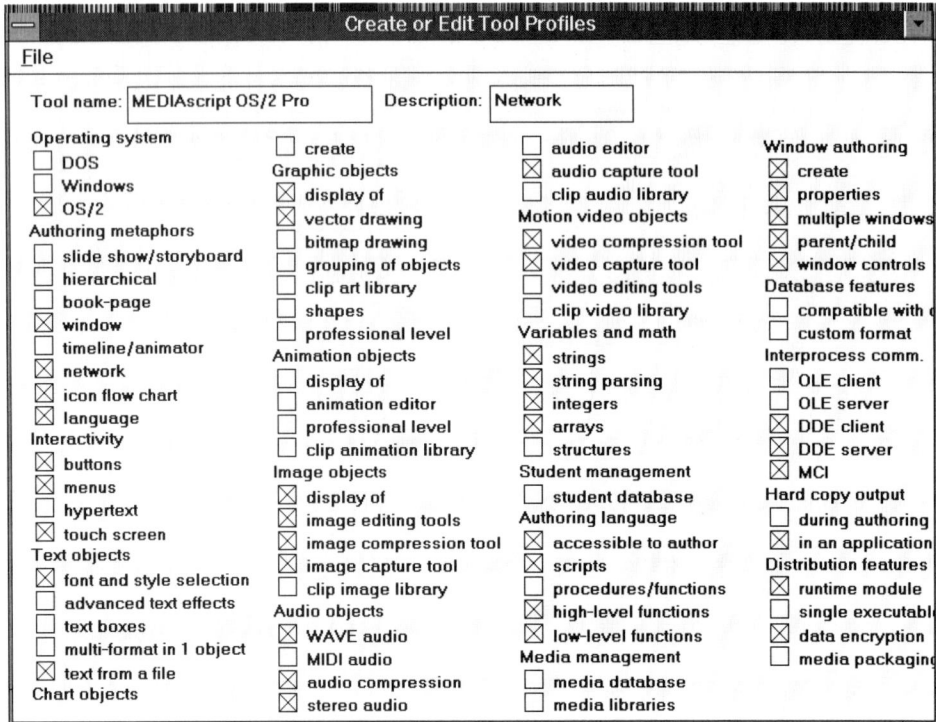

Create or Edit Tool Profiles

File

Tool name: MEDIAscript OS/2 Pro   Description: Network

Operating system
- [ ] DOS
- [ ] Windows
- [x] OS/2

Authoring metaphors
- [ ] slide show/storyboard
- [ ] hierarchical
- [ ] book-page
- [x] window
- [ ] timeline/animator
- [x] network
- [x] icon flow chart
- [x] language

Interactivity
- [x] buttons
- [x] menus
- [ ] hypertext
- [x] touch screen

Text objects
- [x] font and style selection
- [ ] advanced text effects
- [ ] text boxes
- [ ] multi-format in 1 object
- [x] text from a file

Chart objects
- [ ] create

Graphic objects
- [x] display of
- [x] vector drawing
- [ ] bitmap drawing
- [ ] grouping of objects
- [ ] clip art library
- [ ] shapes
- [ ] professional level

Animation objects
- [ ] display of
- [ ] animation editor
- [ ] professional level
- [ ] clip animation library

Image objects
- [x] display of
- [x] image editing tools
- [x] image compression tool
- [x] image capture tool
- [ ] clip image library

Audio objects
- [x] WAVE audio
- [ ] MIDI audio
- [x] audio compression
- [x] stereo audio

- [ ] audio editor
- [x] audio capture tool
- [ ] clip audio library

Motion video objects
- [x] video compression tool
- [x] video capture tool
- [ ] video editing tools
- [ ] clip video library

Variables and math
- [x] strings
- [x] string parsing
- [x] integers
- [x] arrays
- [ ] structures

Student management
- [ ] student database

Authoring language
- [x] accessible to author
- [x] scripts
- [ ] procedures/functions
- [x] high-level functions
- [x] low-level functions

Media management
- [ ] media database
- [ ] media libraries

Window authoring
- [x] create
- [x] properties
- [x] multiple windows
- [x] parent/child
- [x] window controls

Database features
- [ ] compatible with
- [ ] custom format

Interprocess comm.
- [ ] OLE client
- [ ] OLE server
- [x] DDE client
- [x] DDE server
- [x] MCI

Hard copy output
- [ ] during authoring
- [x] in an application

Distribution features
- [x] runtime module
- [ ] single executable
- [x] data encryption
- [ ] media packaging

Figure B.3 The Add Tools editor from ATS

Immediately following the code is the name of the item, which is displayed in the first column of the profiles screen. This is terminated by a vertical bar "|" character. The next item represents the algorithm for how ATS will fill in this profile item based on the Author's Input and the Multimedia Features dialogs.

The algorithm is another code that can contain any number of items from the dialogs combined by logical OR (the "+" character) or logical AND (the "&" character). Each item is represented by a letter and a number. The letter is either "a" for the Author's Input screen or "f" for the Multimedia features screen. The number represents the number of the particular check box you want to read. The numbering of the check boxes is shown in Figures B.1 and B.2. Algorithm codes should contain no spaces. For example, if you want to have a profile item that depends on either Interactive by the General Public or Interactive by Professionals, the algorithm code would be:

```
|a6+a9|
```

As shown above, the algorithm code is contained within two vertical bar characters. These must always be present, even if you have no algorithm.

The final item is the description of the item that appears when you click in the first column of the Profiles screen. This text can be any length, up to as many characters as will fit in the description dialog box. That is about 512 characters, depending on the exact content.

THE TOOL PROFILES

ATS contains an editor (Figure B.3) that can easily modify the tool profile files. However, editing 90 files is a challenge that you probably would not want to face. I don't recommend changing the existing profile list unless you really have an important purpose for doing it. The real reason I included this editor is in case you want to create a profile for a new tool that is not already in the list. You choose the Add Tools item from the File menu of the Profiles window to access the tool profile editor. The use of the editor is very simple; you enter the name of the tool, a description of it, and then check all the items you want in its profile. You save the new tool by selecting Save from the File menu of the editor and entering a file name. The name and description of your new tool will now appear automatically in the Available Tools list when you open the Include Tools dialog in ATS.

Appendix C

Sources of Hardware and Software

This appendix lists some sources of multimedia hardware and software.

THE ULTIMEDIA TOOLS SERIES

The IBM Ultimedia Tools Series is presently .the most comprehensive source for multimedia authoring software. Managed by IBM, it is a competitive mail order marketing operation with several different twists—it specializes in multimedia authoring tools only, and it has a vision of an authoring environment where all the tools work smoothly together. All the tools they are marketing have been qualified against a set of specifications for that vision. There are more than 90 tools in the series, from over 30 vendors (including IBM). In addition, they sell the IBM multimedia hardware, including *ActionMedia II*, CD-ROM drives, and audio and video add-in boards.

Buying software is a risky business because you often cannot try out software before you buy it. The Ultimedia Tools Series has attacked that problem by offering a Sampler CD-ROM disc that contains product information, demonstrations, and *working models* for most of the products. Of course the working models are limited in some ways, but they provide an excellent means for you to try out the product before you commit to buying it. A version of the Ultimedia Tools Series sampler CD is included with this book; it is described in Appendix A. In the list that follows, I will not repeat references to the companies whose products are in the Tools Series, but I will list other companies whose products have been mentioned in the book.

You may contact the IBM Ultimedia Tools Series at:

IBM Ultimedia Tools Series
1055 Joaquin Road
Mountain View, CA 94043
1 800 887-7771 (Voice)
1 800 887-7772 (Fax)

*** IMPORTANT INFORMATION ***

- **800 #s ARE NOT VALID OUTSIDE THE U.S.**
- **PRODUCTS ARE NOT AVAILABLE FROM THE IBM ULTIMEDIA® TOOLS SERIES™ OUTSIDE THE U.S.**
- **SOME PRODUCTS MAY BE AVAILABLE THROUGH LOCAL DISTRIBUTORS IN YOUR COUNTRY OR DIRECTLY FROM THE VENDOR**

OTHER SOURCES OF MULTIMEDIA TOOLS

The list below includes hardware and software vendors whose products are mentioned in this book. Contact information is given for each company along with a list of the relevant products.

Intel Corporation
DVI Technology, ActionMedia II, Smart Video Recorder, Indeo
1-800-548-4725

Aldus Corporation
PhotoStyler
411 First Avenue South
Seattle, WA 98104-2871
1-800-685-3569
1-206-622-5500

Corel Systems
CorelDRAW
1-800-772-6735 x23

Creative Labs, Inc.
Sound Blaster
1-800-998-5227
1-408-428-6600

Media Vision, Inc.
Pro Audio Spectrum 16, Pocket Recorder
3185 Laurelview Court
Fremont, CA 94538
1-800-845-5870

Microsoft
Windows 3.1, Windows NT, Windows for Workgroups, PowerPoint, Video for Windows, Visual Basic
1-800-426-9400

Software Publishing Corp.
Harvard Graphics
1-800-336-8360

Lotus Development Corp.
FreeLance Graphics, SmartPics
55 Cambridge Parkway
Cambridge, MA 02142

Inset Systems
Hijaak PRO
1-800-374-6738

Micrografx, Inc.
Windows Draw!
1303 Arapaho
Richardson, TX 75081
1-800-326-3510
1-214-234-1769

Glossary

accelerator A hardware unit that assists the CPU to speed up a particular process. For example, a graphics accelerator speeds up the processing and display of graphics.

adaptive differential PCM (ADPCM) A compression technique that depends on the incoming data not changing too much from one sample to the next. As a result, fewer bits are necessary to represent the changes between samples that it would take to code the samples themselves. ADPCM is used for audio compression, where it can deliver up to 4:1 compression.

additive color system A color reproduction system in which an image is displayed by mixing appropriate amounts of red, green, and blue lights. It is the color system used by color television and computer displays.

ADPCM *See* adaptive differential PCM

algorithm A group of processing steps that perform a particular operation, such as drawing a line or compressing a digital image.

American National Standards Institute (ANSI) A standardizing body that produces standards for the United States in many different fields.

analog A system in which values are represented by continuous scales.

animation A process for creating artificial video where the computer calculates or assembles the content of each frame as it is displayed.

ANSI *See* American National Standards Institute

API *See* application programming interface

application A computer program written for a specific purpose.

application programming interface (API) The means whereby an application communicates with the system software. An API is usually specified in terms of one or more computer languages, such as C or Pascal.

assembly language A programming language where each statement relates directly to a single instruction of the CPU's instruction set.

assembly tool An authoring tool for building the overall structure of an application.

author One who uses authoring tools to create application programs.

authoring The process of creating an application program by the use of authoring tools.

authoring language A high-level programming language intended specifically for authoring. It contains commands or statements that simplify many of the steps of authoring.

basic input/output system (BIOS) A software module that is built into the computer hardware (usually as ROM). It provides the first level of interface between the hardware and an operating system.

BIOS *See* basic input/output system

bit The fundamental digital data unit. Its value can be either 0 or 1.

bitmap A region of memory or storage that contains the pixels representing an image arranged in the sequence in which they are scanned to display the image.

bits per pixel (bpp) The number of bits used to represent the color value of each pixel in a digitized image.

bits per sample (bps) In a sampling process, the number of bits used to represent the value of each sample.

bpp *See* bits per pixel

bps *See* bits per sample

branching In a computer program, the act of jumping to another location in the program, instead of just continuing with the next instruction in the program.

bus In a computer system, the means for interconnecting the various units of hardware, such as the CPU, RAM, mass storage, etc.

byte A digital value represented by eight bits. A byte can represent decimal values between 0 and 255.

CAD *See* Computer-Aided Design

capture The process of bringing video or audio signals into a digital system. It normally requires conversion to a digital format and storing in the mass storage of the digital system.

CBT *See* Computer-Based Training

CD-ROM *See* Compact Disc Read-Only Memory

cel A building block of animation. It consists of one or more images of a single object that will be displayed as part of the animation.

central processing unit (CPU) The unit that performs system control and computing in a personal computer. The CPU is usually a single microprocessor chip.

chroma keying In television production, the process of placing one image over a second (background) image by making areas of the first image be transparent in the combining process. A specific color (often blue) is used to define the transparent areas.

CISC *See* complex instruction set computer

client A computer program that is requesting services from another computer program (the server).

clip art library A collection of vector drawings or bitmapped images that can be selected, modified, and combined to create screens for an application or presentation. The same library approach is often also used with audio, video, or animations.

Common User Access (CUA) The name given by IBM to their standard for Graphical User Interfaces.

Compact Disc Read-Only Memory (CD-ROM) A digital data version of the audio CD (Compact Disc). The CD-ROM can be inexpensively replicated and holds up to 680 megabytes of data. Because it is read-only, the data cannot be changed by the user.

compiler A computer program that converts a program written in a high-level language into the microprocessor instructions that will perform the tasks represented by the language statements.

complex instruction set computer (CISC) A microprocessor whose instruction set contains a large number of instructions that perform higher-level tasks that require many CPU cycles to complete.

component video A color video signal system that uses more than one signal to describe a color image. Typical component systems are RGB; or S-video.

composite video A color video signal system that contains all of the color information encoded into one signal. Typical composite television systems are NTSC, PAL, and SECAM.

compression A digital process that allows data to be stored or transmitted using fewer than the normal number of bits. For example, video compression refers to techniques that reduce the number of bits required to store or transmit images or motion video.

Computer-Aided Design (CAD) The use of a computer to assist in the design of an object or process. For example, CAD is widely used in the design of mechanical parts or mechanisms.

Computer-Based Training (CBT) The use of a computer to deliver programmed one-on-one personal training.

coordinates On a computer screen, the system of numbers that specifies position relative to an origin point, usually given in the form x,y where x is a horizontal position and y is a vertical position relative to the upper left corner of the screen.

CPU *See* central processing unit

cropping In an image, the process of selecting and cutting out a partial area of the image.

CUA *See* Common User Access

DDE *See* dynamic data exchange

decompression The process of restoring compressed data into its original uncompressed form.

digital A system in which values are represented by a series of bits.

digital signal processor (DSP) A special form of microprocessor designed to be most efficient at doing data processing tasks such as compression or decompression.

direct manipulation In a graphical user interface, the process of "picking up" an object on the screen and moving it (usually with a mouse) over another object to perform a task. This technique is also called "drag/drop."

DLL *See* dynamic link library

DOS The original operating system for the IBM-compatible family of PCs. The name stands for "Disk Operating System," and it is distributed by Microsoft.

dot pitch In a computer display monitor, the size of an individual dot of color on the physical screen. For proper reproduction of an image, the dot pitch must be smaller than the size of a single pixel in the image.

drag/drop *See* direct manipulation

draw tool An authoring tool for creating vector graphic drawings.

driver A software entity that provides an interface to a specific piece of hardware. For example, a video driver provides software access to the video board hardware.

DSP *See* digital signal processor

DVI Technology A hardware and software system developed by Intel and IBM to add audio and motion video capability to personal computers.

dynamic data exchange (DDE) An interprocess communication technique for *Windows* and *OS/2*. Using DDE, applications can send and receive data once a communication path is established.

dynamic link library (DLL) A computer program module that contains routines or functions that may be used by a number of applications.

edit decision list (EDL) In audio or video postproduction, a list of commands and values that defines a series of edits to be made in order to assemble a scene.

EDL *See* edit decision list

EISA *See* extended integrated system architecture

embedding With OLE, the capability for a document to include data from another application along with the ability to use the other application for editing or updating.

engine program A special program or program segment that performs a specific process on a data object. For example, a bullet chart display engine would take a text file and display its lines as a formatted bullet chart.

environment The collection of hardware and software that performs a specified set of tasks for the user for example, an authoring environment.

ESDI *See* extended system disk interface

extended graphics adaptor (XGA) An IBM graphics system that offers resolution modes higher than VGA.

extended integrated system architecture (EISA) This is a high-performance 32-bit system bus.

extended system disk interface (ESDI) This is a hard disk interface standard that offers higher preformance than the Integrated Disk Electronics (IDE) standard that is widely used. ESDI is often used with the larger hard disk sizes.

font A definition for drawing a set of text characters. It may be either in the form of a bitmap for each character or a mathematical description of how to draw each character in the specific style of the font (a vector font).

frame One image of a motion video sequence. In motion video, images are presented typically at 30 frames per second to create the illusion of continuous motion.

graphic accelerator A special-purpose integrated circuit that assists the CPU in performing graphic functions.

graphical user interface (GUI) A computer-user interface that combines a graphical screen capable of displaying graphics and images with a pointing device (such as a mouse). The user makes selections and issues commands by clicking the mouse button(s) while the pointer is over a graphic icon representing the desired task.

GUI *See* graphical user interface

hard disk A mass storage device based on read/write magnetic recording on one or more rigid rotating disks.

high color An alternate name for a color display system using 16 bits per pixel. Such a system can reproduce up to 65,536 unique colors.

high-level language A programming language that encapsulates complex tasks into simple language statements.

hypertext A text display system that allows an author to highlight specific text words or phrases to indicate to the user that he can click on that item for additional information.

icon In a graphical user interface, a graphic or image that visually represents an object in the environment.

IDE *See* integrated disk electronics

image processing Techniques which manipulate the pixel values of an image for some particular purpose. Examples are: brightness or contrast correction, color correction, or changing size (scaling).

Industry Standard Architecture (ISA) The 16-bit system bus introduced in the IBM PC/AT and now used as the basis for most IBM-compatible PCs.

information delivery The process of using a computer to provide the user with specific information. For example, a kiosk in a travel site that provides hotel, restaurant, and entertainment information for the surrounding area.

instance In a multitasking operating system, an instance is a single invocation of a particular program. If a second copy of the same program is started, it is a second instance.

instruction set In a microprocessor, the binary commands that the processor recognizes to control its operation.

integrated circuit (IC) An electronic component based on a semiconductor chip, usually made of silicon. Each IC can contain many individual circuits (sometimes millions) that are connected to perform a useful task or process.

integrated disk electronics (IDE) The most common hard disk interface standard.

interactivity The ability of a user to control the presentation by a multimedia system, not only for material selection, but for the way in which material is presented.

interface In computer software, a connection between two entities; for example, an Application Programming Interface (API) is the software connection between an application program and the system software of a PC. Similarly, a user interface is the way that a user sees, hears, and controls a computer.

interpreter A form of computer program that reads a high-level language and converts it to computer instructions that are immediately executed.

interprocess communication (IPC) In a multitasking operating system, any means of passing data or commands between concurrently running applications.

IPC *See* interprocess communication

ISA *See* Industry Standard Architecture

Joint Photographic Expert Group (JPEG) A working party of the ISO IEC Joint Technical Committee 1, who developed standards for compression of still images, called the JPEG standard.

JPEG *See* Joint Photographic Expert Group

kilobyte 1024 bytes.

kiosk A free-standing interactive computer system used for public access or information delivery.

laser video disc A read-only analog video and audio delivery system utilizing a 12" optical disc. Smaller sizes of the analog disc are also available in some products.

linear presentation Any presentation where the various screens or slides are arranged in straight-line fashion—that is, each slide always follows the same previous slide.

linking In OLE, the process of connecting a data object to a document without making a copy of the data object. This type of connection provides automatic updating of the data object in any documents where it is linked.

local bus In a PC, a special bus that connects directly between the CPU and another unit (such as a video display adaptor) without going through the main system bus.

lossless compression The result of compression followed by decompression is exactly the same as the original.

lossy compression The result of compression followed by decompression is not the same as the original. Normally a lossless compression system will throw away data that the end user will not easily see or hear.

mass storage Nonvolatile (permanent) storage used in a PC. Typically the mass storage is a magnetic hard disk, although floppy disk drives and optical drives are also used.

MCI *See* Media Control Interface (MCI)

Media Control Interface In multimedia computers, a device-independent software standard for communicating control information between applications and the system.

megabyte 1,048,576 (2^{20}) bytes.

megahertz A unit of frequency. One megahertz means that something is happening 1,000,000 times per second.

metafile A special form of data file that contains a mixture of drawing commands and/or bitmapped data, from which an appropriate driver can construct an image.

MIDI *See* Musical Instrument Digital Interface

millions of instructions per second (MIPS) This is a parameter that describes the speed of a microprocessor in terms of how fast (on the average) it executes its instructions.

MIPS *See* millions of instructions per second

morphing A technique where the computer generates a sequence of frames that smoothly transforms one image into another.

Motion Picture Expert Group (MPEG) A working party of the ISO IEC Joint Technical Committee 1, working on algorithm standardization for compression of motion video for use in many industries.

MPC *See* Multimedia Personal Computer

MPEG *See* Motion Picture Expert Group

MS-DOS *See* DOS

multimedia In computers, the presentation of information or training by using audio, motion video, realistic still images, and computer metaphors.

Multimedia Personal Computer (MPC) A PC that contains equipment for multimedia, such as audio, video, and CD-ROM hardware. Standards for MPCs are published by the Multimedia PC Marketing Council, an organization of PC manufacturers.

multitasking In a computer, a technique that allows several processes (programs) to appear to run simultaneously even though the computer has only one CPU. Multitasking is accomplished by sequentially switching the CPU between the tasks, usually many times per second.

multithreading In multitasking, some systems allow multiple concurrent activities (threads) within a single process (program).

Musical Instrument Digital Interface (MIDI) A serial digital bus standard for interfacing of digital musical instruments. MIDI is widely used in the music industry.

National Television Systems Committee (NTSC) The standardizing body that in 1953 created the color television standards for the United States. This system is called the NTSC color television system.

network A system that connects multiple PCs and allows data sharing between them.

nonlinear editing In conventional (linear) audio or video editing, one must rerecord the edited sequence every time a change or addition is made. In nonlinear editing with a computer, the edited sequence is stored as an edit decision list (EDL) that can be played at any time using the random-access capabilities of the computer's mass storage.

non-volatile memory Memory that retains its data when the power is turned off.

NTSC *See* National Television Systems Committee

object A data entity that can be manipulated by the user as a single unit. Objects can have built-in behavior and properties.

Object Linking and Embedding (OLE) An interprocess communication protocol built into multitasking operating systems that supports the inclusion of external data objects into a document. For example, with OLE a word processor document can include a spreadsheet chart that was created by a separate application. OLE also provides for editing of the object without leaving the document application, and (with linking) it provides for automatic updating of all instances of the object.

object-oriented A system of programming or operation based on the concept of objects.

OLE *See* Object Linking and Embedding

operating system In a personal computer, the core program that provides applications with access to all of the hardware resources of the system. Typical operating systems are DOS and OS/2.

OS/2 A multitasking and multithreading operating system supported by IBM.

paint tool A bitmapped editing tool.

palette The collection of colors that can be simultaneously displayed on the screen. Some systems that have a limited number of palette entries because of a low bpp (such as 4 or 8 bpp) support a palette that can be customized from a larger array of colors. However, a single image or single screen still cannot have more colors than will fit into a single palette.

PC Memory Card International Association (PCMCIA) An association that produced standards for a plug-in card interface, primarily intended for portable computers. The PCMCIA interface can be used for memory or mass storage expansion, a modem, or other hardware peripherals.

PCM *See* pulse code modulation

PCMCIA *See* PC Memory Card International Association

pixel A single point of an image, having a single color value.

pixellation The effect produced when there are too few pixels for the size of the image. Pixels become visible as small rectangles or squares of color.

platform In computers, the base architecture of a computer system. Typical computer platforms are IBM PC-compatible or Macintosh.

pointing device A device used by a computer user to point to locations on the screen. For example, a mouse device moves a cursor on the screen and the user clicks buttons on the mouse to make selections at the location of the cursor. Similarly, a touch screen pointing device accomplishes the same thing by the user simply touching the screen at the desired location.

postproduction In video or audio, the process of merging original video and audio from tape or film into a finished program. Postproduction includes editing, special effects, dubbing, titling, and many other video and audio techniques. You can do digital postproduction with a computer.

preemptive multitasking A multitasking system is *preemptive* if it is capable of interrupting any application regardless of what the application may be doing. This prevents a single application from ever hogging all the system resources or hanging the system.

primitives In computer graphics, a set of simple functions for drawing on the screen. Typical primitives are rectangle, line, ellipse, polygon, etc.

process In a multitasking operating system, the name given to an executable entity (typically an application). In some systems, processes can contain subblocks, called *threads.*

production In video, refers to the process of creating programs. In more specific usage, production is the process of getting original video onto tape or film and ready for postproduction.

productivity In computer applications, refers to applications that assist the user in doing his job. Typical productivity applications are word processing, spreadsheets, planning, etc.

pulse code modulation (PCM) The system of sampling an analog waveform and digitizing the samples to produce a digital data stream representing the analog waveform.

RAM *See* random-access memory

random-access memory (RAM) Memory that can be directly accessed at any location, for example, at every byte position. RAM usually refers to the main memory of a computer, which is solid-state read/write memory.

reduced instruction set computer (RISC) A microprocessor that has a simplified instruction set so that every instruction executes in the same period of time (usually a single clock cycle).

render In computer graphics, the process of creating an image or screen from mathematical or computer-language descriptions.

Resource Interchange File Format (RIFF) A file format specifically developed for platform-independent storage of most computer data types.

RIFF *See* Resource Interchange File Format

RISC *See* reduced instruction set computer

runtime module A separate application that only plays back the output of an authoring assembly tool. Runtime modules are distributed at low cost or even sometimes free.

sampling The process of reading the value of an analog signal at evenly spaced points in time.

sampling rate The clock frequency for sampling or the number of samples per second.

scaling A process for changing the size of an image.

scanner A device that converts hard copy images or photographs to a digital image file by moving an image sensing device across the image (scanning).

SCSI *See* Small Computer System Interface

server A program that responds to commands from another application (the client) to provide a service, such as data lookup. Servers exist only in multitasking operating systems and communicate via DDE or OLE.

simulation The process where a computer program behaves like a different object or system.

Small Computer System Interface (SCSI) A special bus for connecting devices to a PC. Most often used to connect CD-ROM or hard disk drives.

source code The code or script in a high-level language that describes a computer program. The source code must be either interpreted or compiled to produce executable instructions for the computer.

spatial redundancy In a digital image, the redundancy that results because of similarity between adjacent pixels. Image compression schemes try to detect this and eliminate repeated pixel values while still allowing the original image to be recreated for display.

storyboard A method of planning the content of a presentation by drawing sketches of each screen with notes about what happens in that scene.

student management In computer-based training (CBT) or education, the process of keeping track of multiple students' progress in using the training or education system. This is a special feature of some authoring assembly programs intended for the training or education markets.

subsampling In video compression, the process of reducing the pixel count for the color components of an image, done by discarding samples in a regular pattern.

subtractive color Color reproduction by mixing appropriate amounts of color paints or dyes on white paper, used for color painting and printing. The color print primaries are red, blue, and yellow. Note that red as used in printing is technically a magenta color, and blue is technically a cyan color.

Super VGA (SVGA) An extension to the VGA specification that offers increased resolution and/or increased number of colors. The use of Super VGA requires increased video memory and higher-performance display monitors.

SVGA *See* Super VGA

syntax In a programming language, the exact details for how statements and their parameters are formed.

Tagged Image File Format (TIFF) A file format for bitmapped images.

teleconferencing The use of electronic communication for holding conferences. This normally involves the two-way transmission of sound and pictures in some form.

temporal redundancy In a motion video stream, the redundancy that results because of similarity between adjacent frames. Motion compression techniques try to detect the temporal redundancy and transmit only the information that actually changes from one frame to the next.

thread In some multitasking operating systems, one or more concurrently executing tasks may exist within a process—these are called *threads*.

TIFF *See* Tagged Image File Format

tool A computer program that performs functions that assist the user in a particular task. For example, if the user is doing authoring, he will benefit from the use of authoring tools.

transparency In a digital image, the process of defining one or more color values that will not be reproduced when the image is copied over another image. Instead, pixels having the transparency values will still display the previous image. This is used to overlay objects over a background, such as the weathercaster standing in front of a weather map background.

treatment A narrative writeup, usually nontechnical, which describes a proposed creative work such as a software application or an audio/video production segment.

true color A digital display system that uses 24 bits per pixel, thus being capable of displaying 16,777,216 colors.

tweening In animation, the process of creating new frames between other frames in order to smooth out the motion displayed by the frames. The original frames are called *key frames*. In computer animation, tweening is often accomplished with a morphing algorithm.

Ultimedia Tools Series (UTS) An IBM initiative to bring together authoring tool vendors to create a series of authoring tools that work together in their environment.

user interface The means by which a user communicates with a computer. It includes not only the devices used (mouse, keyboard, touch), but also the objects on the screen and the sounds made by the computer in response to the user.

UTS *See* Ultimedia Tools Series

variables In an authoring assembly tool, variables are used to store values that are created at runtime, either by the program or by the user. Most assembly tools have built-in variables that keep values created by the system (system variables), and many tools allow the author to create specific variables for things he needs to keep track of in his application.

VCR *See* video cassette recorder

vector drawing The drawing process where drawn objects are represented by mathematical descriptions that are used at runtime to render the bitmap that is displayed. Vector drawings are more efficient in terms of storage, and the runtime rendering can be done for any kind of display resolution and bpp.

VGA *See* Video Graphics Array

video cassette recorder (VCR) Equipment that records and plays back video and audio from a video tape cassette. VCR standards are available for home, professional, and broadcast use.

video disc Usually refers to the laser video disc, which is a read-only analog video system using a 12-inch optical disc.

Video Graphics Array (VGA) This is the standard display type for most PCs. VGA provides many optional formats, but the most common one is 640×480 pixels with 16 colors.

VL bus This is one standard for a local bus that couples the video display adaptor directly with the CPU.

volatile memory Memory that loses its data when the power goes off. The most common volatile memory is the RAM used for the main system memory in PCs.

WAVE A standard for digital audio based on PCM sampling of analog audio without compression.

Windows When capitalized as shown, Windows is the graphical user interface created as a DOS extension by Microsoft.

Windows NT This is a new version of Windows that eliminates the need for DOS (and its limitations) and adds new features such as preemptive multi-tasking, threads, security, networking, etc.

WORM *See* write-once, read many

write-once, read many (WORM) An optical mass storage device that can write new data into storage but cannot change data already stored.

XGA *See* Extended Graphics Adaptor

Bibliography

The following list is not meant to be an exhaustive bibliography of multimedia publications. It is a list of the books and periodicals that I consulted in writing this book.

BOOKS

Bunzel, Mark J., and Morris, Sandra K., *Multimedia Applications Development*, Second edition, New York: McGraw-Hill, 1993.

IBM Corporation, *Object-Oriented Interface Design: IBM Common User Access Guidelines*, Publication SC34-4399. Cary, NC.: IBM, 1993

Luther, Arch C., *Digital Video in the PC Environment*, Second edition, New York: McGraw-Hill, 1991.

Luther, Arch C., *Desiging Interactive Multimedia*, New York: BantamBooks, 1992.

Microsoft Corporation, *Microsoft Windows Multimedia Authoring and Tools Guide*, Redmond, WA: Microsoft Press, 1991.

———, *Microsoft Windows Multimedia Programmer's Workbook*, Redmond, WA: Microsoft Press, 1991.

PERIODICALS

Aldus Magazine. Published by Aldus Corporation, 411 First Ave. S., Seattle, WA 98104-2871.

AV Video. Published monthly by Montage Publishing, Inc., 701 Westchester Ave., White Plains, NY 10604.

Byte. Published monthly by McGraw-Hill, Inc., One Phoenix Mill Lane, Peterborough, NH 03458.

Keyboard. Published monthly by Miller Freeman, Inc., 600 Harrison St., san Francisco, CA 94107.

OS/2 Professional. Published monthly by I. F. Computer Media, Inc., 172 Rollins Ave., Rockville, MD 20852.

PC World. Published monthly by PC World Communications, Inc., 501 Second St. #600, San Francisco, CA 94107.

Videomaker. Published monthly by Videomaker, Inc., PO Box 4591, Chich, CA 995927.

Windows Magazine. Published monthly by CMP Publications, Inc., 600 Community Drive, Manhasset, NY 11030.

CD-ROM

Microsoft Developer Network CD, Disc Five, Microsoft Corporation: Seattle, WA, 1993.

Index